Plant This, Not That

Plant This, Not That

Over 200 Native Plant Swaps for a More Sustainable, Pollinator-Friendly Garden

ELISE HOWARD

WORKMAN PUBLISHING | NEW YORK

Plant descriptions adapted with permission: Native Plant Information Network, NPIN (2024). Published on the internet http://www.wildflower.org/plants/ [accessed throughout 2023 and 2024]. Lady Bird Johnson Wildflower Center at the University of Texas, Austin, TX.

Maps are used with permission: Kartesz, J. T., The Biota of North America Program (BONAP). 2015. *North American Plant Atlas*. (http://bonap.net/napa). Chapel Hill, N.C. [maps generated from Kartesz, J. T. 2015. Floristic Synthesis of North America, Version 1.0. Biota of North America Program (BONAP). (in press)].

Workman
Workman Publishing
Hachette Book Group, Inc.
1290 Avenue of the Americas
New York, NY 10104
workman.com

Workman is an imprint of Workman Publishing, a division of Hachette Book Group, Inc.
The Workman name and logo are registered trademarks of Hachette Book Group, Inc.

Design by Suet Chong
Photo research by Sophia Rieth
Photography credits on page 252

Library of Congress Control Number: 2026006099

ISBN 978-1-5235-2591-1 (paperback), 978-1-5235-3626-9 (ebook)

First Edition January 2026

Printed in the United States of America (VER) on responsibly sourced paper

10 9 8 7 6 5 4 3 2

For my father, William Henry Howard,
who loved everything about gardening, from the soil
to the treetops (except poison oak), and who would
have been delighted and determined to come along for
the native plant journey

And for my sister Megan Eileen Howard,
who loved learning and saying complicated and
beautiful plant names as much as I do

CONTENTS

INTRODUCTION

Why Plant Natives?

If you have arrived on this page, chances are you're curious about the benefits of adding native plants to your landscape. You may have heard that our pollinators, our climate, and our very survival depend on home gardeners planting more natives, for several reasons.

There's no longer enough public land in the United States to sustain the wildlife that creates the food web—the interlocking system of creatures, from insects to birds to mammals, that nourishes much of life on Earth—so it's up to home gardeners to help create wildlife-rich environments. Many of our traditional garden plants don't support the pollinators and other creatures whose survival is fundamental to our ecosystems—in some cases because those plants come from distant countries and thus didn't evolve to be a food source for our local wildlife, and in others because by hybridizing and manipulating them for garden beauty, we reduced their value to the ecosystem.

Additionally, some of the non-native ornamental plants we've introduced to our gardens have escaped their boundaries, and other plants brought to the United States for agricultural uses have behaved the same way. In other words, they've become invasive. These invasive plants have taken over landscapes and crowded out more beneficial natives. They need to come out of our gardens as soon as possible.

The conversation about what's a good (beneficial) or bad (harmful) plant is confused by the fact that a lot of the plants we're now being encouraged to bring into our yards are ones we used to call weeds and worked hard to keep at bay. And perhaps you're wary of the ability of these "weeds" to offer the same joys—high-impact color, fragrance, size, boldness—as the classic nursery plants you're used to.

Rest assured, you don't have to sacrifice garden beauty to support pollinator insects, caterpillars, and birds. Many conversations about the benefits of native plants leave out what may feel like the best news for many gardeners: These plants can be incorporated into whatever style garden you want to create, and they promise better success rates than non-native plants. Native plants are typically the ones best suited for any site, because they have evolved in the local climate, soil, and moisture conditions.

What's more, native plant gardening generally favors an abundance of plants over weeding and mulching, as well as natural balance over high-intervention gardening techniques. This combination means that in a short time (three years or even less), a native or mostly native garden can provide more pleasure and beauty for less money and labor than a traditional garden featuring plants from far away.

As someone who gardened for decades before being introduced to the idea of focusing on native plants, I've seen my plant preferences shift from those of a collector seeking the elegant, the unusual, and the pristine as presented in botanical gardens and design magazines to valuing a garden as a reflection of and contributor to a sense of place.

And the pleasures of gardening with native plants don't end at the boundaries of your own backyard. As our built landscapes look more and more similar from Portland, Maine, to Portland, Oregon, and from Springfield, Maine, to Springfield, Texas, it's heartening to be able to recognize a place through its plants and plantings thanks to the work of gardeners, institutions, and communities getting to know and restore the native plant communities of their regions, from eastern and western forests to the plains, mountains, deserts, and coasts.

Getting Started

Whether you're designing a privacy hedge or a hellstrip garden or even thinking about an eye-catching new specimen tree for your front yard, I hope you've picked up this book because you're ready to add some native plants to your garden. Before you do, we need to answer a critical question: What's a native plant, anyway?

Plant This, Not That begins there, establishes some key principles of gardening with native plants, and then offers specific suggestions for native plants in your region that can fill the places now taken up by familiar, but less-beneficial plants. Ideally, from this jumping-off point, you'll feel empowered to make your own native plant selections, and you'll find plenty of practical information and alternative suggestions to broaden the range of possibilities. In the plant profiles and in the reference pages that follow, you'll also discover additional resources that will help you extend your native plant search and knowledge.

What Is a Native Plant, Anyway?

When it comes to the contiguous United States, there is a consensus that the plants we consider native are those that were present before European colonization.

It's tempting to talk about "North American native plants" (and the conversation about plants and native plant gardens is often framed this way), but in a country as big as the United States this is an oversimplication. A given plant may be native to a wide swath of North America or to a very particular local region. It may grow beyond that region, but it won't necessarily support local pollinators and wildlife elsewhere—which is a main objective of native plant gardening. The plants that animals coevolved with will provide the most benefits to local animal populations. And where plants can attract the most enthusiastic pollinators, those plant populations will thrive.

So how do you determine what plants are locally native? To begin with, rather than focusing on the United States Department of Agriculture (USDA) hardiness zones that commercial nurseries use to identify where a plant *can* grow, climate scientists now talk about *ecoregions*: areas defined by similarities of land, climate, and other natural resources. There are twelve level I (i.e., top level) ecoregions in the continental United States (which excludes Hawai'i), some spanning more than a thousand miles in length and breadth, so these ecoregions are useful but not very precise in talking about native plants. For that, you'd have to go down several levels in the ecoregion map, a complicated exercise. Instead, many commercial native plant nurseries and native plant organizations have

adopted the Biota of North America Program (BONAP) North American Plant Atlas. BONAP has used decades of data and observation to map by genus and species the native ranges of thousands of plants by county and state. You'll find BONAP maps used in this book's plant guide, too.

Along with BONAP maps, local resources can be a huge help in understanding native plants. If you are lucky enough to have a brick-and-mortar (or mud-and-water) native plant nursery nearby, visit, ask questions, and get to know the plants on offer. In addition, state and regional botanical gardens and native plant organizations typically offer a more local point of view on cultural requirements and growing conditions (though many botanical gardens don't limit their collections to native plants). National organizations, like Wild Ones and the National Wildlife Federation, also offer advice at the local level—as local as your zip code, sometimes. Some of these are listed in Further Reading and Additional Resources on page 236.

Principles of a Native Plant Garden

Whether you're a lifelong gardener or new to planting, you may have thought of gardening as a matter of taste and choice, a hobby where what to plant depended on figuring out what shrubs or flowers you like, and then which of those will grow in your area and are easily available. The idea of creating a native plant garden can be daunting if it seems like a practice with a lot of rules to follow, mistakes to make, and even judgments to endure. Keeping in mind the following five basic principles will make native plant gardening approachable and achievable.

1. **Aim for a *mainly* native garden.** You may be asking, *What about my roses? And peonies?* If so, here's some good news: A garden made up of 70 percent native plants can sustain pollinators; provide key food and shelter for insects, birds, and mammals; and establish the wildlife corridors necessary to support animal populations that often live their entire lifespans within yards of where they are born, according to entomologist Douglas Tallamy, the National Wildlife Federation, and other experts. Opinions vary on what percentage of plant matter in your garden must be native to ensure the health of the ecosystem; some experts and studies suggest the number could be as low as 50 percent, but almost all seem to agree that 70 percent will do the job. And every native plant you add will increase the benefits you are providing.

   One important caveat to this guideline: You want to make sure that there are no invasive plants in your garden. These are non-native plants that grow so vigorously where they are introduced that they can crowd out native plants, eliminate food and habitat for local fauna, and even change soil structure, with disastrous effects. Because many nurseries still sell invasive plants, it's always good to double-check the status of a non-native plant you're considering. You'll find how to do this in Beyond Plant Swaps on page 229.

If you remove and avoid invasives, and if 70 percent of what you plant—including the lawn—is locally native trees, shrubs, grasses, and herbaceous flowering plants (aka forbs) that provide nutrition and habitat to local animal populations, up to 30 percent of what you plant can be non-native, including other North American natives and plants introduced from farther away.

2. **Plant for wildlife and for beauty.** Our food web and its supporting ecosystem connect myriad forms of life, from the smallest bugs to the largest mammals: pollinating insects, caterpillars, butterflies, dragonflies, fireflies, toads, bees, songbirds, and birds of prey. Contributing to this food web with a native plant garden means expanding the beauty of your landscape to include more and more of these spectacular creatures. Of course, you don't want to look at your garden and see nothing but munched-up leaves. So plant more than enough to go around. Then the beneficial bugs you've invited in won't go away half full, the critters can take their fair share, and there will be plenty of greenery left behind for you to enjoy. I now get as excited when I see insects nibbling on my leaves as I do when I see a hummingbird sipping nectar.

3. **Build layers.** This book will show you that you can still create a vibrantly colored garden or a white garden or a fragrance garden or a collector's garden using native plants. But you may also find, as I did, that once you begin to consider a garden's potential to house and feed wildlife, it enlarges your awareness and appreciation of garden beauty from flowers and blooms to a more expansive, more dimensional perspective.

If you think for a moment about birds, it's easy to envision how there would be some that nest in tall trees, some that nest in smaller trees and shrubs, and many that feed on the seeds of flowers or forage for insects and other food in the soil and organic litter at ground level. Since a key goal of a native garden is supporting wildlife through food and shelter, you'll want to create a layered landscape to support animals who live at ground level, in shrubs and hedges, and high in the treetops. As the idea of bringing more shrubs into my garden to attract more birds took hold, I started to see beyond blooms, which can be ephemeral indeed, and to contemplate the beauty of leaf patterns, bark, and berries. I began to appreciate the way a layered landscape carries the eye from the flowers near the ground to the rustling of branches to the majesty of the overstory.

In choosing native plants for your garden, keep in mind the importance of creating layers that reflect the natural growth of locally native plants, whether that means trees, shrubs, and ground-level plants or the mixed grasses (or grasslike sedges and rushes) and flowering plants of the prairie—whatever layers reflect the region where you live and garden.

4. **Create plant communities.** In nature, plants grow in communities, and they can do the same thing in the garden. Especially when it comes to residential landscapes, we are used to the idea that a lovely garden features a collection of plants, each one surrounded by a frame of mulch, like family portraits hanging on a living room wall. That's great for ancestors' pictures, but plants want the company of other plants that share similar requirements for light, soil, and moisture. The interplay of growth above- and belowground guides plants in spreading out to fill space or staying in check to make room for their neighors. When growing plants support each other, there's less flopping and breaking of stems—and less time and money spent on stakes or fancy garden supports. Permitting compatible plants to fill the garden space minimizes areas of open soil where weeds like to move in. So out with the framed portraits, in with the collage.

5. **Ditch the mulch and hang up the rake.** Not only do abundant layers of varied plants ensure that you and the local insects can share nicely, they reduce your annual garden maintenance.

   We've been told that mulch holds moisture in the soil, keeps down weeds, and adds nutrients. But mulch can also prevent moisture from getting *to* the soil, and it eventually breaks down and becomes a great medium for weed growth. As this process takes place, it changes the composition of the soil and raises the soil level, which then changes the planting depth of existing plants. Because dense plant cover reduces moisture loss and keeps down weeds, once your native plant garden is established, you can skip the annual applications of mulch.

   Along with ditching the mulch, a native plant garden allows you to skip those aspects of annual spring and fall cleanup that are among gardeners' least favorite chores. Instead of chopping down perennials, you can leave some stems. Flower heads full of seeds and the berries on shrubs provide a reliable food source for winter birds. They can also turn the typical flat, bare winter garden into a tapestry of browns, grays, and soft greens—occasionally punctuated by the bright hues of a visiting finch or cardinal. Leaving flower stems and leaves in your beds and borders over the winter can help insulate soil, filter rain and melting snow, absorb runoff, and provide nesting materials and shelter for overwintering insects and other garden creatures. In spring, your new habit of planting abundantly means leaf litter and plant debris can stay in place to be quickly concealed by new growth and become a valuable source of nutrients and organic matter for soil.

Native Plants and Pollinators

On any given summer day in my Maine garden, within the space of an hour or two, I might encounter dragonflies, hummingbirds, toads, bumblebees, butterflies, grasshoppers, moths, countless songbirds, and often turkeys, hawks, and a soaring bald eagle. It's only since I've been a native plant gardener that I have realized that the dragonfly population is as varied and spectacular as the world of butterflies, for example, and includes darners and dancers and bluets and skimmers and dozens of others in a dazzling array of iridescent colors and shapes. Have you ever purchased a hummingbird feeder to attract that most lovable of birds, only to fill it and forget it? Or set it aside once you read the important warnings about regular cleaning? Guess what: Nature provides the best, most low-maintenance hummingbird feeders available. In much of the Midwest, East, and Southeast, that "feeder" might be a crimson honeysuckle vine. In an even larger part of the country, it's a form of bee balm. The Anna's hummingbird of the Pacific Northwest loves the nectar of local salvias and California fuchsia.

Native plants that have existed in a particular location for millennia both depend on and support the life cycle of locally native fauna—larval and adult insects, birds, mammals, and reptiles. Douglas Tallamy has pioneered work demonstrating that pollinators receive the best nutrition from the plants with which they coevolved, a process he describes in his books, including *Bringing Nature Home*. Insect populations are largest where their most dependable and nutritious food sources thrive.

The effects ripple throughout the food web. The monarch butterfly is one of our best-known and most beautiful examples. A monarch will lay eggs *only* on an asclepias (milkweed) plant. No milkweed, no monarchs. Because agriculture and development have dramatically reduced wild asclepias populations, it's up to private citizens to step in and plant their region's native asclepias species. Many other animals are not quite so specific in their needs, but they often depend on a handful of locally coevolved plants and cannot be sustained by the plants introduced into our gardens from abroad. This can be a double whammy if those introduced plants have become invasive, adapting so well that they escape cultivation to crowd out beneficial native plants.

Take for example the *Buddleja davidii*, or the common butterfly bush, which has been a garden staple for decades. US gardeners (and garden writers and commercial nurseries) will sometimes defend the presence of this colorful and fragrant, but invasive, plant by citing the way it's covered with butterflies and other pollinators all summer long. Yes, butterfly bushes in bloom can be beautiful. But if insects are visiting a butterfly bush instead of native plants for nectar, the native plants are losing out on pollination and reproduction. And while a butterfly bush may supply nectar to *adult* insects, it is not useful to caterpillars or other juvenile insects. Attractive though they may be, the butterflies

swarming non-native plants are masking the larger harm that plant may be doing to the whole ecosystem.

Another example: Clover is sometimes touted as a good choice to replace high-maintenance turf grass in lawns because it grows quickly and easily and appears to attract many bees when in bloom. But clover isn't native to the United States and it evolved with honeybees (not a North American species), so it benefits those bees but provides little for our native bees or for the larger insect populations in the area. Herbaceous plants such as goldenrods, sunflowers, and asters—to name a few—feed and shelter scores of pollinators and insects. Many other plants produce nectar or leaves necessary to feed a specific local insect.

Even when non-native plants provide *some* pollen, nectar, or shelter for local pollinator and animal populations, native plants typically support many more local species. As he describes in *The Nature of Oaks,* Douglas Tallamy counted 897 species of moth caterpillars supported by oak trees across various regions—511 of which live in his own Pennsylvania county. (In contrast to oaks, a non-native Callery pear supported a single caterpillar species.) Caterpillars, an essential source of nutrition for many birds, are at the epicenter of our food web. Plant an oak, feed the world. Choosing native over non-native plants at every level of the landscape ensures that you are a supporting a healthy, vibrant ecosystem where plants and pollinators don't just coexist, but support and sustain one another.

Sourcing Native Plants

Once you identify the native plants you'd like to add to your garden, how you source them is important. Native plant nurseries are sprouting all over the country, but it's going to take a while before they are common and accessible to everyone. If you have a native plant nursery within reach, make it your first stop. The owners and staff are often passionate about the native plant movement, well informed, and invested in matching plants to place and making sure you go home with specimens that will thrive in your garden. They may grow plants on the premises, which is the best way to make sure you know where your native plants are coming from and under what conditions they've been cultivated. There's a good chance you'll leave a native plant nursery with lots of plants and invaluable knowledge.

More traditional commercial growers and nurseries are getting in on the native plant business, too, after years of resistance to it—but it's important to be an educated buyer when shopping with these retailers to make sure you are getting plants that will bring the biggest benefits to your ecosystem.

One way large commercial plant producers are joining the native plant movement is by "improving" on the straight native species of plants to create cultivated varieties (called cultivars in the trade), just as they have done for non-native plants for many decades, in order to trademark the new cultivars and profit from their reproduction and sale. In some cases, those cultivars modify features like plant height or the intensity of fall color in ways that seem not to diminish their ecological benefits. But other changes reduce a plant's environmental value. Altering bloom color, for instance, can confuse insects who use color to identify a high-value food source. Double flowers are created by turning a flower's reproductive parts into petals, so these flower forms cannot produce pollen or seeds. Recent studies have shown that manipulating green summer leaves to turn them red all season makes them less attractive and less nutritious to the animals that feed on them.

Even if alterations are benign in terms of plant characteristics (say, height), trademarked cultivars must be reproduced by cloning. Genetically identical, cloned plant populations are less disease resistant than populations that contain the variations of plants grown from seed. And be aware that if you do plant cultivars and let them volunteer via seeds, their offspring may be different in height, bloom color, and other ways.

If you are fortunate enough to have a local nursery that sells native plants, look for seed-grown, straight species plants rather than cultivars (or the cutely labeled "nativars").

There is plenty of evidence that even more benefit comes from planting local ecotypes—plants grown from the seed of local plants rather than seed from a plant in another part of the native range. For example, if you want to grow an *Acer rubrum* (red maple), you will have the best outcome with a locally sourced plant, since maples imported from the northern part of the range to the south don't do as well as those from the southern part, and vice versa. It's also important to make sure plants are ethically grown and not harvested from the wild. Your nursery should be able and willing to identify the source of their stock.

As the adoption of native plants grows, brick-and-mortar nurseries of all kinds can't yet meet the demand. There are great mail-order native plant nurseries that fill the gap, offering a wide variety of native plants supported by websites and catalogs that make it easy to figure out what plants are a match for your site. You'll find some of these listed in Further Reading and Additional Resources on page 236.

How to Use the Guide

This is a book of recommendations for the native plant curious. Maybe you're starting from scratch in a part of the yard in need of a little attention. Maybe that old privet hedge has seen better days, and you'd like to replace it with something native. Or maybe you've read about the need to remove invasives from your yard and you wonder what native plants can offer the same great fragrance or fall color. You have come to the right place.

This book is divided into chapters that reflect the way we typically think of a residential garden and its functions. Each section presents some of the most commonly used non-native plants in American gardens, with suggestions for substitutes that are either widely native or else fill a specific role in the garden particularly well.

Each native is introduced with the plant's Latin name, including genus and species. Most native plant advocates encourage getting to know and use Latin names, for a few reasons. One plant may have many common names, and sometimes the same common name is used (often in different regions) for more than one plant, which can be confusing. No matter which names you're using, if you hear that one variety of a plant is native in your region, whether it's a common name like "laurel" or a Latin one like *Prunus* or *Viburnum* or *Rhododendron*, it doesn't mean that other plants sharing that name are also native in your region—or that they are even native to North America. The best way to be sure you source plants native to your landscape is to use the fuller Latin name, including genus and species. But while I encourage you to learn the Latin, in this guide I also include the most widely known common names, since they may be more familiar to many gardeners.

After the names, along with a photograph of each plant, you'll find an at-a-glance list of states where the plant is native in at least *some* counties. From there, you can use the BONAP maps that appear alongside the more detailed listings that follow to find out if a plant is native to *your* county. (The nonprofit BONAP gathers data from a variety of sources to document the native range of thousands of plants in continental North America.)

In addition to the BONAP map, these more detailed listings contain information about

BONAP MAP KEY

- (light green) Native to North America and present in county
- (dark green) Native to North America and present in some counties (in light green or teal) in state
- (teal) Native to North America, adventive but not native in state, present in county (plants described as adventive, or naturalized, have been introduced to an area—by humans, animals, or even the wind—and can now be found growing in the wild)
- (orange) Native to North America, historically present but extirpated/no longer found in state or county
- (yellow) Native to North America, present but rare in county and state
- (purple) Native or non-native to North America, present and noxious in county and state
- (hatched dark green) Questionable Presence

the plant's native range and requirements, as follows:

- Plant type and growth habit.
- Ornamental features including bloom time and color, berries or fruit, and fall color.
- Requirements for sun (full sun: six or more hours per day; part shade: under five hours; or full shade: less than an hour); soil (dry: fast draining, potential for drought; moist: retaining some water but well drained; or wet: consistently wet, occasionally saturated); and special cultural characteristics.
- Workhorse or pollinator plants as designated by the Ecoregional Revegetation Application (ERA) tool of the US Environmental Protection Agency. A workhorse plant is one that is hardy, durable in a garden, and widely commercially available. Plants essential to certain pollinators or plants whose pollen is used by a high number of species are designated as high pollinator value (HPV) or very high pollinator value (VHPV). All the listings include categories of pollinators known to depend on each plant.
- Deer-resistant plants have low palatability to deer and other browsing mammals and are especially recommended for areas with high deer pressure or large populations of other browsing mammals. (Ideally, the balance in a native plant garden will allow it to tolerate some browsing. But with so many factors at play in an ecosystem, deer pressure may be so high in local areas that it's important to understand which plants are most resilient to it.)

Each native plant is discussed in full where it is first featured in the guide. Because many of the plants listed are versatile and can be swapped for a number of non-natives or fill a variety of roles in the garden, they may appear in the lists entitled "More great native choices," especially where they are native to a range not found among the featured plants.

With hundreds (if not thousands) of native plants available to purchase or grow from seed, many beautiful and beneficial plants didn't make it into this guide—including some excellent garden plants native to such a small area that it wasn't practical to list them here. You will discover them at native plant nurseries, so consider this book a starting place for understanding the beauty, versatility, and benefits of plants native to your region. And if you see a plant that appeals to you but isn't shown as native to your region, it's worth checking nurseries and other resources to find out if there is a related locally native plant. Just make sure that the native species of any plant has characteristics similar to the one featured here, since there can be great variety within any given plant genus.

It was not possible to cover some regions of the contiguous United States (aka the Lower 48)—particularly the mountain deserts and California and the Southwest—as thoroughly as others because of their particularities of climate and growing conditions and the limited ranges of plants native to these regions. I've done my best to include them where I can, and to feature plants that suggest the beauty of typical native plants most used in these areas.

Sometimes there's no perfect one-to-one swap of a native plant for an introduced one. If you are truly committed to gardening with locally native plants, you might first consider what your aim is for the space, then look for another plant that meets this criterion (evergreen, vigorous enough to hold invasives at bay, winter interest, etc.). Browsing through this guide should acquaint you with many plants native to your area, and you'll likely find one that works for your landscaping needs.

The native plant descriptions are adapted with permission from wildflower.org, the website of the Lady Bird Johnson Wildflower Center. Cultural requirements are based mainly on the ERA tool. The zone numbers noted in plant descriptions refer to the USDA plant hardiness zones. And because a plant can be reclassified by scientists and its genus and/or species name changed, I also include the synonym when a plant may still be sold by that older Latin name.

In the case of shrubs, when the ERA tool varied from other sources I consulted, primarily the Lady Bird Johnson Wildflower Center and *Native Trees, Shrubs, and Vines* by William Cullina, I tended to rely on Cullina's estimates, since he distinguishes between typical garden growth and growth in the wild. That said, plant growth may vary a great deal from site to site depending on soil condition, sun, heat, and rain. In my Maine garden, for instance, *Aronia melanocarpa* grew taller than any estimate I have seen in the references I used.

CHAPTER ONE

The Foundation Garden

There's nothing more classic than the American foundation garden. It blends the house with its surrounding lawn and softens the edges of the built structure, which is usually box shaped and almost always made up of hard angles. In many cases, the foundation garden conceals that line where a basement emerges from the earth, rising a few feet above the soil.

A handful of plants remains steadfastly on the top hits list for foundation gardens, maybe because these plants are often installed by builders or developers of whole communities. The classics include rhododendron and azalea, hydrangea, boxwood, roses, barberry, euonymus, Japanese or English holly, and andromeda, among others. Of course, they found their way into American gardens because of their distinctive features and appeal. These plants provide a combination of graceful shape, concealing growth habit, seasonal bloom—often abundant and stunning—winter brightness, and even fragrance. Unfortunately, they don't provide support for pollinators or, in many cases, food for the insects at the heart of our food web or for local birds. But for every traditional choice, there's a native plant that's just as appealing—and beneficial, too.

INSTEAD OF THIS:

Buxus sempervirens

BOXWOOD

Native to southern Europe, Asia, and Africa, boxwood is one of the most familiar plants in North American gardens. One of its common names is even American boxwood, though it is *not* a native American plant. Its somewhat formal evergreen shape gives a neat appearance to a foundation or hedge, particularly due to its ability to take pruning. An unpruned boxwood can get messy quickly, however. While a boxwood in good health is a beautiful plant with a pleasant fragrance, it can be finicky and prone to pests—and in recent years, a fungal disease known as boxwood blight has become a problem. There's nothing sadder looking than a brown or naked boxwood in the middle of an otherwise healthy garden. Boxwood prefers a mostly sunny site, with afternoon shade in hotter climates, and is usually grown in Zones 5 to 8.

PLANT THESE:

Ilex glabra

INKBERRY HOLLY

AL, AR, CT, DE, FL, GA, LA, MA, MD, ME, MS, NC, NH, NJ, NY, OH, PA, RI, SC, TX, VA

Ilex verticillata

WINTERBERRY HOLLY

AL, AR, CT, DC, DE, FL, GA, IA, IL, IN, KY, LA, MA, MD, ME, MI, MN, MO, MS, NC, NH, NJ, NY, OH, PA, RI, SC, TN, TX, VA, VT, WI, WV

Mahonia aquifolium

OREGON GRAPE HOLLY

CA, ID, MT, OR, WA

Paxistima myrsinites

OREGON BOXWOOD, MYRTLE BOXLEAF

AZ, CA, CO, ID, MT, NM, OR, UT, WA, WY

Ilex glabra

INKBERRY HOLLY

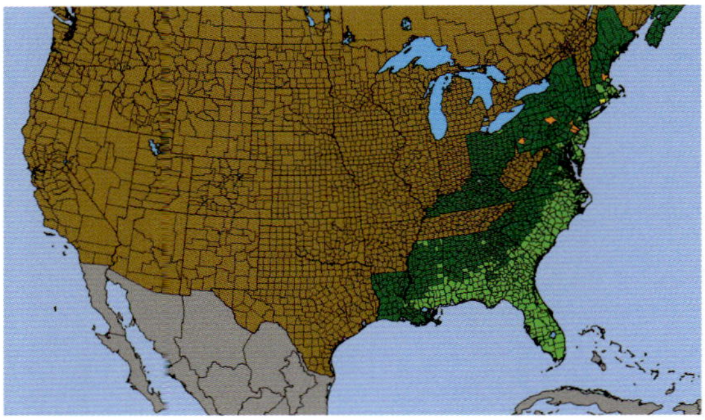

- Evergreen shrub; 3 to 5 feet.
- Spring white flowers followed by small, dark berries.
- Sun to part shade; wet to moist acidic soil, with consistently wet soil in full sun. Salt tolerant.
- Workhorse. VHPV: Pollinated by native bees, butterflies, other insects. Host to moth and butterfly caterpillars. Berries feed birds.
- Deer and rabbit resistant.

Ilex glabra makes a great substitute for a number of non-native garden plants, in particular the boxwood. Inkberry holly is a relatively slow grower that can be pruned to fit well into a foundation planting. One male plant will pollinate many females, producing gradually darkening berries that will feed birds throughout winter or sometimes last until spring. The glossy, dark green, oval leaves brighten the winter garden. Inkberry is easily pruned at any time, unless you want to encourage berry production—in that case, since inkberries bloom on old wood, you'll want to prune after the spring bloom. If planting your inkberry in a foundation, cut back suckers to prevent spreading. *I. glabra* is dioecious, meaning male and female plants are required for berry production: One male is needed to pollinate one or more female plants.

Ilex verticillata

WINTERBERRY HOLLY

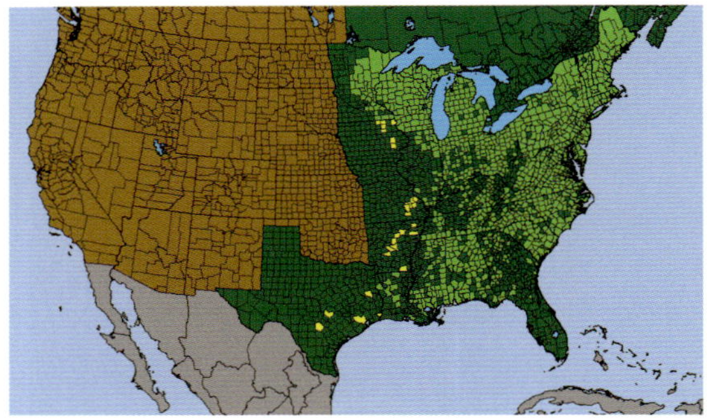

- Deciduous shrub; 4 to 10 feet.
- Spring insignificant white flowers followed by bright red berries.
- Sun to part shade; wet to moist acidic soil. Compacted soil, salt, and pollution tolerant.
- Workhorse. VHPV: Pollinated by native bees, butterflies, other insects, birds. Host to moth and butterfly caterpillars. Berries feed birds.
- Deer and rabbit resistant, though both may browse its berries.

Unlike some other familiar hollies, *Ilex verticillata* is deciduous, with small, spineless green leaves. However, bright red berries persist on its branches through winter (or until the birds have done feasting), making winterberry a plant perhaps most beautiful in its leafless state—especially under a light blanket of new snow. There are cultivars with gold berries, which birds seem to like as well as the red ones. Avoid other cultivars, as some are hybrids with other non-native hollies, which could affect their pollinator value (see pages 10–11). *I. verticillata* is dioecious: One male is required to pollinate one or more female plants, and berries appear only on female plants.

Mahonia aquifolium

OREGON GRAPE HOLLY

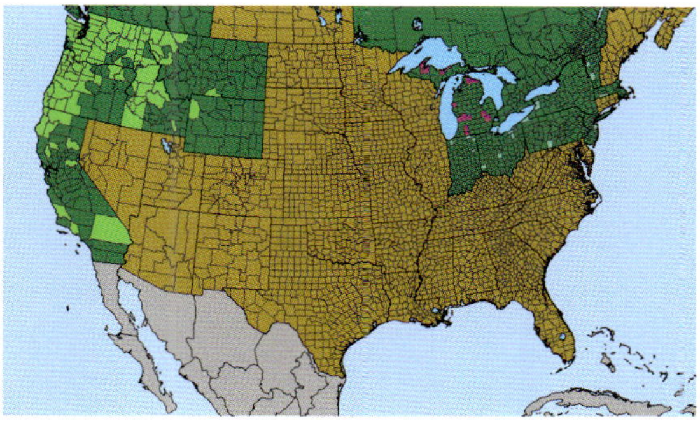

- Evergreen shrub; 3 to 6 feet.
- Spring yellow flowers followed by blue berries.
- Part shade to shade; moist to dry acidic soil. Drought tolerant.
- Workhorse. Pollinated by native bees, hummingbirds. Berries feed birds, small mammals.
- Deer and rabbit resistant, though both may browse its berries.

Oregon grape holly, which is famously neither a grape nor a holly, is shorter at maturity than either the medium-sized Chinese holly (8 to 15 feet) or the slow-growing English holly (30 to 50 feet). What it lacks in mature height it makes up for in four-season interest, with its persistent leaves putting on a show as reddish new spring foliage turns bright green in summer and then a deeper red in fall. In spring, old leaves may drop as new ones appear to replace them, accompanied by clusters of delicate yellow flowers. The berries of *Mahonia aquifolium*, which go from a powdery blue when new to a deep purple-blue, are edible, but it may be tough to harvest them because you'll be competing with many animals that find them delicious; plant more bushes close together to help them fruit more abundantly. Prune suckers to prevent colonizing.

Paxistima myrsinites

OREGON BOXWOOD, MYRTLE BOXLEAF

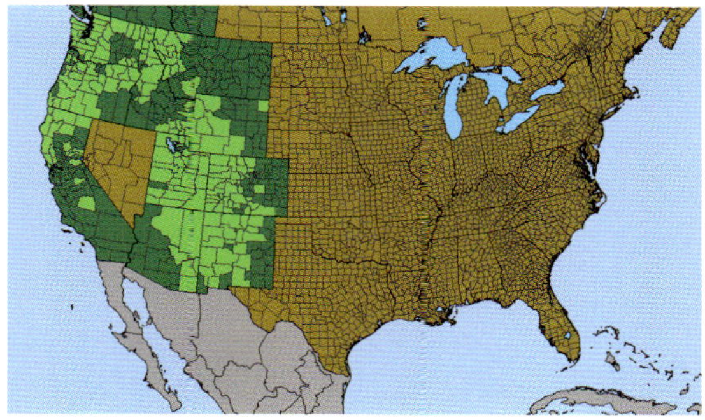

- Evergreen shrub; 1 to 3 feet.
- Late-spring to early-summer red flowers.
- Sun to shade. Dry soil.
- Host to moth caterpillars.

As its common name suggests, this native boasts leaves that bear a close resemblance to boxwood's. But paxistima's new leaves are light green, maturing to a glossy darker green, with some leaves developing a red color in fall. The red flowers that appear in summer are tiny but abundant. Once established, the plant grows in dry soil with little to no care. Like boxwood, *Paxistima myrsinites* is easily used for low hedges.

More great native choices: *Kalmia latifolia* (page 42), *Arctostaphylos glandulosa* (page 43), *Morella* spp. (pages 50–53)

INSTEAD OF THESE:

Berberis thunbergii

JAPANESE BARBERRY

Berberis vulgaris

EUROPEAN BARBERRY

Gardeners have grown these plants for their color, their easy care, and their thorns, which protect them and the areas around them from foot traffic and deer browsing. But these Eurasian barberries are among the most invasive plants disrupting our ecosystems, with seeds distributed over wide distances by birds, so that barberries crowd out beneficial natives in woods, along roadsides, and in fields. In addition, the conditions within and beneath the branches of the Japanese barberry make it a welcoming home to black-legged (deer) ticks, the Lyme disease host, and the mice that often carry these ticks and spread their populations.

As the sale of invasive barberry becomes forbidden in more states, some nurseries have promoted a sterile form of barberry, which doesn't produce seeds, as a noninvasive alternative. However, sterile plants do not attract pollinators (no pollen!).

PLANT THESE:

Physocarpus opulifolius

EASTERN NINEBARK, COMMON NINEBARK

AL, AR, DC, DE, FL, GA, IA, IL, IN, KS, KY, MD, MI, MN, MO, NC, ND, NE, NJ, NY, OH, OK, PA, SC, SD, TN, VA, WI, WV

Hypericum prolificum

SHRUBBY SAINT-JOHN'S-WORT

AL, AR, DC, DE, FL, GA, IA, IL, IN, KY, LA, MD, MI, MO, MS, NC, NJ, NY, OH, OK, PA, SC, TN, TX, VA, WI, WV

Physocarpus capitatus

PACIFIC NINEBARK

CA, ID, OR, WA

Swida sericea (syn. *Cornus sericea*)

RED OSIER DOGWOOD, RED TWIG DOGWOOD

AZ, CA, CO, CT, DE, IA, ID, IL, IN, MA, MD, ME, MI, MN, MT, ND, NE, NH, NJ, NM, NV, NY, OH, OR, PA, RI, SD, UT, VA, VT, WA, WI, WV, WY

Physocarpus opulifolius
EASTERN NINEBARK, COMMON NINEBARK

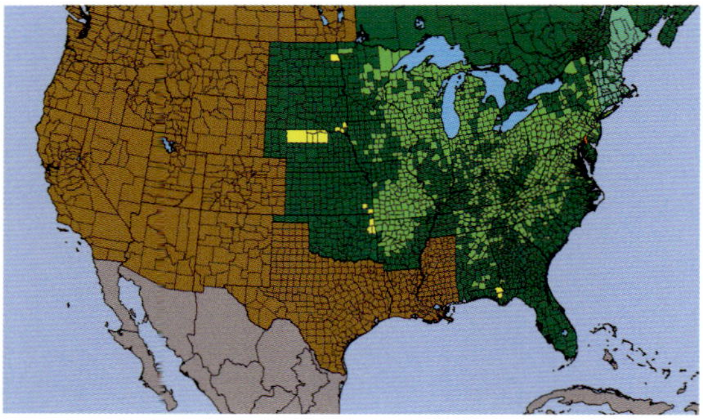

- Deciduous shrub; 3 to 10 feet.
- Spring to summer small, white to pinkish flowers. Yellow fall foliage.
- Sun to part shade; moist acidic soil. Drought tolerant once established.
- Workhorse. VHPV: Pollinated by native bees, butterflies (including monarchs), other insects. Host to butterfly caterpillars.
- Deer and rabbit resistant.

Physocarpus capitatus
PACIFIC NINEBARK

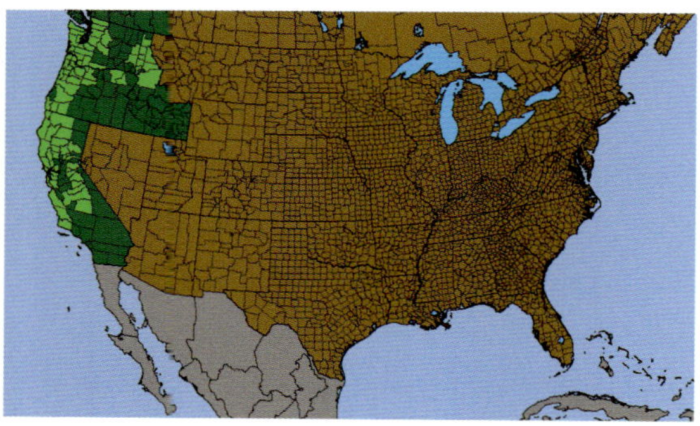

- Deciduous shrub; 3 to 8 feet.
- Spring to summer small, white to pinkish flowers. Red to brown fall foliage.
- Sun to shade; wet to dry acidic soil.
- Workhorse. HPV: Pollinated by native bees, butterflies, other insects. Host to moth and butterfly caterpillars.
- Deer and rabbit resistant.

Ninebark (both *Physocarpus opulifolius* and *P. capitatus*) is a popular native substitute for barberry because of its similar graceful, fountainlike growth habit. Its flower clusters, which are 2 to 3 inches wide, appear in spring and are followed by clustered red seedpods. The peeling bark that is the source of the plant's name (because it was believed to be nine layers in shades from dark brown to pale tan) gives ninebark beauty through all seasons, especially winter. This versatile shrub is also good in hedges and as a specimen.

NOTE: Many nurseries sell cultivars of ninebark with burgundy leaves. Some research suggests that insects avoid red leaves as a food source, making these varieties less beneficial in the native plant garden.

Hypericum prolificum

SHRUBBY SAINT-JOHN'S-WORT

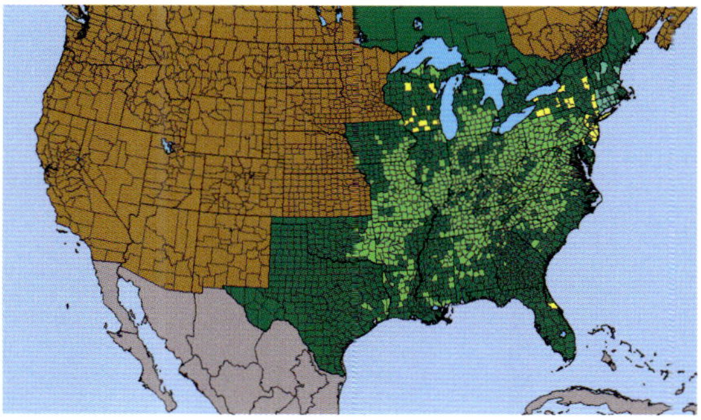

- Deciduous shrub; 1 to 6 feet
- Summer yellow flowers. Yellow fall foliage.
- Sun to part shade; moist to dry soil.
- Workhorse. HPV: Pollinated by native bees, butterflies, other insects. Host to moth caterpillars.

The leaf shape and dense branching structure of *Hypericum prolificum* make it a good substitute for barberry, but in all other ways, it's a more cheerful and appealing plant. It's adaptable to many soils; its large yellow flowers bloom throughout summer, giving way to yellow fall foliage; and it adds winter interest to the garden with its exfoliating red to purple bark.

Swida sericea (syn. *Cornus sericea*)

RED OSIER DOGWOOD, RED TWIG DOGWOOD

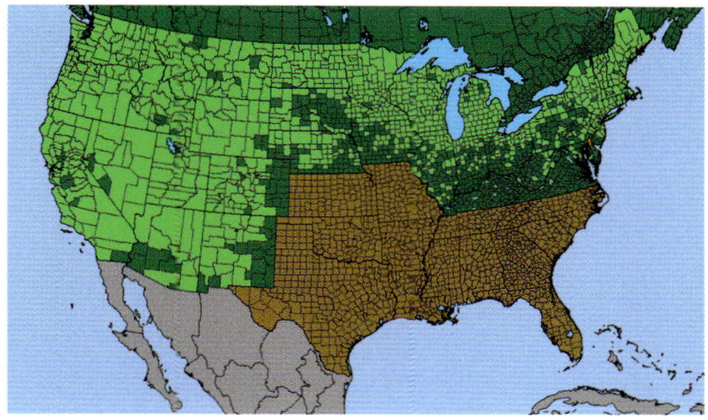

- Deciduous shrub; 3 to 9 feet.
- Spring white flowers followed by white berries.
- Sun to part shade; wet to moist soil.
- Workhorse. VHPV: Pollinated by native bees, moths, butterflies, other insects. Host to moth and butterfly caterpillars. Berries feed birds.

Swida sericea puts on a spectacular winter show like few other shrubs—not with foliage, but with stems that grow brilliant scarlet as the temperatures fall. This multistemmed shrub throws up abundant shoots covered in dense foliage in spring and summer, which makes it easy to prune a third or more of the stems to the ground each spring, a practice that encourages new growth (which has the best red color). Both the flowers and berries are modest, but pollinators can't get enough of them.

More great native choices: *Arctostaphylos glandulosa* (page 43), *Morella* spp. (pages 50–53)

INSTEAD OF THIS:

Euonymus alatus

BURNING BUSH, WINGED EUONYMUS

No commonly planted shrub says "fall is here" more emphatically than burning bush (also widely known as winged euonymus) with its scarlet autumn leaves. Unfortunately, it's also one of the most invasive plants introduced to the American landscape, jumping garden boundaries and colonizing roads and forests. In fact, once you can identify burning bush, every fall you'll be struck by what a problem it has become, as its foliage lights up the side of highways and glows from within the woods along roadsides. Because birds are the ones spreading the seeds, the plant can appear well behaved in a single garden, but its progeny may be spreading miles away from their source. Several states have prohibited this plant's sale, and if you have it in your garden, you should consider eliminating it as soon as possible.

PLANT THESE:

Aronia arbutifolia

RED CHOKEBERRY

AL, AR, CT, DC, DE, FL, GA, KY, LA, MA, MD, ME, MI, MS, NC, NH, NJ, NY, OH, OK, PA, RI, SC, TN, TX, VA, WV

Aronia melanocarpa

BLACK CHOKEBERRY

AL, AR, CT, DC, DE, GA, IA, IL, IN, KY, MA, MD, ME, MI, MN, MO, MS, NC, NH, NJ, NY, OH, PA, RI, SC, TN, VA, VT, WI, WV

Aronia arbutifolia

RED CHOKEBERRY

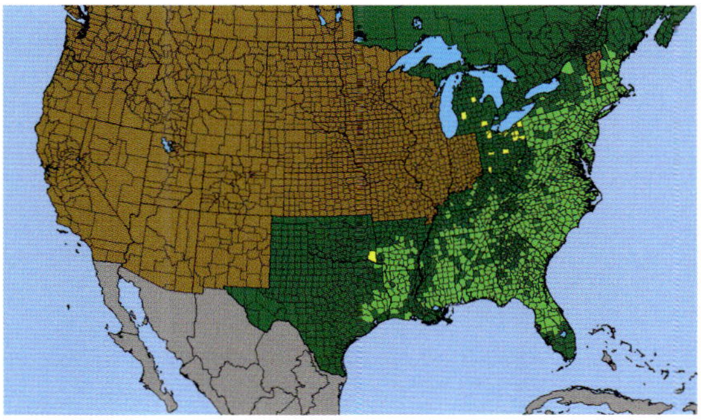

- Deciduous shrub; 6 to 15 feet.
- Spring white blossoms followed by red berries. Red to orange fall foliage.
- Sun to part shade; wet to moist acidic soil.
- Workhorse. HPV: Pollinated by native bees, moths, butterflies, other insects.
- Deer resistant.

Aronia melanocarpa

BLACK CHOKEBERRY

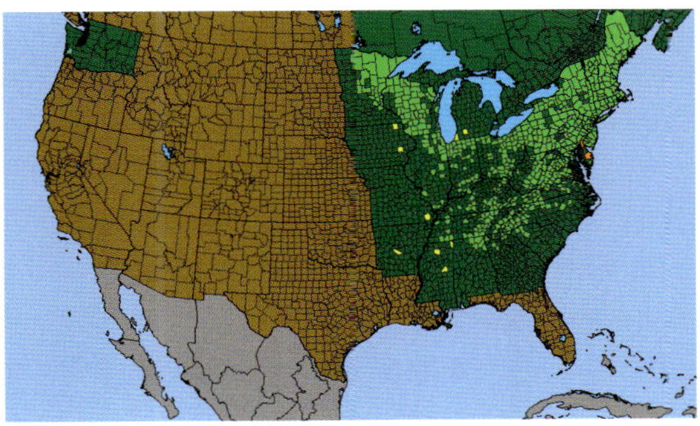

- Deciduous shrub; 5 to 8 feet.
- Spring white blossoms followed by dark berries. Red to orange fall foliage.
- Sun to part shade; moist to dry acidic soil.
- Workhorse. VHPV: Native natives bees, moths, butterflies, other insects. Host to moth and butterfly caterpillars. Berries feed birds.
- Deer resistant.

For some native plant gardeners, the choice between *Aronia arbutifolia* (red chokeberry) and *A. melanocarpa* (black chokeberry) may be determined by the plants' different native ranges. Otherwise, both make great foundation plants, with black chokeberry slightly smaller at maturity—though both of these are easily pruned to stay in proportion in a foundation bed. Their tendency to sucker is easily kept in check by early-spring pulling or pruning. The round, plump, astringent summer berries grow in easy-to-spot clusters. Winter freeze-and-thaw cycles mellow the flavor, making chokeberries an excellent food source for overwintering birds when most other berries are gone. The glossy green summer leaves give way to early and brilliant fall color, in shades from scarlet to a deep, purplish red.

More great native choices: *Swida sericea* (page 25), *Viburnum prunifolium* (page 92), *Amelanchier alnifolia* (page 53), *Clethra alnifolia* (page 73), *Itea virginica* (page 73), *Rhus aromatica* (page 165)

INSTEAD OF THESE:

Hydrangea macrophylla

BIGLEAF HYDRANGEA, MOPHEAD HYDRANGEA, LACECAP HYDRANGEA

Hydrangea paniculata

PANICLE HYDRANGEA

It's no wonder North American gardeners across many generations have relied on hydrangeas. These prolific bloomers bear large flowers in colors from white to pale pink to purple to light blue, in some varieties the color depending on the acidity of the soil where they grow. But virtually all the commercially available mophead and lacecap *Hydrangea macrophylla* in the United States are cultivated varieties of a parent native to Japan, and mopheads are sterile, providing no benefits to pollinators. Lacecaps feature a mix of sterile and fertile flowers, but they produce far fewer of the blooms attractive to pollinators than native hydrangeas; most varieties of non-native hydrangea bloom on one-year-old wood, meaning an unusually cold winter can greatly reduce flower production, making these plants fussier and more fragile than native alternatives.

Non-native panicle hydrangeas (*H. paniculata*), which are cousins to the mophead, typically bloom later in the season, with cone-shaped flower clusters, sometimes trained into a small tree form, growing in shade to sun in moist soil. The white panicles change color as they age, from white in summer to russet in fall and then brown in winter. When grown as specimen plants, these more cold-hardy hydrangeas can reach up to 8 feet tall.

PLANT THESE:

Hydrangea arborescens

SMOOTH HYDRANGEA, WILD HYDRANGEA

AL, AR, DC, DE, FL, GA, IL, IN, KY, LA, MD, MO, MS, NC, NJ, NY, OH, OK, PA, SC, TN, VA, WV

Hydrangea quercifolia

OAKLEAF HYDRANGEA

AL, DC, FL, GA, LA, MS, TN, VA

Ceanothus americanus

NEW JERSEY TEA, REDROOT

AL, AR, CT, DC, DE, FL, GA, IA, IL, IN, KS, KY, LA, MA, MD, ME, MI, MN, MO, MS, NC, NE, NH, NJ, NY, OH, OK, PA, RI, SC, TN, TX, VA, VT, WI, WV

Ceanothus velutinus

SNOWBRUSH CEANOTHUS, REDROOT

CA, CO, ID, MT, NV, OR, SD, UT, WA, WY

Hydrangea arborescens

SMOOTH HYDRANGEA, WILD HYDRANGEA

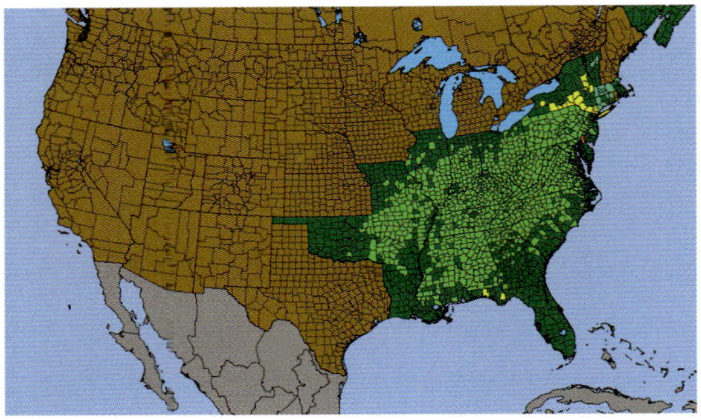

- Deciduous shrub; 3 to 6 feet.
- Summer white flowers.
- Part shade to shade; dry soil.
- Workhorse. VHPV: Pollinated by native bees, moths, butterflies, other insects. Host to moth caterpillars.

Hydrangea arborescens is a straightforward native substitute for *H. macrophylla* thanks to a similar growth habit. Its white blooms are not as flashy as those of bigleaf hydrangeas, but the wide native range and high wildlife benefits make smooth hydrangea a great addition to your garden. The flowers appear over a long summer period and often remain (lightly) in bloom into September. These white blossoms fade to an attractive beige in fall and make great dried flowers.

Since this plant blooms on new wood, some or all of the branches can be pruned to the ground each spring to maintain a pleasing shape and size, but only damaged or diseased branches must be removed. The peeling bark of the canes provides winter interest after the leaves have fallen.

NOTE: The popular 'Annabelle' cultivar has bigger blooms than the straight species, but they are sterile and do not support pollinators or birds.

Hydrangea quercifolia

OAKLEAF HYDRANGEA

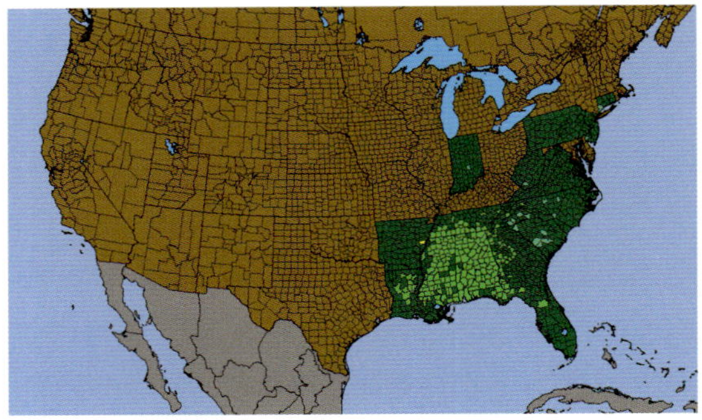

- Deciduous shrub; 4 to 8 feet.
- Spring to summer off-white flowers. Red fall foliage.
- Sun to part shade; moist soil. Somewhat drought tolerant once established.
- Workhorse. HPV: Pollinated by native bees, other insects. Host to moth caterpillars.

The large, dramatic panicles of *Hydrangea quercifolia* first appear in shades of white or cream, sometimes tinted with green, framed by the equally dramatic, deeply lobed large, deep green leaves that give the plant its name. The flowers gradually change color over the course of the summer to pink, then russet, then brown, usually persisting through winter. After a show of deep red fall color, the leaves drop, and the plant's shaggy, peeling bark provides winter interest in shades of beige and brown.

Ceanothus americanus

NEW JERSEY TEA, REDROOT

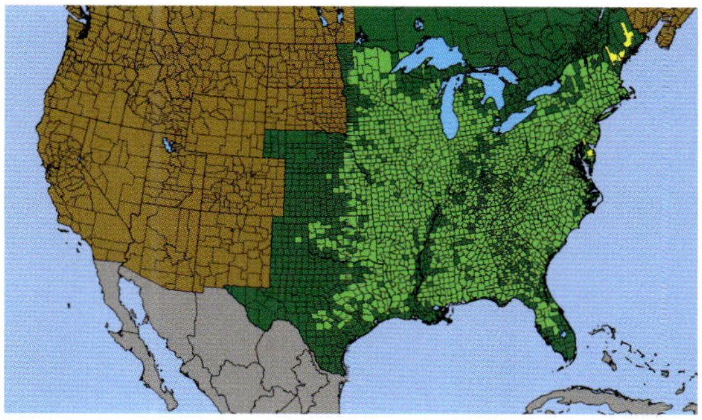

- Deciduous shrub; 3 to 4 feet.
- Summer white to pale pink flowers.
- Sun to part shade; moist to dry soil. Drought tolerant.
- Workhorse: VHPV: Pollinated by native bees, other insects, hummingbirds. Host to moth and butterfly caterpillars.

The low growth habit of *Ceanothus americanus* makes it a great option where a short, durable, low-maintenance plant is wanted. It tops out under 4 feet, with a rounded shape, so it's especially useful for tucking into blank spots in the garden. In summer, rounded clusters of sweetly fragrant tiny white flowers draw an abundance of pollinators. The leaves, sometimes used to make a tea substitute, have a light wintergreen fragrance. In areas where rainfall is unpredictable, the deep, drought-tolerant root system of New Jersey tea makes it an especially good substitute for the more finicky mophead hydrangeas.

Ceanothus velutinus

SNOWBRUSH CEANOTHUS, REDROOT

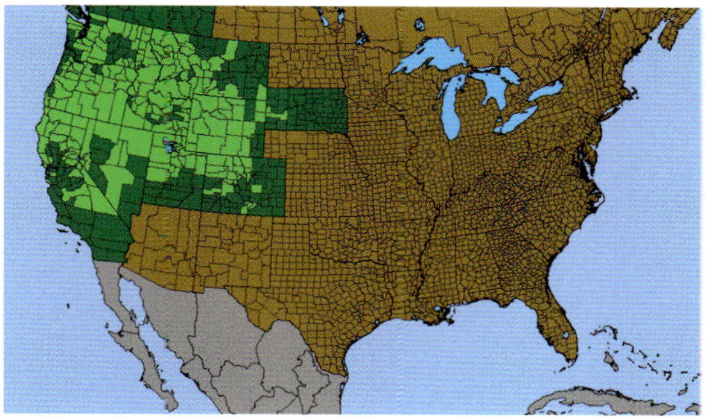

- Evergreen shrub; 3 to 10 feet.
- Summer white to blue flowers.
- Sun to shade; dry to moist soil. Drought tolerant.
- VHPV: Natives bees, moths, butterflies, other insects, hummingbirds. Host to moth and butterfly caterpillars.
- Deer resistant.

Long clusters of white flowers recommend *Ceanothus velutinus* as a hydrangea substitute, but it has an appeal all its own. The flowers have a sweet smell and the foliage a light balsam scent, and the plant is adaptable to a range of habitats and soils, as long as the soil is always well drained. Its evergreen leaves and full, sturdy stems make *C. velutinus* a good hedge plant, too. Along with this white-flowered variety, there are many other appealing western native *Ceanothus* species to consider in a range of hues.

More great native choices: *Physocarpus* spp. (page 24), *Viburnum prunifolium* (page 92)

INSTEAD OF THESE:

Ilex cornuta
CHINESE HOLLY

Ilex aquifolium
ENGLISH HOLLY

Chinese and English holly have been widely adopted for their glossy, spined leaves, which are an effective deer and rabbit deterrent, and for their bright red berries, which persist through winter. Chinese holly is often pruned for shape and size in hedges but can be found as a 25-foot specimen tree. Hardy in Zones 7 to 9, it is sometimes grown farther north with the help of elaborate burlap wrapping in winter. English holly, hardy to Zone 5, can slowly reach a mature height of 30 or more feet but is often pruned to a lower height for hedges. The branches of both have been a mainstay of the winter holiday season, but we now know that in the Pacific Northwest, English holly has become an invasive pest, displacing native understory plants. Luckily, there are great American plants to use in your garden and for holiday cheer. As natives, they may also provide better nutritional benefits to the birds and small animals that browse their winter berries.

PLANT THESE:

Ilex opaca

AMERICAN HOLLY, CHRISTMAS HOLLY

AL, AR, CT, DC, DE, FL, GA, IL, IN, KY, LA, MA, MD, ME, MO, MS, NC, NJ, NY, OH, OK, PA, RI, SC, TN, TX, VA, WV

Juniperus scopulorum

ROCKY MOUNTAIN JUNIPER, ROCKY MOUNTAIN CEDAR, WESTERN RED CEDAR

AZ, CO, ID, KS, MT, ND, NE, NM, NV, OK, OR, SD, TX, UT, WA, WY

Frangula californica

CALIFORNIA BUCKTHORN, CALIFORNIA COFFEEBERRY

AZ, CA, NM, NV, OR

Ilex opaca

AMERICAN HOLLY, CHRISTMAS HOLLY

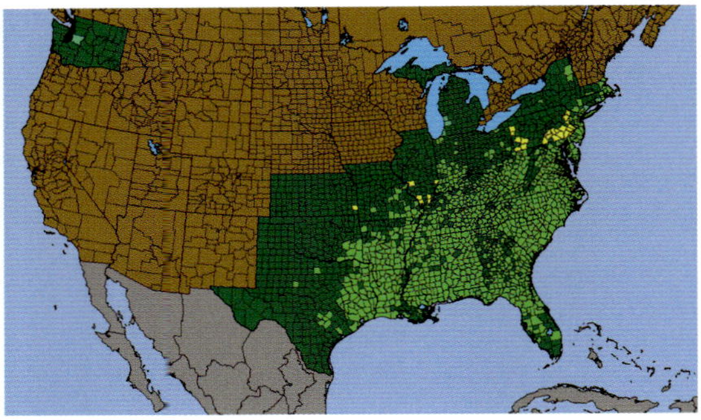

- Evergreen shrub/tree; 15 to 40 feet.
- Spring white flowers followed by red berries.
- Sun to shade; wet to dry acidic soil.
- Workhorse. VHPV: Pollinated by native bees, butterflies, other insects. Host to moth and butterfly caterpillars. Berries feed birds, small mammals.
- Deer and rabbit resistant.

Although one of the earliest cultivated plants in the United States, *Ilex opaca* lost ground as a commercial landscaping plant to its faster-growing Chinese and English cousins. But its habit of growing only 6 inches a year makes it a better choice for foundation beds, where it can also be pruned to size in summer—or in winter, when the cuttings can be brought indoors for holiday decorating. Because of its slow growth, you may want to start with a plant close to the mature size you envision. The dark green spined leaves provide a great high-contrast background for the plant's bright red berries. Like other evergreen shrubs, *I. opaca* is an important winter cover plant for birds and small mammals. *I. opaca* is dioecious: One male is required to pollinate one or more female plants, and berries appear only on female plants.

Juniperus scopulorum

ROCKY MOUNTAIN JUNIPER, ROCKY MOUNTAIN CEDAR, WESTERN RED CEDAR

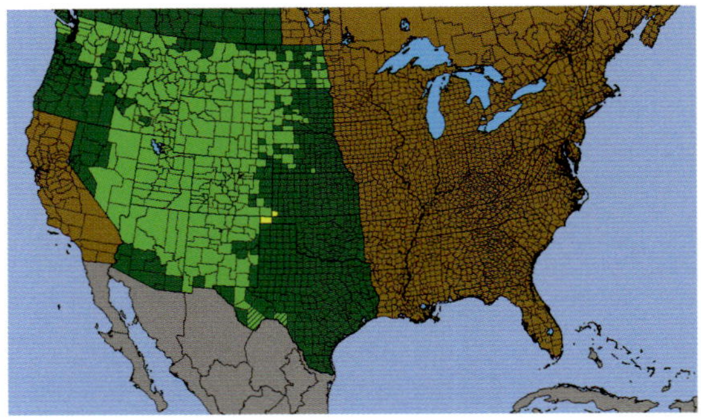

- Evergreen shrub/tree; 10 to 25 feet.
- Spring inconspicuous yellow flowers followed by berrylike blue cones on female plants.
- Sun to part shade; dry soil. Drought tolerant.
- Workhorse. Host to moth and butterfly caterpillars. Berries feed birds, small mammals.

Hollies are not western natives, but other evergreen plants offer different kinds of winter interest just as striking. *Juniperus scopulorum* features scalelike foliage that lights the sleeping landscape with a spectrum of greens, from dark to bluish to light, often taking on a reddish color in fall. Both the leaves and berries are aromatic—the berries are used to flavor gin. *J. scopulorum* can be gently pruned for shape but usually grows with a pleasantly rounded crown. This plant is occasionally monoecious but most often dioecious, meaning male is required to pollinate one or more female plants. The males have small yellow or brown cones, and the females produce a blue fruit that is commonly called a berry but is really a modified cone.

Frangula californica

CALIFORNIA BUCKTHORN, CALIFORNIA COFFEEBERRY

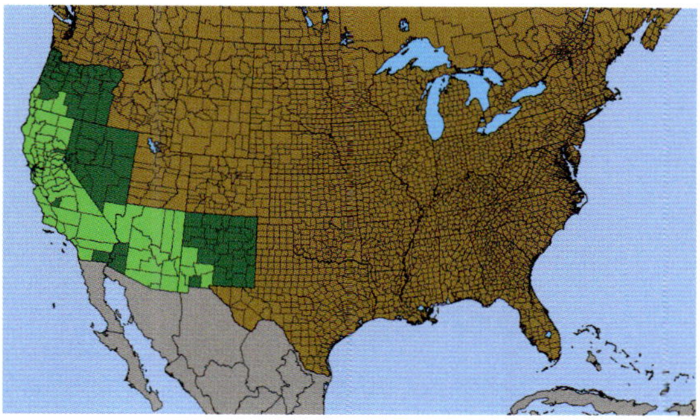

- Evergreen shrub; 4 to 15 feet.
- Spring greenish white flowers followed by berries that go from red to purple to black.
- Sun to shade; moist to dry soil. Drought tolerant; not tolerant of wet soils.
- Workhorse. Pollinated by native bees, other insects, butterflies. Host to moth and butterfly caterpillars.
- Deer resistant.

Although its leaves are quite different from a holly's, *Frangula californica* produces dense clusters of small flowers followed by showy berries, just as a holly does. *F. californica*'s somewhat larger berries begin as an apple red that turns to purple then black. Mature height estimates vary widely for this plant, but its attractive red branches are easily pruned.

More great native choices: *Mahonia aquifolium* (page 21), *Morella californica* (pages 52–53)

INSTEAD OF THIS:

Nandina domestica

HEAVENLY BAMBOO

Nandina domestica, called heavenly bamboo (though it's not a bamboo), has been widely used in mid-Atlantic, southern, and West Coast gardens for its easy growth and evergreen or semi-evergreen foliage, which emerges with a reddish hue, followed by clusters of red berries. Nandina is now considered invasive in the Southeast, where it has displaced natives in woodlands, and it's a nuisance plant as far north as Virginia. Though a relatively low-toxicity plant, nandina has nonetheless proven lethal to cedar waxwings, as the birds' habit of gorging on a food source compounds nandina's toxic effects.

PLANT THESE:

Euonymus americanus

AMERICAN STRAWBERRY BUSH, WAHOO

AL, AR, DC, DE, FL, GA, IL, IN, KY, LA, MD, MO, MS, NC, NJ, NY, OH, OK, PA, SC, TN, TX, VA, WV

Callicarpa americana

AMERICAN BEAUTYBERRY

AL, AR, FL, GA, LA, MD, MO, MS, NC, OK, SC, TN, TX, VA

Ribes aureum

GOLDEN CURRANT

AR, AZ, CA, CO, ID, KS, MA, MO, MT, ND, NE, NM, NV, OK, OR, SD, TX, UT, VT, WA, WY

Heteromeles arbutifolia

TOYON, CHRISTMASBERRY, CALIFORNIA HOLLY

CA, OR

Euonymus americanus

AMERICAN STRAWBERRY BUSH, WAHOO

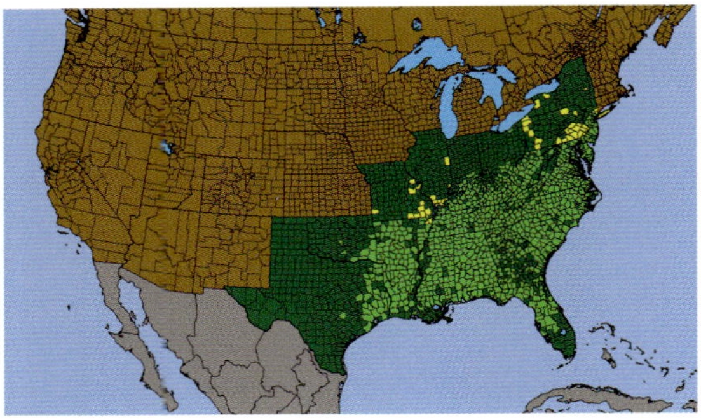

- Deciduous shrub; 6 to 10 feet.
- Late-spring to early-summer greenish flowers followed by red fruits. Red fall foliage.
- Part shade to shade; wet to moist acidic soil.
- Workhorse. Pollinated by native bees, other insects. Host to moth caterpillars.
- Deer resistant.

Euonymus americanus is a particularly important example of the need to distinguish among the various species of a genus when choosing plants. Some other kinds of euonymus (see page 26) are among the most invasive species and should be removed from gardens immediately, yet they are still frustratingly available at nurseries in many states. But if you buy only this native, you'll be rewarded with a lovely, red-twigged shrub whose red fruits and large orange seeds are some of the most attractive and distinct among native plants.

Callicarpa americana

AMERICAN BEAUTYBERRY

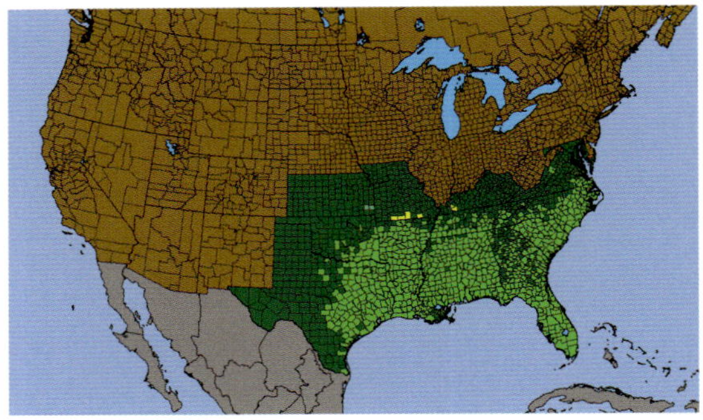

- Deciduous shrub; 3 to 6 feet.
- Summer pink flowers followed by purple berries. Yellow fall foliage.
- Sun to part shade; moist to dry soil.
- Workhorse. VHPV: Pollinated by native bees, butterflies, other insects. Host to moth caterpillars. Berries feed birds, small mammals.

The unique color of *Callicarpa americana*'s stunning bright purple berries make it a standout among North American natives. Those bright orbs, clustered at the leaf axils, persist into fall, when they complement the plant's yellow foliage and are a favorite food of the northern bobwhite. The slight downside to this exceptional beauty: Deer do love to graze the foliage.

NOTE: There is a very similar non-native, *Callicarpa japonica*, often misidentified as *Callicarpa americana*. But it's relatively easy to spot once you know what you're looking for: That plant's berries hang away from the stem, rather than wrapping around it as the native version's do.

Ribes aureum

GOLDEN CURRANT

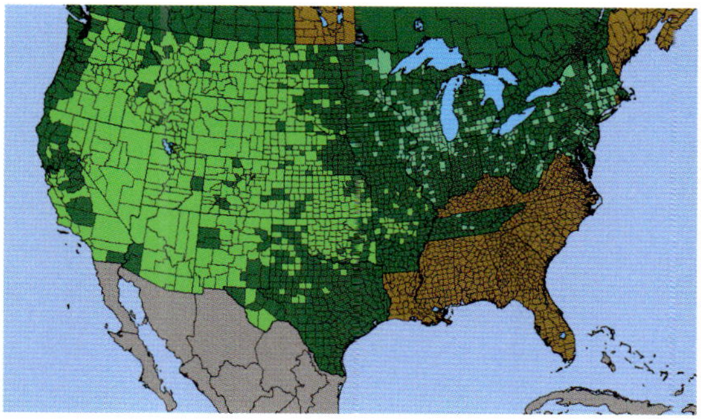

- Deciduous shrub; 3 to 10 feet.
- Spring yellow flowers followed by red to black berries.
- Sun to part shade; moist to dry soil.
- Workhorse. VHPV: Pollinated by native bees, moths, butterflies, other insects, hummingbirds. Host to moth and butterfly caterpillars. Berries feed birds, small mammals.

Virtually every description of *Ribes aureum* mentions its heady fragrance, variously described as spicy, clovy, or like vanilla, which announces this plant from a distance. After the clouds of yellow flowers with pink to white centers fade, edible berries follow. Some call them sweet and some call them tart; they're popular for cooking and preserving, but they're equally as delicious to birds and mammals as to humans, so they must be picked when just ripe—or it'll be too late.

Heteromeles arbutifolia

TOYON, CHRISTMASBERRY, CALIFORNIA HOLLY

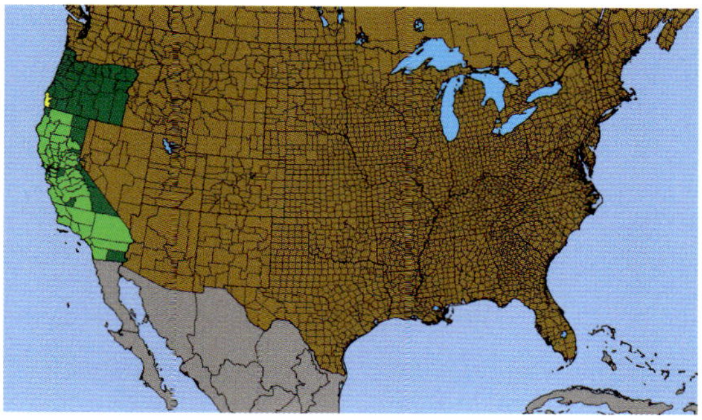

- Evergreen shrub; 5 to 15 feet.
- Spring to late-summer white flowers followed by red berries.
- Sun to shade; dry soil. Drought tolerant.
- VHPV: Pollinated by native bees, other insects, hummingbirds. Host to moth and butterfly caterpillars. Berries feed birds, small mammals.

Although it sometimes grows taller, in the garden *Heteromeles arbutifolia* typically reaches 6 to 8 feet tall and spreads 4 to 5 feet, making it a great choice for foundation beds or hedges. Prolific blooms precede plentiful, long-lasting clusters of bright red fall and winter berries, both of which stand out vividly against dark green, leathery leaves, giving the plant year-round interest.

INSTEAD OF THIS:

Pieris japonica

ANDROMEDA

Pieris is an evergreen foundation plant widely used for its relatively slow but full growth habit and its early-blooming drooping clusters of white bells. Although pieris's curving, twisting branches make it a graceful plant, it can be finicky, sometimes growing to 4 or 6 feet or more only to quickly decline and die, seemingly unsavable by a gardener's interventions.

PLANT THESE:

Eubotrys racemosus

(syn. *Leucothoe racemosa*)

SWAMP DOGHOBBLE, SWEETBELLS

CT, DC, DE, FL, GA, LA, MA, MD, MS, NC, NJ, NY, PA, RI, SC, TN, TX, VA

Kalmia latifolia

MOUNTAIN LAUREL

AL, CT, DC, DE, FL, GA, IN, KY, LA, MA, MD, ME, MS, NC, NH, NJ, NY, OH, PA, RI, SC, TN, VA, VT, WV

Vaccinium ovatum

EVERGREEN HUCKLEBERRY, CALIFORNIA HUCKLEBERRY

CA, OR, WA

Arctostaphylos glandulosa

EASTWOOD MANZANITA

CA, OR

Eubotrys racemosus

(syn. *Leucothoe racemosa*)

SWAMP DOGHOBBLE, SWEETBELLS

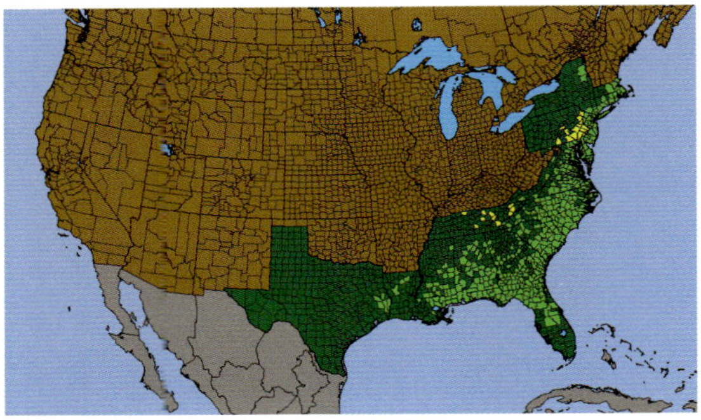

- Semi-evergreen shrub; 4 to 6 feet.
- Early-spring to late-summer white flowers. Yellow, orange, red fall foliage.
- Sun to shade; wet to moist acidic soil.
- Pollinated by native bees. Host to moth caterpillars.
- Deer resistant.

The fragrant, long-blooming flowers of *Eubotrys racemosus* bear a strong resemblance to the flowers of *Pieris japonica*, but its attractive, shiny leaves are larger and more prominent, and this plant has a more horizontal habit than Pieris. Evergreen in the southern part of its range, *E. racemosa* may be completely deciduous farther north. As its range suggests, this plant thrives in hot, humid locations. It requires consistently wet soil when planted in a sunny location.

Kalmia latifolia

MOUNTAIN LAUREL

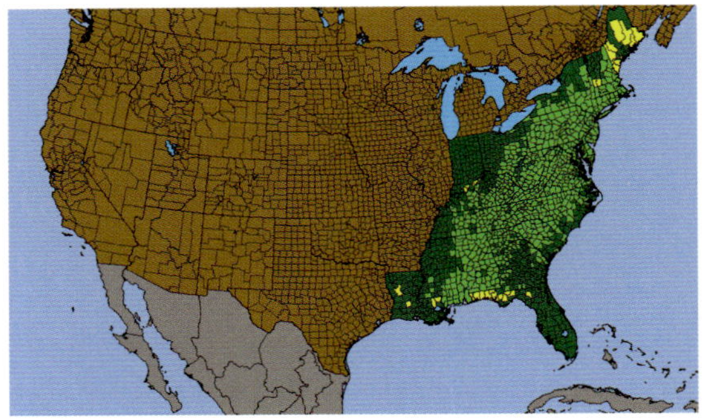

- Evergreen shrub; 5 to 15 feet.
- Spring white to pink flowers.
- Part shade to shade; moist to dry acidic soil. Drought tolerant.
- VHPV: Pollinated by native bees, butterflies, other insects, hummingbirds. Host to moth caterpillars.

One reason North American gardeners have relied on non-native evergreen shrubs is that there just aren't as many native ones. Even fewer native evergreens thrive in the shade. *Kalmia latifolia* is a great native choice for a shadier area. The abundant blossoms' fused petals pop open in spring to reveal blooms from white to pale pink with darker pink interior markings. Mountain laurel is a relatively slow grower whose irregular branching structure is sturdy enough to stay relatively formal in a foundation planting. Its eventual mature size is large, but it tolerates heavy pruning.

Vaccinium ovatum

EVERGREEN HUCKLEBERRY, CALIFORNIA HUCKLEBERRY

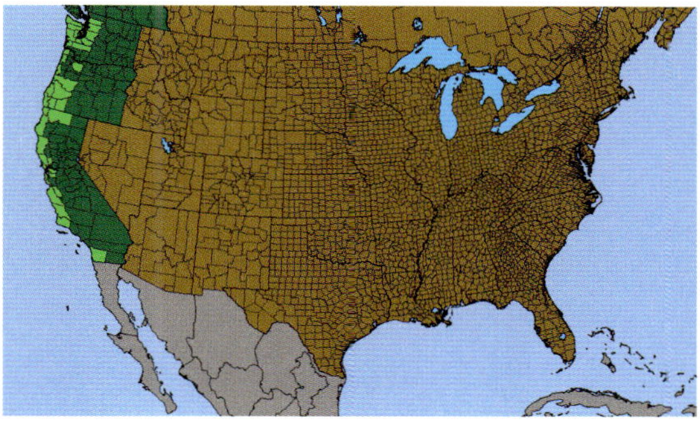

- Evergreen shrub; 2 to 8 feet.
- Spring pink flowers followed by dark blue berries.
- Sun to shade; moist to dry acidic soil.
- Workhorse.

The reddish new leaf growth of *Vaccinium ovatum* matures to a glossy, leathery green. Plants can grow to 8 feet but typically are shorter. Though this shrub is native only along the West Coast, there are other, mostly deciduous, *Vaccinium* species native elsewhere in the country that could work as a Pieris substitute.

Arctostaphylos glandulosa

EASTWOOD MANZANITA

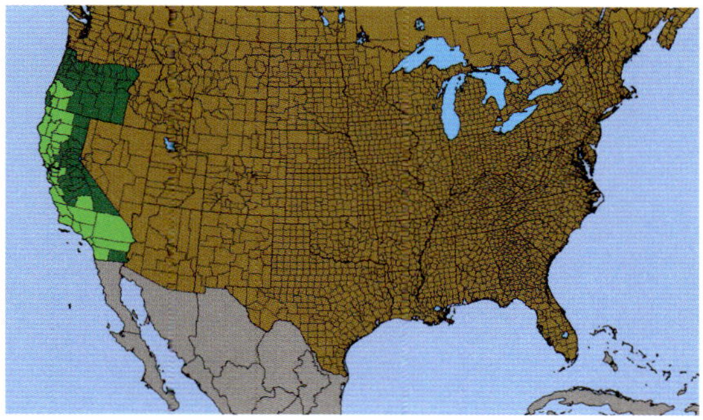

- Evergreen shrub; 3 to 8 feet.
- Winter to spring white to pink blooms followed by red fruits.
- Part shade; dry soil.
- Pollinated by native bees, other insects.

Arctostaphylos glandulosa is one of many species in a complex genus; *A. glandulosa* has one of the widest native ranges, and its erect habit, reddish stems, and velvety oval leaves make it especially good for foundation use. Some manzanita species have naturally occurring subspecies and varieties, and a number of the highly local species can be found in native plant nurseries, so it pays to consult with a local nursery to find a manzanita that will work in your garden.

More great native choices: *Swida sericea* (page 25), *Ilex opaca* (page 34), *Ribes aureum* (page 39), *Morella* spp. (pages 50–53)

INSTEAD OF THESE:

Weigela florida

WEIGELA

Abelia × grandiflora

ABELIA

Both weigela and abelia are medium-sized shrubs at maturity, grown primarily for their flowers, which bloom over a long period. Weigela's trumpet-shaped flowers in shades of pink, red, or white, along with colorful foliage ranging from green to purple, make this native of China, Japan, and Korea a foundation standard. It's adaptable to different soils, growing to 4 to 5 feet with its branches loosely arching, or pruned to a more compact shape.

Abelia shrubs typically grow 3 to 6 feet tall in acidic to neutral soil, flowering best in sunny spots. This heavily hybridized collection of semi-evergreen shrubs now listed in the honeysuckle family is known for its hardy, drought-tolerant nature and fragrant flowers that bloom throughout summer.

Without watchful, carefully timed pruning to maintain their shape, weigela and abelia may revert to their underlying parent form.

PLANT THESE:

Symphoricarpos albus

SNOWBERRY

CA, CO, DC, IA, ID, IL, MD, MI, MN, MT, ND, NE, NH, NM, NY, OH, OR, PA, SD, UT, VA, VT, WA, WI, WV, WY

Symphoricarpos orbiculatus

CORALBERRY, BUCKBRUSH

AL, AR, DC, FL, GA, IA, IL, IN, KS, KY, LA, MD, MN, MO, MS, NC, NE, OH, OK, PA, SC, SD, TN, TX, VA, WV

Diervilla lonicera

BUSH HONEYSUCKLE

AL, CT, DE, IA, IL, IN, MA, MD, ME, MI, MN, NC, ND, NH, NJ, NY, OH, PA, RI, TN, VA, VT, WI, WV

Symphoricarpos albus

SNOWBERRY

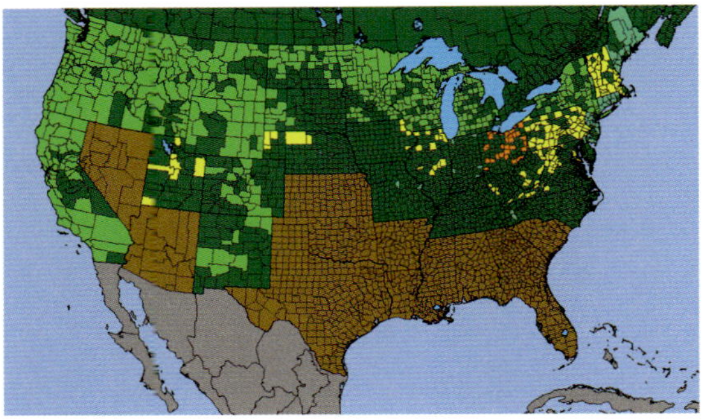

- Deciduous shrub; 2 to 6 feet.
- Spring pink to white flowers followed by white berries.
- Sun to shade; moist to dry soil.
- Workhorse. VHPV: Pollinated by native bees, butterflies, other insects, hummingbirds. Host to moth and butterfly caterpillars.

Symphoricarpos orbiculatus

CORALBERRY, BUCKBRUSH

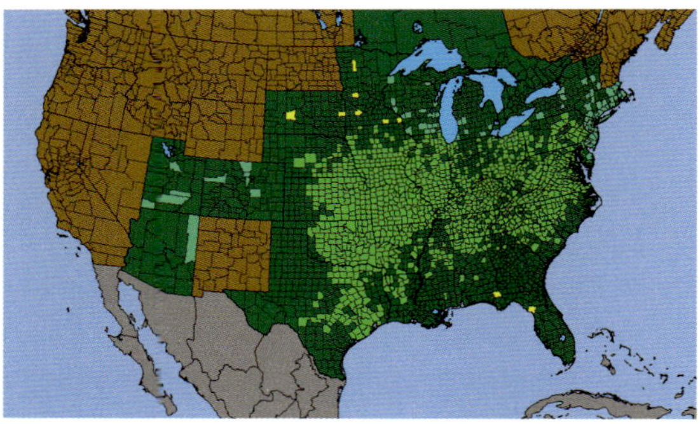

- Deciduous shrub; 2 to 4 feet.
- Late-spring to early-summer pink to white flowers followed by pink to red berries.
- Sun to part shade; moist to dry soil.
- Workhorse. VHPV: Pollinated by native bees, butterflies, other insects, hummingbirds. Host to moth and butterfly caterpillars.

It's the showy, purplish red berries that make *Symphoricarpos albus* and *S. orbiculatus* decorative substitutes for shrubs like weigela and abelia, although their wiry branches grow somewhat more sparsely. Native to slightly different ranges, coralberry and snowberry are similarly sized shrubs, both easy to care for, tolerating a wide range of light and moisture conditions, and appealing to a wide range of pollinators, including hummingbirds. The berries of *S. orbiculatus*, in particular, put on a showstopping later-season display.

Diervilla lonicera

BUSH HONEYSUCKLE

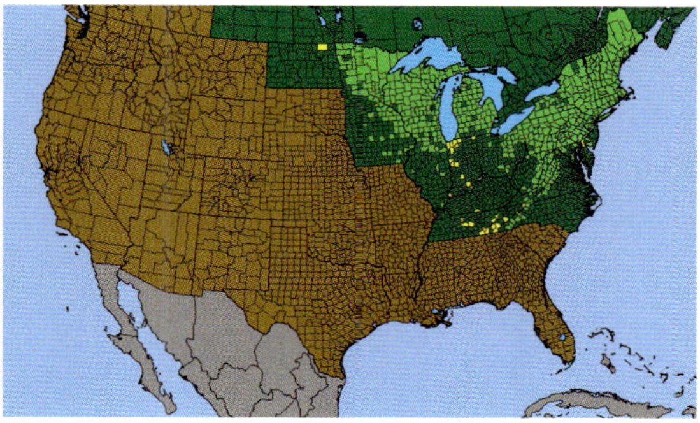

- Deciduous shrub; 2 to 4 feet.
- Late-spring to early-summer yellow flowers turning orange or red. Red fall foliage.
- Full sun to shade; moist to dry acidic soil. Drought tolerant once established.
- VHPV: Pollinated by native bees, moths, butterflies, other insects. Host to moth and butterfly caterpillars.

Although this shrub is popularly called honeysuckle, it's not in the same family as the more well-known honeysuckle shrubs and vines, many of which are invasive (see page 000). *Diervilla lonicera* may not be a long-lived shrub, but it's easy to propagate from either soft, new growth or older, hardwood cuttings, which will root quickly when in contact with soil. This habit also makes diervilla a spreading shrub. The new spring foliage is tinted red before turning fully green; some commercial varieties have been bred to keep the orange or reddish leaf color all season, but this may affect the plant's nutritional value to insects. The leaves of the straight native species turn brilliant dark red in fall. When grown in full sun, diervillas require constant moisture.

More great native choices: *Ceanothus* spp. (page 20), *Aronia melanocarpa* (page 27), *Callicarpa americana* (page 38), *Amelanchier alnifolia* (page 53)

CHAPTER TWO

The Hedge

There are two broad categories to consider when thinking about hedges: tall or short, and deciduous or evergreen. Because a hedge is such a major part of a landscape, and sometimes intended to separate or conceal, we often want it to mature quickly. That has led us to introduce non-native plants that have turned out to be more aggressive than we bargained for, and many invasives have escaped from hedges. Happily, many native plants can do the work of a hedge and provide more benefits to your yard and the local ecosystem.

Maybe you've heard arguments for avoiding monoculture planting in order to serve the broadest range of wildlife. When choosing natives, you may vary species for more benefits to the ecosystem—and for a more natural look. Remember, however, that each element of your garden is part of the larger whole. Aesthetically massed plants are pleasing to the eye and can create a calmer as well as a more formal impression. Planting a number of the same shrub can help keep the health of plants and the needs of animals who rely on them for food or shelter in balance. If using a diverse group of plants with similar cultural needs appeals to you, great. But a hedge of one sort of plant that's part of a varied garden or landscape can work, too.

INSTEAD OF THESE:

Ligustrum species

PRIVET

Privet is one of the most widely used and well-known hedge plants. It grows in sun or part shade in all but the coldest and hottest parts of the United States. It grows fast, it stands up to pollution and salt, and, in more southern regions, it's semi-evergreen. But privet is one of those plants that has been too adaptable in North America. It has escaped the bounds of gardens to become invasive, especially Chinese privet in the Southeast from Maryland west to Texas and south to Florida, where it tolerates shade and can be found deep in forests where birds have deposited its seeds, displacing local plants that offer far more benefit. Privet is on the list of noxious plants in many states and is set to be banned for sale in some. If you already have this one in your yard, strongly consider removing it.

PLANT THESE:

Morella pensylvanica

NORTHERN BAYBERRY, CANDLEBERRY

CT, DC, DE, MA, MD, ME, MI, NC, NH, NJ, NY, OH, PA, RI, VA, VT

Morella cerifera

SOUTHERN WAX MYRTLE

AL, AR, DE, FL, GA, LA, MD, MS, NC, NJ, OK, SC, TX, VA

Morella californica

PACIFIC WAX MYRTLE, PACIFIC BAYBERRY, CALIFORNIA BAYBERRY

CA, OR, WA

Amelanchier alnifolia

SASKATOON SERVICEBERRY, WESTERN SERVICEBERRY, JUNEBERRY

CA, CO, IA, ID, MN, MT, ND, NE, NV, OR, SD, UT, WA, WY

Cornus drummondii

ROUGHLEAF DOGWOOD

AL, AR, GA, IA, IL, IN, KS, KY, LA, MI, MN, MO, MS, NE, NY, OH, OK, PA, SD, TN, TX, WI

Sambucus canadensis

BLACK ELDERBERRY, AMERICAN ELDERBERRY

AL, AR, CT, DC, DE, FL, GA, IA, IL, IN, KS, KY, LA, MA, MD, ME, MI, MN, MO, MS, NC, ND, NE, NH, NJ, NY, OH, OK, PA, RI, SC, SD, TN, TX, VA, VT, WI, WV, WY

Corylus americana

AMERICAN HAZELNUT, AMERICAN FILBERT

AL, AR, CT, DC, DE, GA, IA, IL, IN, KS, KY, LA, MA, MD, ME, MI, MN, MO, MS, NC, ND, NE, NH, NJ, NY, OH, OK, PA, RI, SC, SD, TN, VA, VT, WI, WV

Corylus cornuta

BEAKED HAZELNUT, BEAKED FILBERT

AL, CA, CO, CT, DE, GA, IA, ID, IL, MA, MD, ME, MI, MN, MO, NC, ND, NH, NJ, NY, OH, OR, PA, RI, SC, SD, TN, VA, VT, WA, WI, WV, WY

Morella pensylvanica

NORTHERN BAYBERRY, CANDLEBERRY

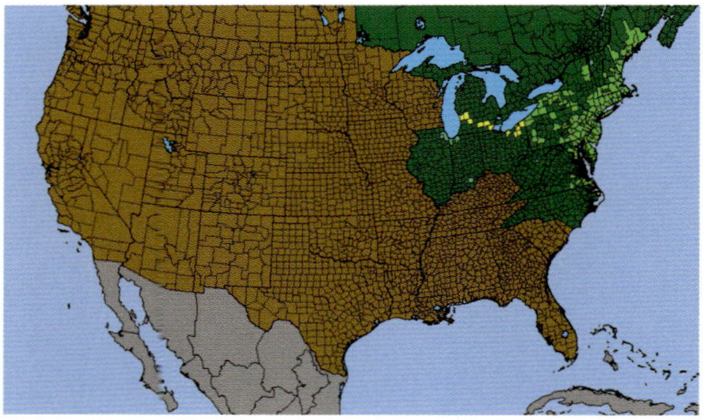

- Deciduous to semi-evergreen shrub; 3 to 6 feet.
- Spring insignificant flowers followed by gray-blue berries.
- Sun to part shade. Wet to dry soil. Drought and salt tolerant.
- Workhorse. Host to moth caterpillars.
- Deer resistant.

Morella cerifera

SOUTHERN WAX MYRTLE

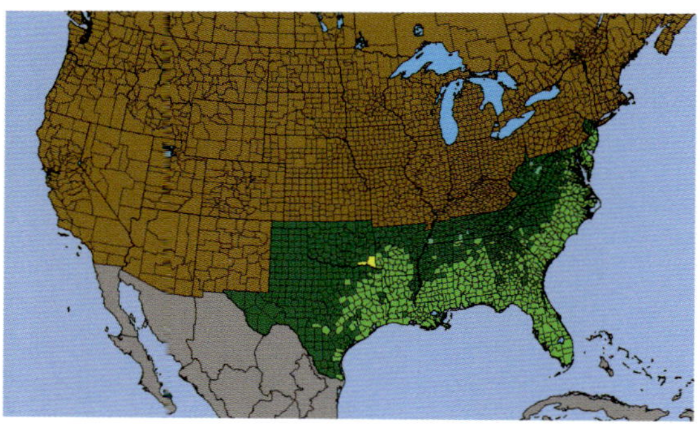

- Evergreen shrub; 8 to 12 feet.
- Spring insignificant flowers followed by gray-blue berries.
- Sun to part shade. Wet to dry soil. Drought and salt tolerant.
- Workhorse. Pollinated by native bees. Host to moth and butterfly caterpillars. Berries feed birds.
- Deer resistant.

Morella californica

PACIFIC WAX MYRTLE, PACIFIC BAYBERRY, CALIFORNIA BAYBERRY

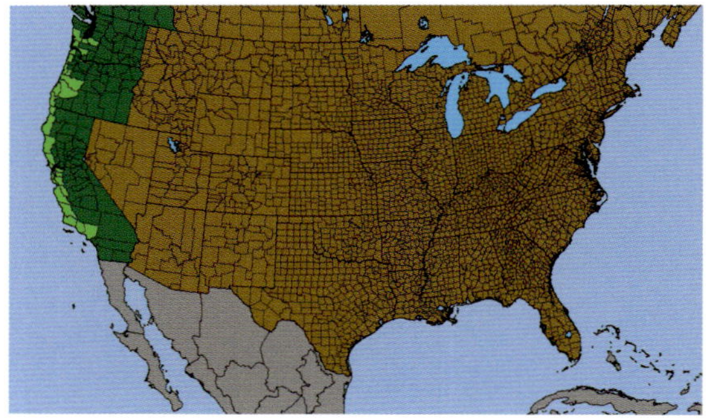

- Evergreen shrub; 6 to 20 feet.
- Summer insignificant flowers followed by purple berries.
- Sun to part shade; wet to moist soils. Salt tolerant.
- Workhorse. Host to moth and butterfly caterpillars.
- Deer resistant.

Morella is a group of shrubs and small trees native to several regions. The leaves, when crushed, have a distinct spicy, and some say mood-elevating, fragrance.

In the Northeast, *M. pensylvanica*, commonly known as northern bayberry, is an ideal substitute for a privet hedge because of its dense, compact growth habit. It can handle a wide range of soils and is drought tolerant, so it's especially useful in coastal gardens. *M. pensylvanica* may retain some of its leaves in the southern part of its zone. The berries' wax coating is high in fat and protein, which makes bayberries an especially attractive source of nutrition to wildlife.

In the mid-Atlantic and across the South, *M. cerifera* is similar to northern bayberry, with a somewhat taller and wider mature size and evergreen leaves. This is the plant from which bayberry candles are made. Both *M. pensylvanica* and *M. cerifera* are dioecious, with male and female plants needed for pollination and berries appearing only on female plants.

M. californica is the only monoecious variety in the *Morella* genus, with male and female flowers on the same plant. The color of the berries is somewhat variable, perhaps because of their variable wax content. Although it is fragrant, this taller relative of eastern bayberries isn't used for candle making. Its shape is more rounded than that of its eastern relatives.

Amelanchier alnifolia

SASKATOON SERVICEBERRY, WESTERN SERVICEBERRY, JUNEBERRY

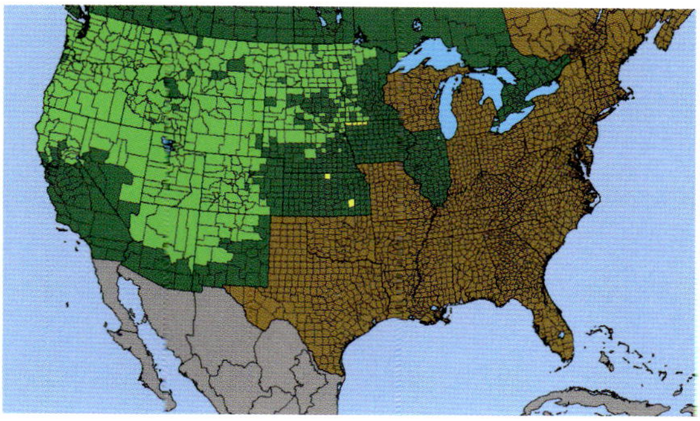

- Deciduous shrub; 4 to 10 feet.
- Spring to summer white flowers followed by purple berries. Yellow to red fall foliage.
- Sun to part shade; moist to dry soil.
- Workhorse. HPV: Pollinated by native bees, butterflies, other insects. Host to moth and butterfly caterpillars.

Amelanchier species appear across some part of all forty-eight contiguous states, and they are amazingly valuable plants—beautiful berries, flowers, and foliage, with many benefits to wildlife and the environment. In the West, *A. alnifolia* has an upright habit that makes it a good privet hedge replacement; it's also easily shaped or renewed by pruning. It's covered in delicate, fragrant white blossoms in early spring; these are followed by berries that ripen from red to blue and are delicious to humans, other mammals, and birds alike. While all amelanchier berries are edible, *A. alnifolia* are consistently described as among the most delicious of wild berries.

Cornus drummondii

ROUGHLEAF DOGWOOD

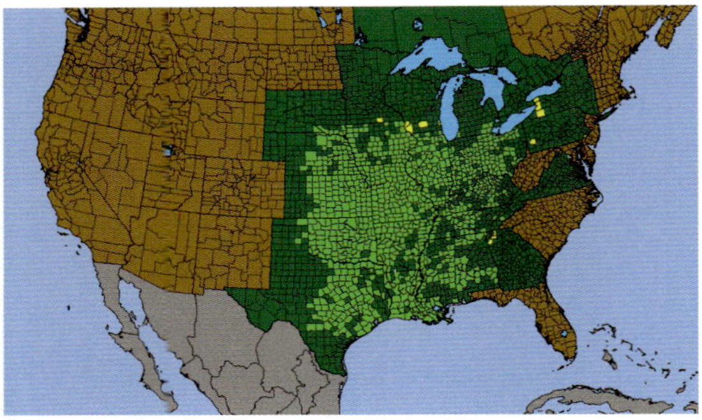

- Deciduous shrub; 8 to 15 feet.
- Spring white flowers followed by white berries. Red fall foliage.
- Sun to part shade; wet to dry soils.
- HPV: Pollinated by native bees, butterflies, other insects. Host to moth caterpillars. Berries feed birds, mammals.

Cornus drummondii grows as a multistemmed shrub or small tree, with the long, oval, deeply veined leaves typical of the genus. Its suckering habit can be useful for filling in a hedge, and unwanted suckers are easily pruned. Roughleaf dogwood is a four-season standout, with creamy white flat flower heads followed by white berries and burgundy fall foliage; in winter, the reddish brown to gray branches take center stage.

Sambucus canadensis

BLACK ELDERBERRY, AMERICAN ELDERBERRY

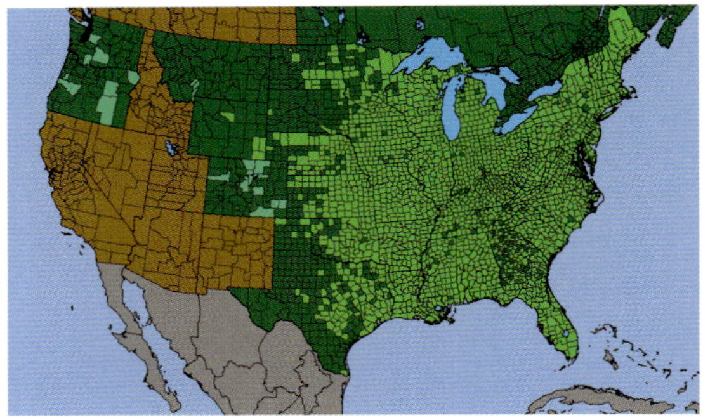

- Deciduous shrub; 5 to 10 feet.
- Spring white flowers followed by dark berries.
- Sun to part shade; wet to dry soil.
- Workhorse. VHPV: Pollinated by native bees, moths, butterflies, other insects. Host to moth caterpillars. Berries feed birds, mammals.

Sambucus canadensis is a widely native plant that grows in a variety of conditions *and* is durable *and* of very high value to pollinators and to wildlife *and* produces antioxidant-rich berries prized by wildlife and delicious to humans. (Note that the reddish black fruits—technically drupes rather than berries—must be cooked for human consumption.) Wildlife browses the young plants aggressively, so it's good practice to protect them for a few years with cages until they can tolerate some munching. The shrubs' unwanted suckers can be pruned. Left unpruned, the plants form thickets.

Corylus americana

AMERICAN HAZELNUT, AMERICAN FILBERT

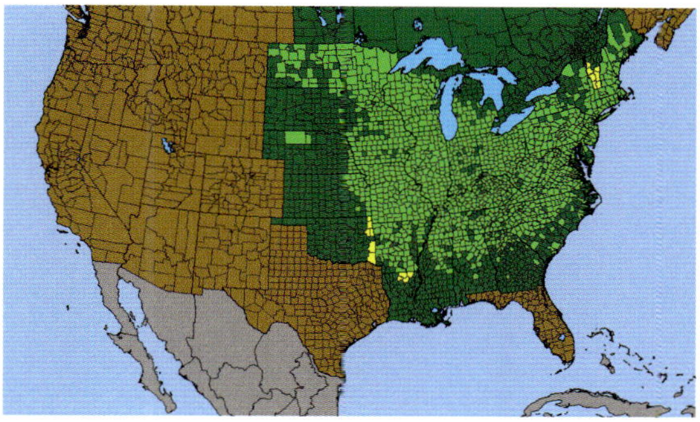

- Deciduous shrub; 5 to 12 feet.
- Late-winter to early-spring yellowish male catkins, inconspicuous red female flowers, followed by husked nuts. Bright yellow to deep red fall foliage.
- Part shade to shade; moist to dry soil.
- Workhorse. Host to moth caterpillars. Nuts feed birds, mammals.

Corylus cornuta

BEAKED HAZELNUT, BEAKED FILBERT

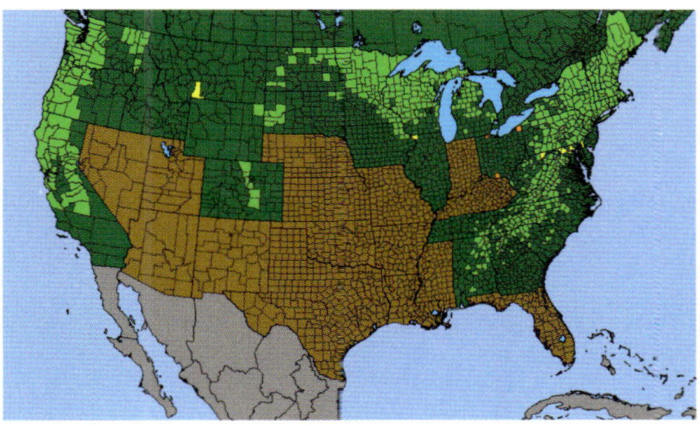

- Deciduous shrub or small tree; 5 to 14 feet.
- Late-winter to early-spring yellowish male catkins, inconspicuous red female flowers, followed by husked nuts. Bright yellow to deep red fall color.
- Part shade to shade; moist to dry soil.
- Host to moth and butterfly caterpillars. Nuts feed birds, mammals.

These two corylus forms grow quickly, with an upright arching form and spreading habit. Both are also adaptable to an especially wide variety of light and soil conditions. The catkins are followed by edible nuts, both of which are covered in a distinct extended husk. *Corylus americana*'s husk is fringed, almost fluffy; *C. cornuta* has a longer, pointier husk. Squirrels and turkeys (and other large birds) love the nuts, so it takes some vigilance to harvest them—but if you're looking for a plant to support bigger birds and small mammals, you can't ask for better.

More great native choices: *Ceanothus* spp. (page 20), *Ilex glabra* (page 20), *Physocarpus* spp. (page 24), *Frangula californica* (page 35), *Heteromeles arbutifolia* (page 39), *Cephalanthus occidentalis* (page 92), *Prunus virginiana* (page 213)

INSTEAD OF THESE:

Prunus laurocerasus

CHERRY LAUREL

Cupressus × leylandii

LEYLAND CYPRESS

Non-native *Taxus* species

JAPANESE YEW, ENGLISH YEW

Euonymus japonicus

JAPANESE EUONYMUS

Because the shrubs or trees of a hedge are on view year-round, a number of non-native evergreens have shared popularity as the go-to plants for defining boundaries or creating privacy.

Cherry laurel is densely evergreen, it will grow in shade and even in the woods, and it doesn't mind dry soil. But these qualities allow it to escape gardens and displace native plants.

Most often used where a tall screen is wanted, Leyland cypress can grow 3 to 4 feet a year and reach 70 feet at maturity. Balancing that quick-fix appeal is its susceptibility to fungus, canker, and needle blight, which tend to occur when plants grow close together—which they inevitably do in a hedge, given this plant's growth rate.

Long-lived plants, these yews require pruning to keep them from outgrowing garden spaces.

The evergreen *Euonymus japonicus* has an almost stereotypically shrubby shape with dense growth and shade tolerance that has made it a go-to plant for screening and privacy; it's an otherwise unremarkable plant.

PLANT THESE:

Thuja occidentalis

ARBORVITAE, NORTHERN WHITE CEDAR

CT, IL, IN, KY, MA, MD, ME, MI, MN, NH, NJ, NY, OH, RI, TN, VA, VT, WI, WV

Taxus canadensis

CANADA YEW, AMERICAN YEW

CT, IA, IL, IN, KY, MA, MD, ME, MI, MN, NC, NH, NJ, NY, OH, PA, RI, TN, VA, VT, WI, WV

Juniperus virginiana

EASTERN RED CEDAR

AL, AR, CO, CT, DC, DE, FL, GA, IA, IL, IN, KS, KY, LA, MA, MD, ME, MI, MN, MO, MS, NC, ND, NE, NH, NJ, NY, OH, OK, PA, RI, SC, SD, TN, TX, VA, VT, WA, WI, WV

Taxus brevifolia

PACIFIC YEW

CA, ID, MT, OR, WA

Thuja occidentalis

ARBORVITAE, NORTHERN WHITE CEDAR

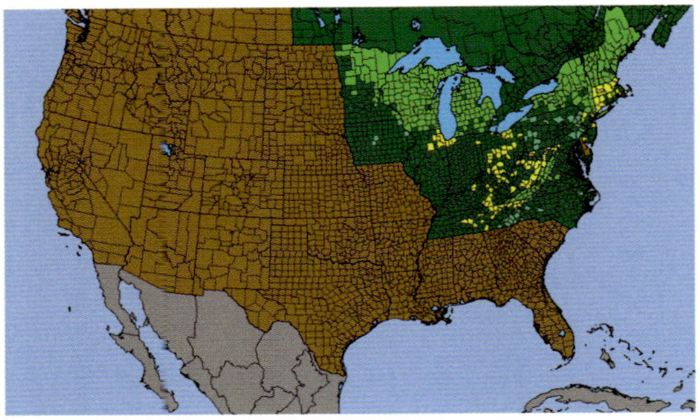

- Evergreen tree; 20 to 30 feet.
- Spring inconspicuous flowers followed by small, brownish cones.
- Sun to part shade; wet to moist soil.
- Workhorse. Host to moth and butterfly caterpillars.

Thuja occidentalis is highly aromatic and fast growing. It has a pyramidal form, and a row—or sometimes two, staggered—of arborvitae will soon make an impressive formal boundary or privacy screen. The bright green leaves are browsed by deer, particularly in winter, when evergreens are the primary food source, which sometimes results in a bare lower trunk where deer pressure is high. Making *T. occidentalis* one element of a mixed hedge is a good way to address this issue.

Juniperus virginiana

EASTERN RED CEDAR

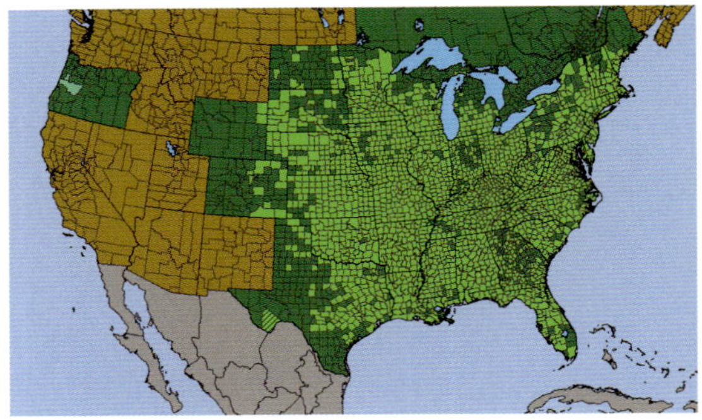

- Evergreen tree; 30 feet.
- Spring insignificant flowers followed by berrylike cones.
- Sun to part shade; dry soil. Drought tolerant.
- Workhorse. Host to moth and butterfly caterpillars.
- Deer resistant.

Juniperus virginiana makes a great evergreen hedge or screen, but due to its ultimate mature size, it is not suitable for tight spaces. Although eastern red cedar grows tall when left to its own devices, it can be pruned for size and shape in spring before new growth emerges. The flowers, leaves, and fruit—small dark blue cones with a berrylike appearance—are all aromatic, with a fragrance often described as piney or peppery. Junipers are dioecious; male and female plants are required for pollination. The cedar waxwing, which feasts on the fruit, is named for this plant.

Taxus canadensis

CANADA YEW, AMERICAN YEW

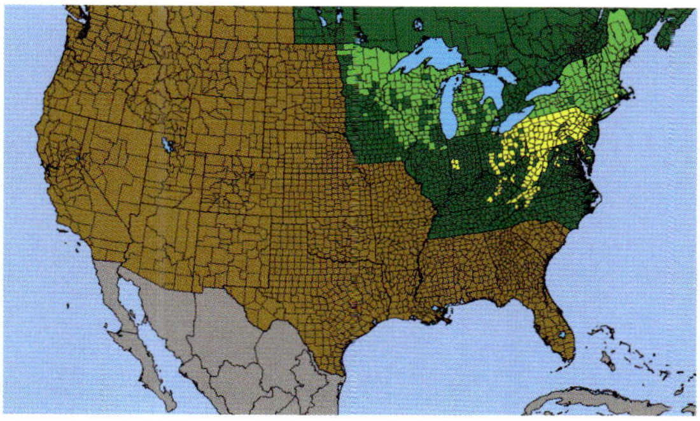

- Evergreen shrub; 3 to 5 feet.
- Spring inconspicuous yellow flowers followed by red, berrylike cones.
- Sun to shade; moist to dry soil.

Taxus brevifolia

PACIFIC YEW

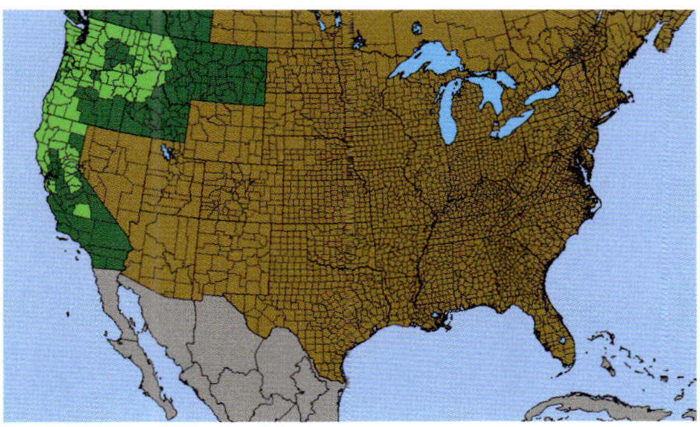

- Evergreen tree; 10 to 40 feet.
- Spring inconspicuous yellow spring flowers followed by red, berrylike cones.
- Shade to part shade; moist to dry soil.
- Host to moth caterpillars.

Taxus canadensis looks like its introduced relatives but is much smaller at maturity. *T. brevifolia* is closer to its overseas cousins in mature size than *T. canadensis*, and it tolerates pruning well; it can even be cut back to the ground if serious reshaping is wanted. Yews do well where there's low to no deer or moose pressure. They are a favorite food of both these animals, though, so where they browse, consider installing cages or deer fencing, or try another native alternative.

More great native choices: *Mahonia aquifolium* (page 21), *Ilex opaca* (page 34), *Juniperus scopulorum* (page 34), *Morella* spp. (pages 50–53)

INSTEAD OF THIS:

Forsythia

Fast-growing forsythia is one of the first shrubs to bloom every year, with its yellow flowers appearing even before leaves. Forsythia is not picky about soil or light, tolerating some shade, and can withstand hard pruning after blooming. It also spreads via stolons, and because its branches will root wherever they touch the ground, it's potentially invasive in some areas, crowding out more beneficial natives.

PLANT THESE:

Hamamelis virginiana

COMMON WITCH HAZEL

AL, AR, CT, DC, DE, FL, GA, IA, IL, IN, KY, LA, MA, MD, ME, MI, MN, MO, MS, NC, NH, NJ, NY, OH, OK, PA, RI, SC, TN, TX, VA, VT, WI, WV

Lindera benzoin

SPICEBUSH

AL, AR, CT, DC, DE, FL, GA, IA, IL, IN, KS, KY, LA, MA, MD, ME, MI, MO, MS, NC, NH, NJ, NY, OH, OK, PA, RI, SC, TN, TX, VA, VT, WV

Hamamelis virginiana
COMMON WITCH HAZEL

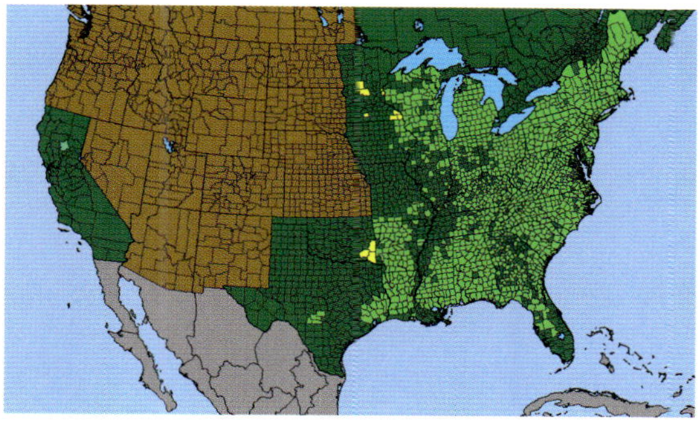

- Deciduous shrub/tree; 12 to 20 feet.
- Late-fall yellow flowers.
- Sun to shade; moist to dry soil.
- Workhorse. HPV: Pollinated by native bees, moths, other insects. Host to moth caterpillars.

From late fall into early winter, when there's little other color, *Hamamelis virginiana* lights up the garden with its fragrant, yellow, ribbonlike blooms—a bright reminder of things to come. It's also a valuable source of nectar for insects when virtually no other plants are blooming. This highly adaptable plant grows in a variety of soils and light conditions but dislikes very dry soil in full sun. It's easily pruned to stay in scale in a garden setting.

Lindera benzoin
SPICEBUSH

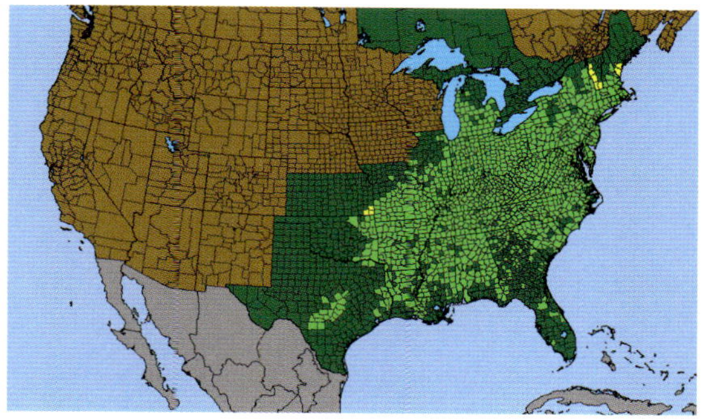

- Deciduous shrub; 6 to 15 feet.
- Early-spring yellow flowers followed by red berries. Fall yellow foliage.
- Sun to shade; wet to moist soil.
- Workhorse. VHPV: Pollinated by native bees, butterflies, other insects. Host to moth and butterfly caterpillars.

The small yellow blooms of *Lindera benzoin* appear up and down its bare stems, announcing spring's arrival before the plants leaf out. Small red berries sometimes follow, but the real pleasures of this shrub are its citrusy twigs and leaves and its bright fall foliage. *L. benzoin* is dioecious; both male and female plants flower, but the two must be present for berries to appear on the female plants later in the season. Spicebush plants are rarely tagged for sex at the nursery, so the best way to guarantee berry production is to plant several shrubs.

More great native choices: *Ribes aureum* (page 39); *Amelanchier alnifolia* (page 53)

INSTEAD OF THESE:

Phyllostachys, *Bambusa*, and *Fargesia* species

BAMBOO

American gardeners were initially attracted to bamboo's rapid growth and adaptability to various soils and light conditions, but these three species are now widely acknowledged to be destructive, taking over landscapes and invading driveways, homes, and roads. Some nurseries have addressed this by promoting clumping bamboos, but these non-natives do not contribute much, if anything, to local ecosystems. Running bamboos are generally used in Zones 5 to 8, and some clumping bamboos (*Fargesia* spp.) are hardy to Zone 4. Here are some native grasses that provide a look and screening effect similar to bamboos; for a more traditional shrub alternative, consider the recommendations elsewhere in this chapter.

PLANT THESE:

Andropogon gerardi

BIG BLUESTEM

Throughout the contiguous US, except CA, ID, NV, OR, WA

Sorghastrum nutans

INDIAN GRASS

Throughout the contiguous US, except CA, ID, NV, OR, WA

Andropogon gerardi
BIG BLUESTEM

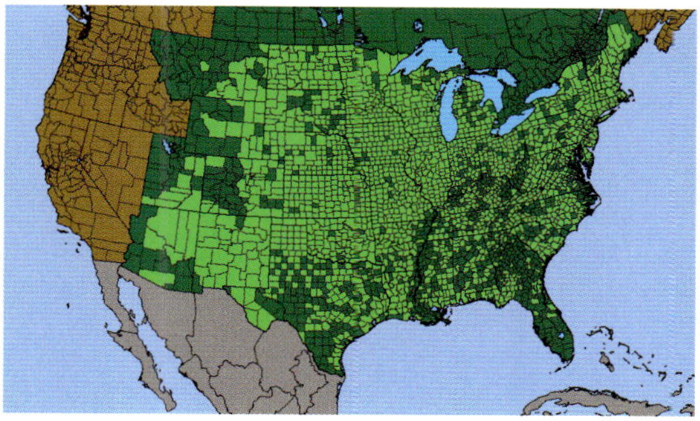

- Deciduous grass; 4 to 8 feet.
- Late-summer to fall seed heads. Red fall foliage.
- Sun to part shade; moist to dry soil. Drought tolerant.
- Workhorse. HPV: Feeds butterflies. Host to moth and butterfly caterpillars.
- Deer resistant.

This widely native grass grows in a bunching habit, which makes it well suited for garden settings. It self-sows freely, so is best used where some spreading is acceptable. The blue-green foliage is topped by ornamental seed heads in late summer and turns deep red in fall, persisting through winter and providing late-season interest in the garden.

Sorghastrum nutans
INDIAN GRASS

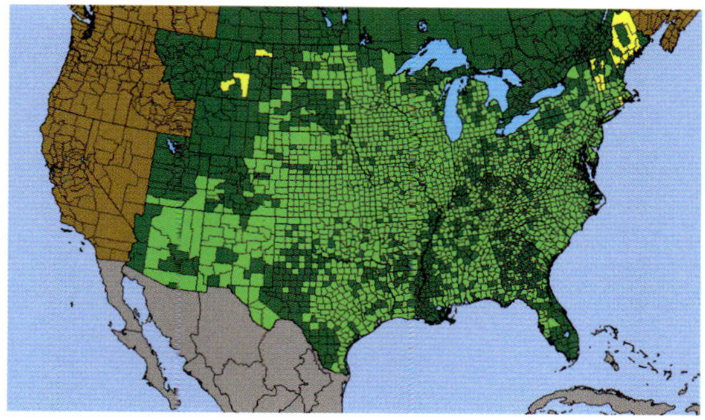

- Deciduous grass; 3 to 8 feet.
- Late-summer to fall seed heads. Yellow fall foliage.
- Sun; moist to dry soil.
- Workhorse. Host to moth and butterfly caterpillars.
- Deer resistant.

This long-lived warm-season grass is most distinguished by its showy late-summer flowers, which feature bright yellow stamens. The show's second act is in the tall, feathery, golden brown seed heads. It self-sows, which makes it best for a site where some spreading is okay. The blue-green summer foliage turns a warm gold in fall.

More great native choices: *Swida sericea* (page 25), *Heteromeles arbutifolia* (page 39), *Morella* spp. (pages 50–53)

INSTEAD OF THIS:

Non-native *Rosa* species

SHRUB ROSES

Roses have long been considered the most classic of garden plants. They offer a profusion of fragrant blooms and continuous color throughout the growing season along with a tolerance of pruning that has made them useful for low hedges. There are varieties that grow in every zone of the contiguous United States. Most of the modern roses sold for gardens, however, are hybrids and have been manipulated. One of the most common manipulations is selective breeding that transforms the flower's reproductive organs into petals—usually rendering them sterile and non–pollen producing, so of no value to pollinators. Commercial non-native roses are also typically high maintenance plants, requiring heavy use of fertilizers and pesticides to grow and bloom well and not succumb to fungal diseases or pests (many of which, like the Japanese beetle, are also non-native). Luckily, there are roses native to almost every part of North America.

PLANT THESE:

Rosa carolina

CAROLINA ROSE, PASTURE ROSE

AL, AR, CT, DC, DE, FL, GA, IA, ID, IL, IN, KS, KY, LA, MA, ME, MI, MN, MO, MS, NC, NE, NH, NJ, NY, OH, OK, PA, RI, SC, TN, TX, VA, VT, WI, WV

Rosa arkansana

ARKANSAS ROSE, PRAIRIE ROSE

AR, CO, DC, IA, ID, IL, IN, KS, MI, MN, MO, MT, ND, NE, NM, OH, OK, SD, TX, WI, WY

Rosa woodsii

WOODS' ROSE, WESTERN WILD ROSE

AZ, CA, CO, IA, ID, KS, MN, MT, ND, NE, NM, NV, OK, OR, SD, TX, UT, WA, WI, WY

Rosa carolina

CAROLINA ROSE, PASTURE ROSE

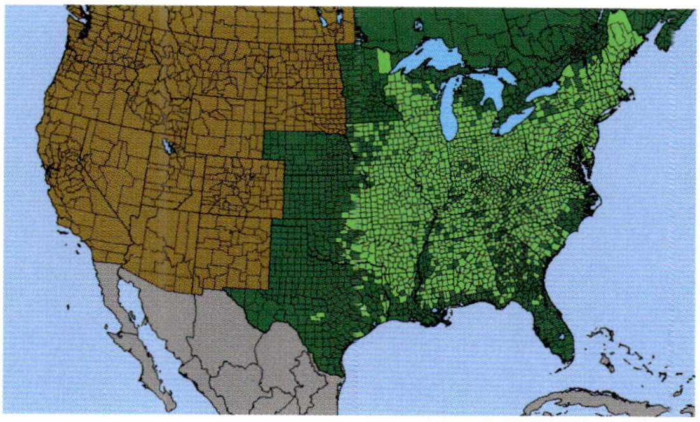

- Deciduous shrub; 3 to 6 feet.
- Late-spring to summer pink flowers followed by red rose hips in fall.
- Sun to part shade; moist to dry soil.
- Workhorse. VHPV: Pollinated by native bees, moths, butterflies, other insects. Host to moth and butterfly caterpillars. Rose hips feed birds, mammals.

Rosa arkansana

ARKANSAS ROSE, PRAIRIE ROSE

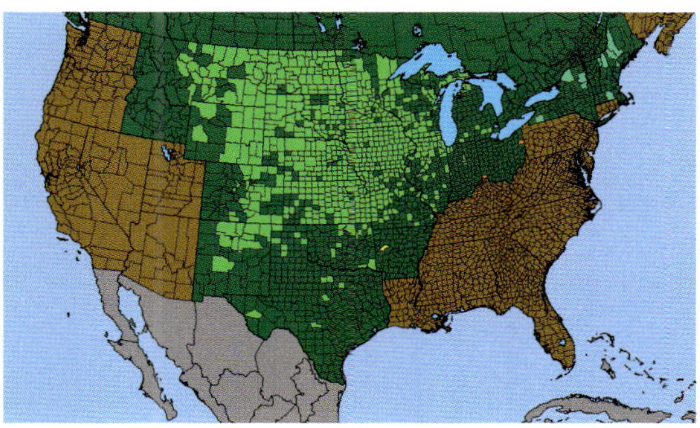

- Deciduous shrub; 2 to 5 feet.
- Late-spring to summer pink flowers followed by red rose hips in fall.
- Sun to part shade; moist to dry soil.
- Workhorse. VHPV: Pollinated by native bees, moths, butterflies, other insects. Rose hips feed birds, mammals.

Rosa woodsii

WOODS' ROSE, WESTERN WILD ROSE

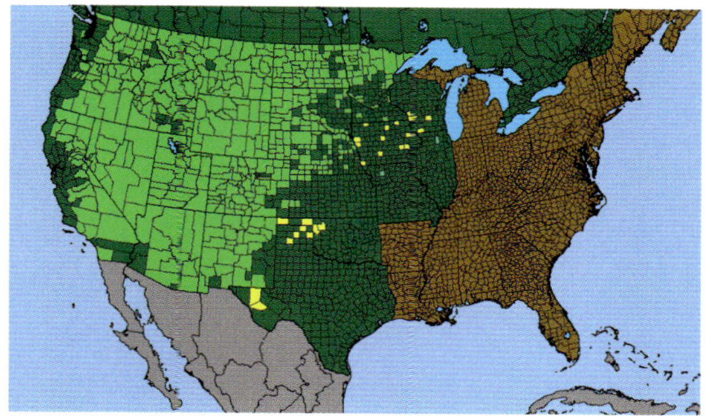

- Deciduous shrub; 3 to 6 feet.
- Late-spring to summer pink flowers followed by red rose hips in fall.
- Sun to part shade; moist to dry soil.
- Workhorse. VHPV: Pollinated by native bees, butterflies, other insects, hummingbirds. Host to moth and butterfly caterpillars. Rose hips feed birds, mammals.

Generally looser and more relaxed in form than non-natives, locally native roses typically offer long bloom times and lifespans, as well as liberation from high maintenance and the high risk of plant failure found with most introduced roses. The natives' single flowers, blooming in colors ranging from white to deep pink and exuding a soft classic rose fragrance, will win you over to their more subtle charms. Many native rose species are available nationwide; the ones shown here represent some of the most widely native and adaptable species in a variety of ranges.

More great native choices: *Rosa blanda* (page 67), *R. nutkana* (page 67)

INSTEAD OF THESE:

Rosa rugosa

RUGOSA ROSE, BEACH ROSE

Rosa multiflora

MULTIFLORA ROSE

Both of these roses were initially introduced for their thicket-forming value, deer-detering thorns, and ornamental appeal. In the case of *Rosa rugosa*, its ability to withstand salt spray and poor soils led to wide adaptation among coastal gardeners. *R. rugosa* prefers acidic soil and is found mainly in the Northeast and Pacific Northwest, where it has become highly invasive, taking over shorelines and roadsides. Similarly, *R. multiflora* has overtaken roadsides, meadows, and woodlands. Amazingly, while these plants are listed as invasive and banned from commerce in several states, many nurseries continue to offer them for sale. The popular appeal of *R. rugosa* has even kept it from being banned in states where it has been identified as noxious.

PLANT THESE:

Rubus odoratus

PURPLE-FLOWERING RASPBERRY, THIMBLEBERRY

AL, CT, DC, DE, GA, IL, IN, KY, MA, MD, ME, MI, NC, NH, NJ, NY, OH, PA, RI, TN, VA, VT, WI, WV

Rosa blanda

MEADOW ROSE, SMOOTH WILD ROSE

CT, IA, IL, IN, KS, MA, MD, ME, MI, MN, MO, MS, MT, ND, NE, NH, NJ, NY, OH, PA, SD, VA, VT, WI, WV

Rosa nutkana

NOOTKA ROSE

CA, CO, ID, MT, NM, NV, OR, UT, WA, WY

Rubus odoratus

PURPLE-FLOWERING RASPBERRY, THIMBLEBERRY

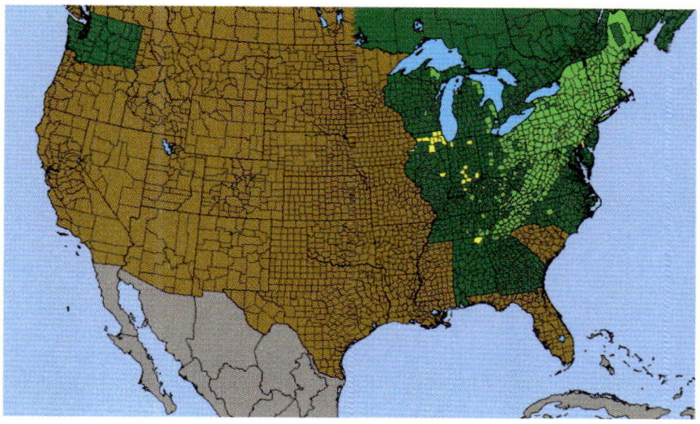

- Deciduous shrub; 3 to 6 feet.
- Late-spring to early-summer pink flowers followed by red to purple berries in late summer. Yellow fall foliage.
- Sun to shade; moist to dry soil.
- VHPV: Feeds bees, moths, butterflies, and other insects. Host to moth caterpillars.
- Deer resistant.

In the Northeast, where *Rosa rugosa* is prolific, especially along shorelines, perhaps the best native replacement is not a rose at all but the local *Rubus odoratus*. Its large, fragrant blooms, ranging from true pink to almost purple, stand out among its fellow *Rubus* species for their size and vivid color. The purple-flowering raspberry's large, deep green leaves are also unusually attractive, and it produces edible fruits, too. Like *R. rugosa*, this plant has a dense growth habit and prickly stems that provide protective cover for birds and make it resistant to deer.

> **More great native choices:** *Rosa arkansana* (page 65), *Rosa carolina* (page 65), *Rosa woodsii* (page 65)

Rosa blanda

MEADOW ROSE, SMOOTH WILD ROSE

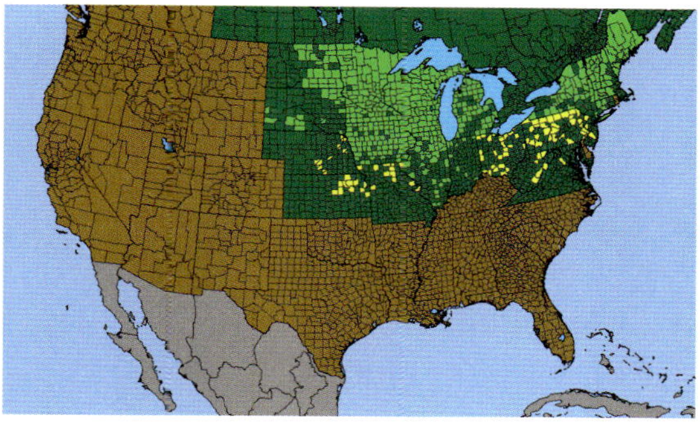

- Deciduous shrub; 2 to 6 feet.
- Late-spring to early-summer pink flowers.
- Full sun; moist to dry soil.
- VHPV: Feeds bees, moths, butterflies, other insects. Host to moth and butterfly caterpillars.

Rosa nutkana

NOOTKA ROSE

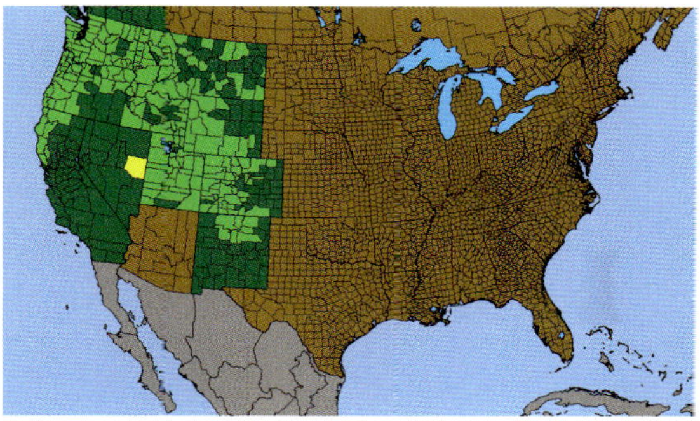

- Deciduous shrub; 3 to 9 feet.
- Spring to early-summer pink flowers.
- Sun to part shade; moist to dry soil.
- VHPV: Feeds bees, moths, butterflies, other insects. Host to moth and butterfly caterpillars.

Both of these native roses feature large, fragrant pink blooms. Flowers are followed by attractive edible rose hips loved by birds and mammals.

CHAPTER THREE

The Entrance Garden and Mixed Border

If the foundation garden exists to mask and soften the place where a building meets the earth, the entrance garden's role is a little broader. Its shape is less rigidly defined, and it may include areas along a walkway or driveway. While there's no single way to plant an entrance garden, it typically has a wider mix of plants than a foundation garden, with more perennials and more variation in the size and texture of plants. It may include a mix of small and large shrubs, perennials, ground covers, and even trees.

A border garden may mark a boundary, but we also use the term for any long garden bed. Once upon a time, a formal border garden might have been almost entirely perennial plants, but the mixed border, with many shrubs among perennials in groups or in drifts, is more modern and lower maintenance. This approach suits a native plant garden especially well. As Douglas Tallamy writes in *The Layered Landscape*, a natural landscape has plants at a variety of levels from the tallest trees to the lowest ground covers. This arrangement supports animals who live at all those heights. By planting densely, as discussed on page 7, you'll make the garden that much more low maintenance, as specimens support one another and crowd out the weeds.

INSTEAD OF THIS:

Buddleja davidii

BUTTERFLY BUSH

"But my butterfly bush is covered with butterflies!" is a common defense of these fragrant, showy, but invasive shrubs. Considerable research suggests that while the plant's nectar attracts insects, including butterflies, it is of lower nutritive value than that of the locally native plants with which North American insects, including butterflies, coevolved. The butterfly bush produces panicles of buds in white, pink, or purple on arching branches, which must be pruned in late winter or early spring to keep from getting spindly or out of bounds. Sterile varieties that are promoted as "not invasive" produce no nectar, so they are definitely not feeding pollinators.

PLANT THESE:

Eutrochium fistulosum

JOE-PYE WEED, TALL JOE-PYE WEED

AL, AR, CT, DC, DE, FL, GA, IL, IN, KY, LA, MA, MD, ME, MI, MO, MS, NC, NH, NJ, NY, OH, OK, PA, RI, SC, TN, TX, VA, WV

Eutrochium maculatum

SPOTTED JOE-PYE WEED

AZ, CO, CT, GA, IA, ID, IL, IN, KS, KY, MA, MD, ME, MI, MN, MO, MT, NC, ND, NE, NH, NJ, NM, NY, OH, PA, RI, SC, SD, TN, UT, VA, VT, WA, WI, WV, WY

Clethra alnifolia

SUMMERSWEET, SWEET PEPPERBUSH

AL, CT, DE, FL, GA, LA, MA, MD, ME, MS, NC, NH, NJ, NY, PA, RI, SC, TN, TX, VA, VT

Itea virginica

VIRGINIA SWEETSPIRE

AL, AR, DC, DE, FL, GA, IL, IN, KY, LA, MD, MO, MS, NC, NJ, OK, PA, SC, TN, TX, VA

Asclepias incarnata

SWAMP MILKWEED, PINK MILKWEED

Throughout the contiguous US, except CA, WA

Asclepias speciosa

SHOWY MILKWEED

AZ, CA, CO, IA, ID, IL, KS, MI, MN, MT, ND, NE, NM, NV, OK, OR, SD, TX, UT, WA, WI, WY

Amorpha canescens

LEADPLANT

AR, CO, IA, IL, IN, KS, MI, MN, MO, MT, ND, NE, NM, OK, SD, TX, WI, WY

Eutrochium fistulosum

JOE-PYE WEED, TALL JOE-PYE WEED

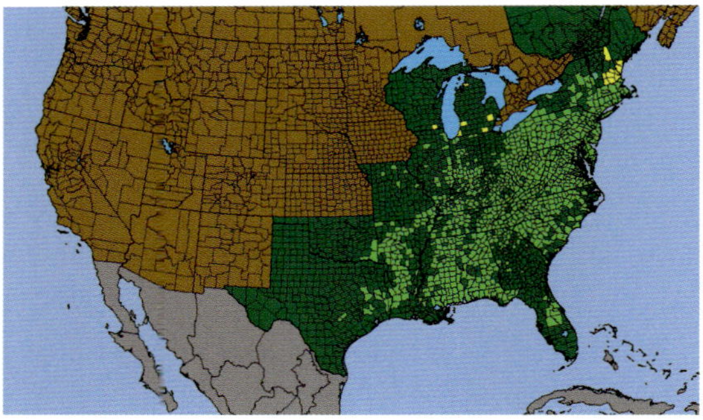

- Herbaceous perennial; 3 to 8 feet.
- Late-summer to early-fall pink flowers.
- Sun to part shade; wet to moist acidic soil.
- Workhorse. VHPV: Pollinated by native bees, butterflies (including monarchs), other insects. Host to moth caterpillars.
- Deer resistant.

Eutrochium maculatum

SPOTTED JOE-PYE WEED

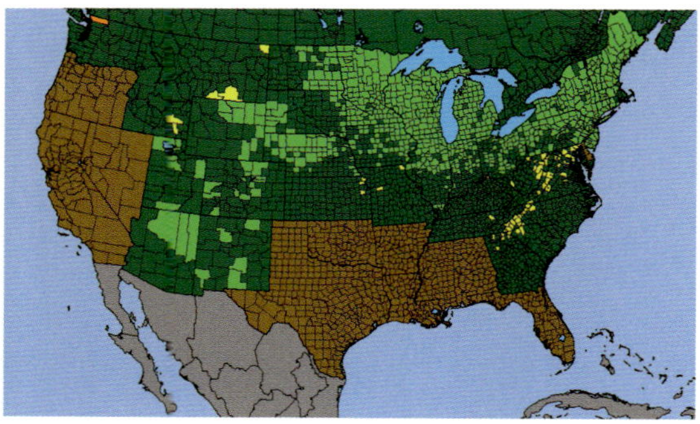

- Herbaceous perennial; 3 to 7 feet.
- Late-summer to early-fall clusters of pink to mauve flowers.
- Sun, part shade; wet, moist acidic soil.
- Workhorse. VHPV: Pollinated by native bees, butterflies (including monarchs), other insects. Host to moth caterpillars.
- Deer resistant.

Of these two joe-pye weeds, *Eutrochium fistulosum* is generally taller and will tolerate somewhat drier soil. *E. maculatum* has a looser, flatter flower shape. Both are tall, majestic plants with showy compound flowers that stand out in the summer garden and against blue skies. They will attract swarms of pollinators and butterflies when other flowers are mostly through, including adult monarchs, who feed on their nectar. Other *Eutrochium* species, with native ranges that overlap the two discussed here, are also available and are equally good choices.

Clethra alnifolia

SUMMERSWEET, SWEET PEPPERBUSH

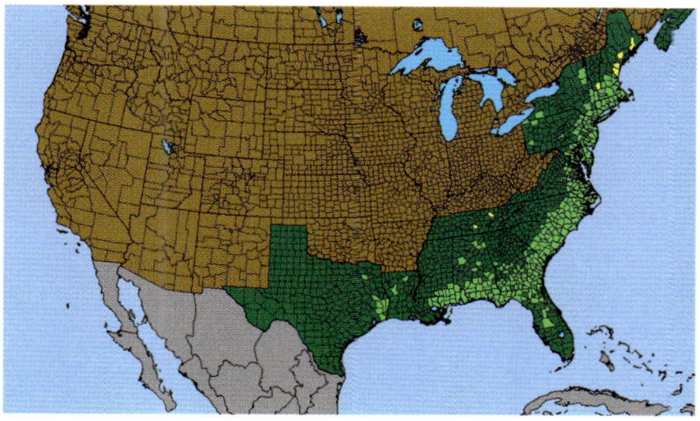

- Deciduous shrub; 3 to 6 feet.
- Summer white to pink flowers.
- Sun to part shade; wet to moist acidic soil. Drought tolerant once established. Salt tolerant.
- Workhorse. VHPV: Feeds bees, butterflies, other insects. Host to moth caterpillars.

This eye-catching plant features white bottle-brush blooms that stand out against glossy, deep green foliage. When flowers are in bloom, the breeze announces *Clethra alnifolia*'s presence from yards away. Summersweet hums with pollinators throughout its bloom time, especially those planted in consistently moist soil that receive some afternoon shade. Persistent brown seed heads follow the spiky flowers for winter interest.

Itea virginica

VIRGINIA SWEETSPIRE

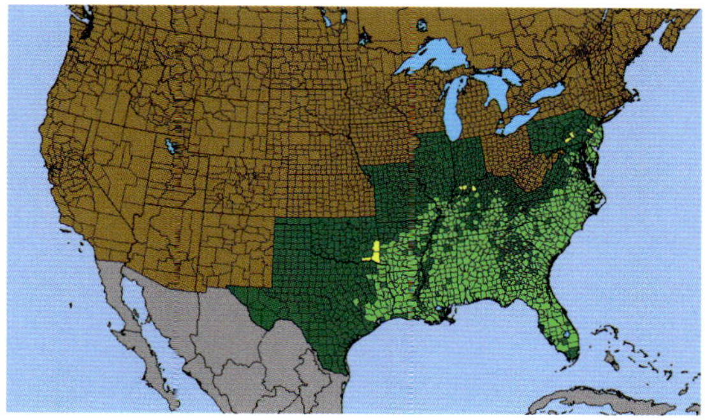

- Deciduous shrub; 3 to 6 feet.
- Spring to early-summer white flowers. Red fall foliage.
- Sun to part shade; wet to moist soil. Salt tolerant.
- Workhorse. HPV: Pollinated by native bees, butterflies.

In early to mid-spring, *Itea virginica* is covered with deliciously fragrant white bottle-brush flowers. When these blooms have faded, the bright green leaves of this mounded, multistemmed shrub hold their own until fall. Earlier than most others, the leaves turn a brilliant scarlet and are among the most prized natives for seasonal color. Its modest growth habit, strong fragrance, and relatively small stature makes *I. virginica* a great plant for dotting throughout the border as a multi-season accent plant.

Asclepias incarnata

SWAMP MILKWEED, PINK MILKWEED

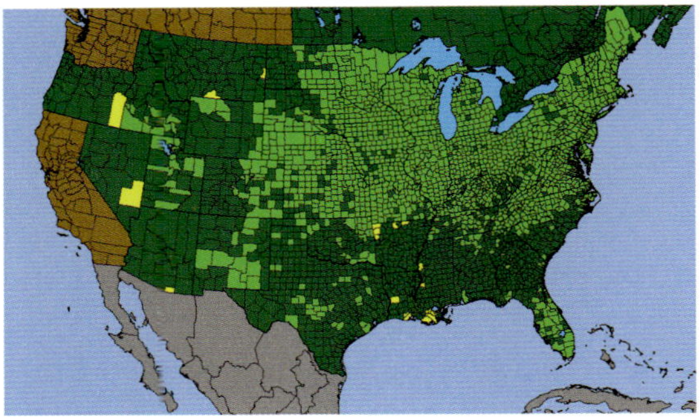

- Herbaceous perennial; 3 to 5 feet.
- Summer deep pink flowers.
- Sun to part shade; wet to moist soil.
- Workhorse. VHPV: Pollinated by native bees, butterflies (including monarchs), other insects. Host to moth and butterfly caterpillars, including monarchs.
- Deer resistant.

Asclepias speciosa

SHOWY MILKWEED

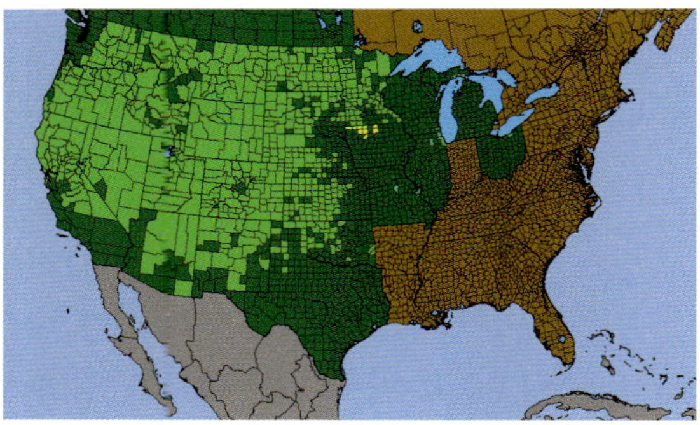

- Herbaceous perennial; 2 to 4 feet.
- Spring to summer white to pink flowers.
- Sun; moist to dry soil.
- Workhorse. VHPV: Pollinated by native bees, butterflies (including monarchs), other insects, hummingbirds. Host to butterfly caterpillars, including monarchs.
- Deer resistant.

There are scores of *Asclepias* species widely or narrowly native to various areas. *Asclepias* is now well known as the only plant on which monarchs lay their eggs and on which monarch caterpillars develop. Many varieties spread too vigorously to work in a typical residential garden, but these two are cordial neighbors to other plants and are widely native, which is important in the support of local monarch populations. Besides having fragrant, bright pink summer flowers, these two *Asclepias* species have eye-catching upright seedpods that open to release the downy floss that distributes their seeds. Beyond these two species, most native plant nurseries offer a variety of local milkweed plants to suit varying growing requirements—just remember to always confirm native range. *Asclepias* exemplifies why it's important to mainly use *locally* native plants—even some North American natives, including a few *Asclepias* species, can be invasive and disrupt ecosystems beyond their locally native boundaries.

Amorpha canescens
LEADPLANT

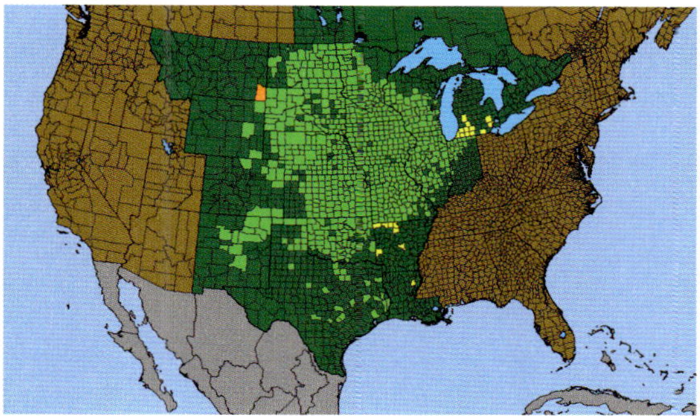

- Deciduous shrub; 1 to 3 feet.
- Summer purple flowers.
- Sun to part shade; moist to dry soil.
- Workhorse. VHPV: Feeds bees, butterflies (including monarchs), other insects. Host to moth caterpillars.

The showy flowers of *Amorpha canescens*, tiny purple blooms assembled in bottle-brush spikes, rival those of the butterfly bush. Orange stamens add complementary beauty. *A. canescens* is slow to mature but eventually develops a deep taproot, reaching down 4 feet or more, which makes it a great border plant but one not suited for foundation gardens or spots near plumbing or other underground materials.

More great native choices: *Ceanothus* spp. (page 31), *Callicarpa americana* (page 38)

INSTEAD OF THESE:

Hibiscus syriacus

ROSE OF SHARON

Paeonia species

PEONY

Both of these plants, as likely to be found in your grandparent's garden as your own, are known for their large, colorful blooms.

Hibiscus syriacus, a deciduous shrub native to Asia, has showy late-summer blooms ranging from white to pink to purple, often accented by a deep red center. Rose of Sharon blooms and self-sows prolifically, which has made it invasive in some areas, especially the Southeast. Even in a garden where it's wanted, rose of Sharon can require vigilant removal of seedlings to stay under control.

Though they are not invasive, the peonies in our gardens, both herbaceous and woody varieties, are highly hybridized non-natives that offer few benefits to the ecosystem and require intensive care for a short period of beauty. Herbaceous peonies usually need staking or other support and are subject to powdery mildew, *Botrytis*, and other diseases that can affect their blooming.

PLANT THESE:

Hibiscus laevis

HALBERDLEAF ROSEMALLOW

AL, AR, DC, FL, GA, IA, IL, IN, KS, KY, LA, MD, MI, MN, MO, MS, NC, NE, NY, OH, OK, PA, SC, TN, TX, VA, WI, WV

Hibiscus moscheutos

CRIMSON-EYED ROSEMALLOW

AL, AR, CA, CT, DC, DE, FL, GA, IL, IN, KS, KY, LA, MA, MD, MI, MO, MS, NC, NJ, NM, NY, OH, OK, PA, RI, SC, TN, TX, VA, VT, WV

Hibiscus laevis

HALBERDLEAF ROSEMALLOW

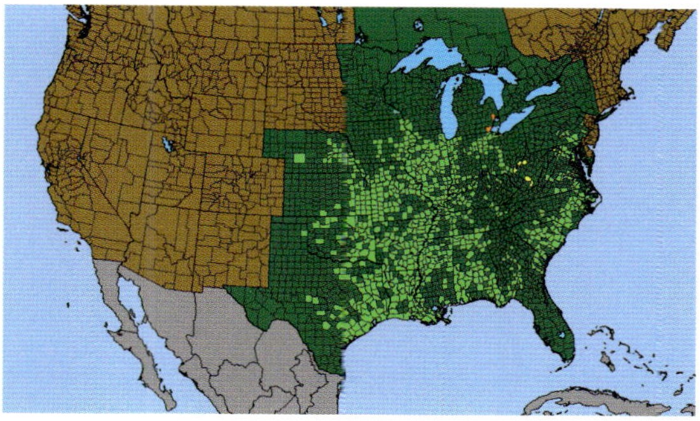

- Herbaceous perennial. 4 to 7 feet.
- Summer white or pink flowers.
- Sun to part shade; wet to moist soil.
- Workhorse. HPV: Pollinated by native bees, hummingbirds. Host to moth caterpillars.
- Deer resistant.

Hibiscus moscheutos

CRIMSON-EYED ROSEMALLOW

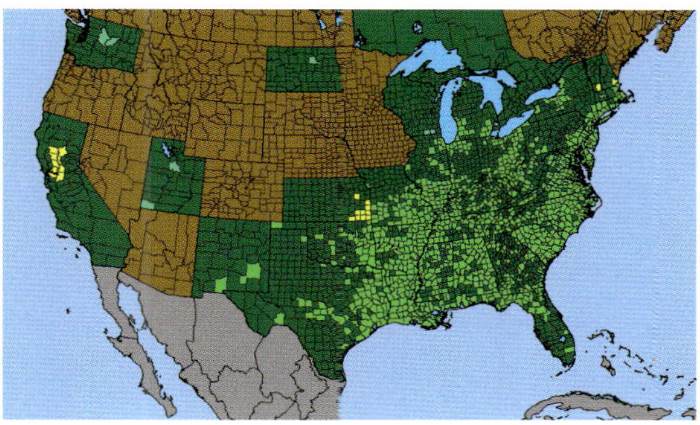

- Herbaceous perennial; 4 to 6 feet.
- Mid- to late-summer white or pink flowers.
- Sun to part shade; wet to moist soil.
- Workhorse. VHPV: Pollinated by native bees, butterflies, other insects, hummingbirds. Host to moth caterpillars.
- Deer resistant.

These two native hibiscus plants are shrubby and may keep their leaves year-round in the southern end of their range. They do not have the tall, woody growth of rose of Sharon, but they do have more spectacular blooms, 5 inches or more across, in colors ranging from white to deep red, with lighter-colored blooms showing a deep red center. The life of individual blooms is brief, but new flowers continually form over a relatively long bloom period. These wetland plants will tolerate saturated soil but must not be allowed to dry out.

Another great native choice: *Magnolia virginiana* (page 209)

INSTEAD OF THESE:

Lonicera morrowii
BUSH HONEYSUCKLE

Lonicera maackii
AMUR HONEYSUCKLE

Lonicera tatarica
TATARIAN HONEYSUCKLE

Several varieties of shrub honeysuckle first entered the United States in the nineteenth century as attractive garden plants that also made good windscreens and erosion control. Unfortunately, the same qualities that recommend them for that work contribute to their invasive nature: Many new plants emerge from their complex root systems, which spread far from the parent. Their seeds are also dispersed by the birds who consume their plentiful berries. These days the distinct upward-facing yellow and white blooms of introduced honeysuckles can be spotted along roadsides and deep in forests, where they've crowded out more beneficial native plants in sunny sites from Zones 3 to 8. Non-native honeysuckles are now banned from sale and propagation in a number of states. Happily, a number of North American native *Lonicera* species offer greater beauty and benefits.

PLANT THESE:

Lonicera dioica

LIMBER HONEYSUCKLE

AL, AR, CT, GA, IA, IL, IN, KS, KY, MA, MD, ME, MI, MN, MO, NC, ND, NE, NH, NJ, NY, OH, OK, PA, R , SD, TN, VA, VT, WI, WV, WY

Lonicera involucrata

TWINBERRY HONEYSUCKLE

AZ, CA, CO, ID, MI, MT, NM, NV, OR, UT, WA, WI, WY

Lonicera dioica

LIMBER HONEYSUCKLE

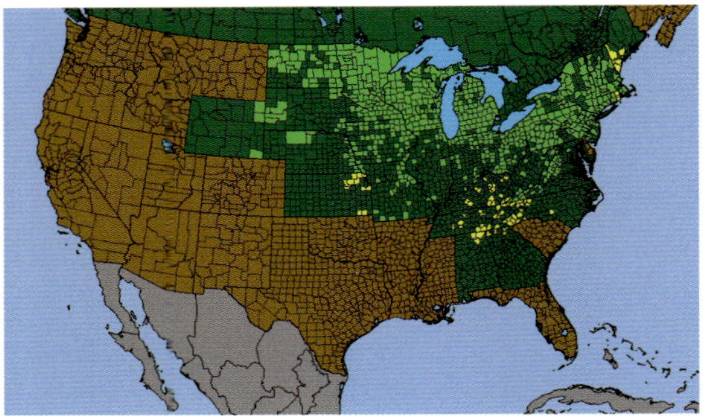

- Deciduous shrub; 3 to 10 feet.
- Late-spring to early-summer yellow to red flowers followed by red berries.
- Sun to shade; moist to dry soil.
- HPV: Pollinated by native bees, butterflies, hummingbirds. Host to moth caterpillars.

Lonicera dioica is sometimes classified as a shrub and sometimes as a vine—its growth is shrublike, while its stems are vining. It's highly adaptable to a range of soil types and light conditions. The final pair of leaves below the flowers is fused, making a frame that shows off bright, highly fragrant flowers and the bright red berries that appear later.

Lonicera involucrata

TWINBERRY HONEYSUCKLE

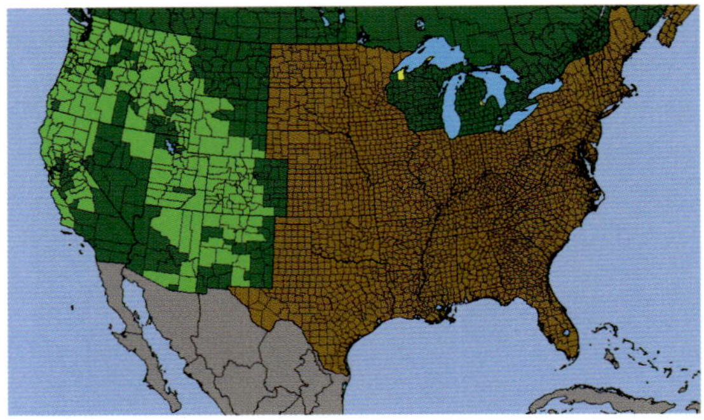

- Deciduous shrub; 3 to 10 feet.
- Late-spring to early-summer yellow to red flowers followed by dark berries.
- Sun to part shade; moist soil. Salt tolerant.
- Workhorse. VHPV: Pollinated by native bees, butterflies, hummingbirds. Host to moth and butterfly caterpillars.

Lonicera involucrata has a more formal (you might even say glamorous) look than some other honeysuckles, with paired flowers appearing from leaf axils that emerge yellow green and turn scarlet red as they mature, followed by dark berries. Although this plant is happy in wet soil, it thrives in a garden with average soil that doesn't dry out.

> **More great native choices:** *Symphoricarpos* spp. (page 46); *Diervilla lonicera* (page 47); and, for fragrance, *Rosa* spp. (pages 65–67) and *Rubus odoratus* (page 67)

INSTEAD OF THESE:

Non-native *Rhododendron* species

EVERGREEN ASIAN AND EUROPEAN RHODODENDRONS

Many non-native rhododendrons are popular garden plants for their dense, evergreen structure, showy spring blooms, and ease of cultivation. There are hundreds of rhododendrons from around the world, and many of the plants we find in US garden centers are hybrids developed through many generations. In general, evergreen rhododendrons require little pruning except to keep their size in check. Rhododendrons thrive in well-drained, acidic soil. While they will grow in full sun in the northern part of their range, they prefer filtered light and require some afternoon shade in southern gardens.

Opposite are two suggestions for evergreen North American native rhododendrons, but they have an admittedly limited native range. So if you have your heart set on a rhododendron and neither of these is native to your region, this might be the time to keep in mind entomologist Douglas Tallamy's recommendation for 70 percent native plants. If you're meeting that goal, perhaps you'll plant one of these anyway (as long as their cultural requirements will allow them to thrive in your garden). You might also consider the evergreen *Rhododendron catawbiense* and *R. minus*, which are commercially available but native to an even smaller range.

PLANT THESE:

Rhododendron macrophyllum

PACIFIC RHODODENDRON, CALIFORNIA RHODODENDRON, WESTERN ROSEBAY

CA, OR, WA

Rhododendron maximum

ROSEBAY RHODODENDRON, GREAT LAUREL, WILD RHODODENDRON

AL, CT, DC, GA, KY, MA, MD, ME, NC, NH, NJ, NY, OH, PA, RI, SC, TN, VA, VT, WV

Rhododendron macrophyllum

PACIFIC RHODODENDRON, CALIFORNIA RHODODENDRON, WESTERN ROSEBAY

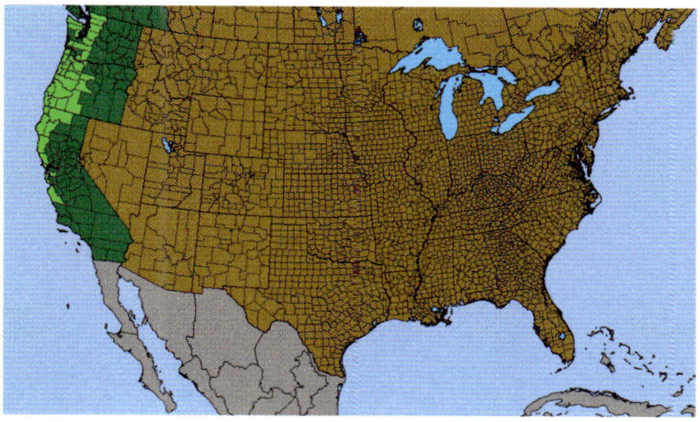

- Evergreen shrub; 5 to 15 feet.
- Spring white to dark pink flowers.
- Part shade to full shade; moist to dry soil.
- Pollinated by native bees. Host to moth caterpillars.

Rhododendron maximum

ROSEBAY RHODODENDRON, GREAT LAUREL, WILD RHODODENDRON

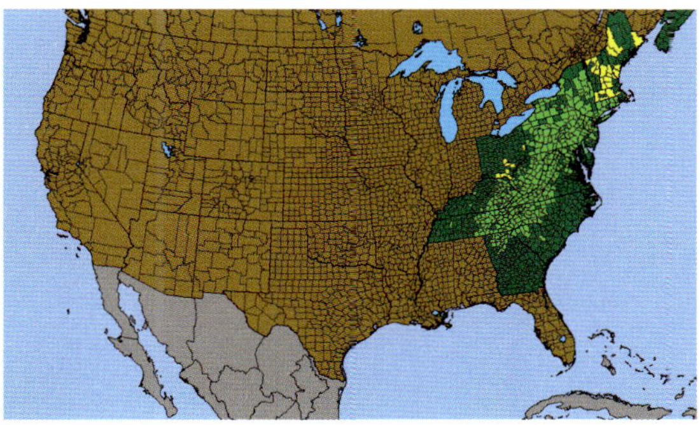

- Evergreen shrub; 4 to 15 feet.
- Spring white to pale purple flowers.
- Part shade to shade; wet to dry soil.
- VHPV: Pollinated by native bees, moths, butterflies, other insects. Host to moth and butterfly caterpillars.

Both these native varieties have a classic rhododendron appearance. Their rounded growth habit makes them highly useful where a formal appearance is wanted. In summer, the terminal clusters of big, pink, tubular flowers can be seen from far away. In winter, the glossy, large, deep green, leathery leaves brighten even the barest landscape or grayest day.

More great native choices: *Ilex glabra* (page 20), *Mahonia aquifolium* (page 21), *Juniperus* spp. (pages 34, 58), *Frangula californica* (page 35), *Kalmia latifolia* (page 42), *Morella* spp. (pages 50–53)

INSTEAD OF THESE:

Rhododendron japonicum and other deciduous non-native *Rhododendron* species

ASIAN AZALEAS

Smaller in stature than the plants we commonly call rhododendrons, azaleas are grown for their abundance of spring blooms in a range of colors from whites and pastel pinks to hot yellows and reds. Azaleas can be evergreen or deciduous, but they are typically compact plants marketed for their spring flowers. As with other highly hybridized garden plants, much of the benefit to the larger ecosystem has been been bred out of the azaleas widely available for sale. Our native azaleas, coevolved with local pollinators and other fauna, are plentiful and offer more benefits.

PLANT THESE:

Rhododendron canescens

MOUNTAIN AZALEA, WILD AZALEA, SOUTHERN PINXTERFLOWER

AL, AR, DE, FL, GA, IL, KY, LA, MD, MS, NC, OK, SC, TN, TX, VA

Rhododendron periclymenoides

PINKSTER AZALEA

AL, CT, DC, DE, GA, KY, MA, MD, NC, NJ, NY, OH, PA, RI, SC, TN, VA, VT, WV

Rhododendron columbianum

(syn. *Ledum glandulosum*)

WESTERN LABRADOR TEA

CA, ID, MT, NV, OR, UT, WA, WY

Rhododendron canescens

MOUNTAIN AZALEA, WILD AZALEA, SOUTHERN PINXTERFLOWER

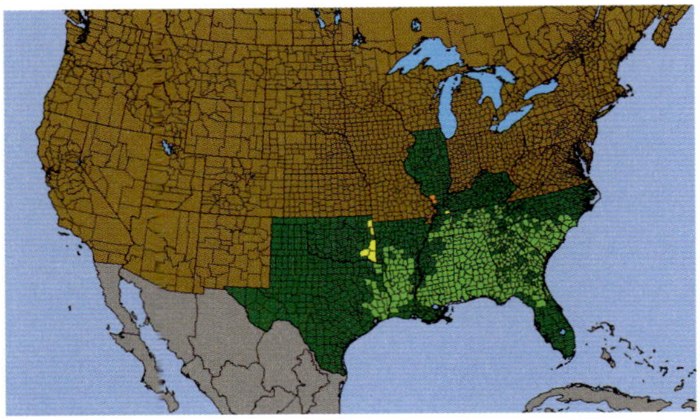

- Deciduous shrub; 4 to 8 feet.
- Spring pink flowers.
- Part shade; wet to moist acidic soil.
- HPV: Pollinated by native bees, butterflies, hummingbirds.
- Deer resistant.

Rhododendron periclymenoides

PINKSTER AZALEA

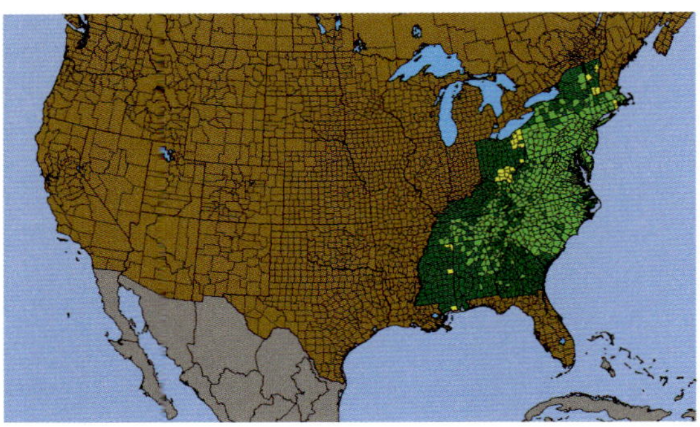

- Deciduous shrub; 3 to 10 feet.
- Spring to summer pink to white flowers.
- Sun to shade; wet to dry acidic soil.
- Workhorse. VHPV: Pollinated by native bees, moths, butterflies, other insects. Host to moth and butterfly caterpillars.
- Deer resistant.

Both of these azaleas are deciduous but put on a high-spring show of abundant, mildly but deliciously fragrant flowers. The small individual blossoms appear in clusters, with exceptionally long stamens that appear from within the plants almost like long, curved eyelashes. In the case of *Rhododendron canescens*, the flowers appear even before the plant leafs out in spring. Both thrive in moist to wet soil; pinkster azalea will tolerate somewhat drier conditions.

Rhododendron columbianum

(syn. *Ledum glandulosum*)
WESTERN LABRADOR TEA

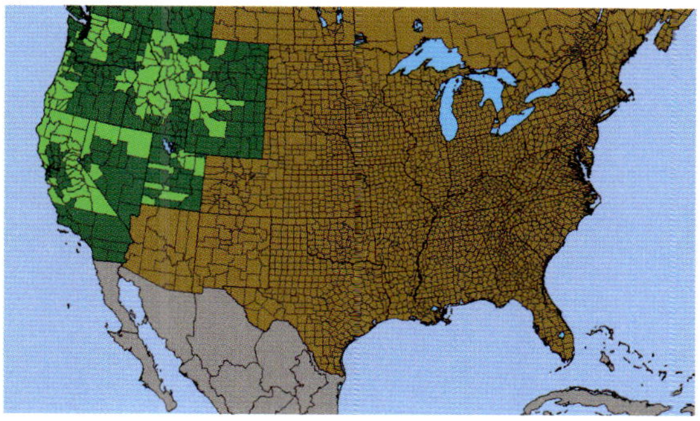

- Evergreen shrub; 4 to 6 feet.
- Spring white to pink flowers.
- Sun to shade; wet acidic soil.
- VHPV: Pollinated by native bees. Host to moth caterpillars.

Here's an azalea-like native evergreen to fill a spot in a western garden. The Latin name has recently changed, and the commercial nursery trade can be slow to catch up, so look for *Ledum glandulosum*, the older name, too. These flowers are not quite as dramatic as others in the rhododendron family, and they are flat rather than tubular, but the plants are reliably and cheerfully evergreen. They do best with consistently wet soil.

More great native choices: *Ceanothus* spp. (page 20); *Cornus drummondii* (page 54); *Cephalanthus occidentalis* (page 92); and, for evergreen foliage, *Ilex glabra* (page 20) and *Kalmia latifolia* (page 42)

INSTEAD OF THIS:

Spiraea japonica

JAPANESE SPIREA

Spiraea japonica became a popular North American garden plant thanks to its prolific blooms and adaptability to a variety of conditions. This deciduous shrub grows best in full sun to partial shade and moist, well-drained soil in Zones 4 to 8. Unfortunately, Japanese spirea has proven to be a little too adaptable here, leaping beyond garden boundaries to become invasive, particularly throughout the eastern United States. There are great native alternatives for most regions, including our own native spireas.

PLANT THESE:

Spiraea tomentosa

STEEPLEBUSH

AL, AR, CT, DE, GA, IL, IN, KS, KY, MA, MD, ME, MI, MN, MO, MS, NC, NH, NJ, NY, OH, PA, RI, SC, TN, VA, VT, WA, WI, WV

Spiraea alba

WHITE MEADOWSWEET

CT, DC, DE, IA, IL, IN, KY, MA, MD, ME, MI, MN, MO, NC, ND, NH, NJ, NY, OH, PA, SD, TN, VA, VT, WI, WV

Spiraea douglasii

ROSE SPIREA

CA, CO, ID, MT, OR, TN, WA

Spiraea tomentosa
STEEPLEBUSH

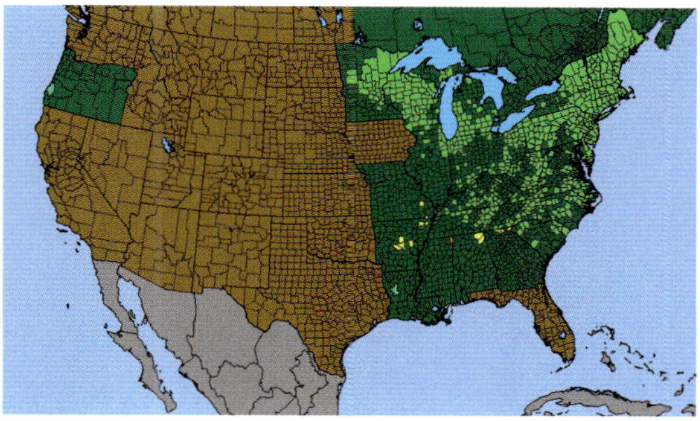

- Deciduous shrub; 2 to 4 feet.
- Mid- to late-summer pink flowers.
- Sun to part shade; wet to moist acidic soil.
- VHPV: Pollinated by native bees, butterflies, other insects. Host to moth caterpillars.
- Deer resistant.

Spiraea alba
WHITE MEADOWSWEET

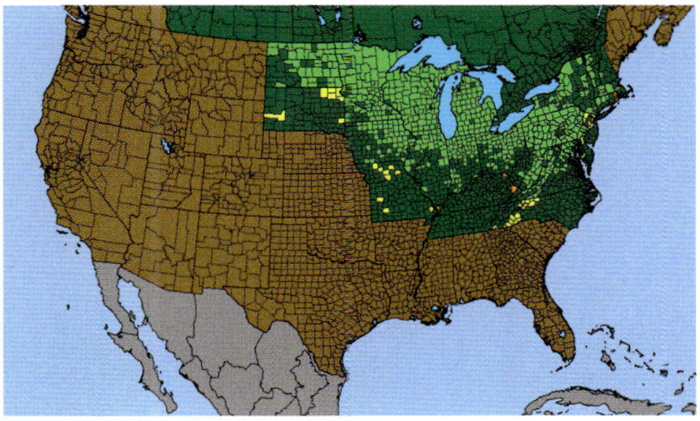

- Deciduous shrub; 2 to 4 feet.
- Early- to midsummer white flowers.
- Sun to part shade; wet to moist acidic soil.
- VHPV: Pollinated by native bees, butterflies, other insects. Host to moth and butterfly caterpillars.
- Deer resistant.

Spiraea douglasii
ROSE SPIREA

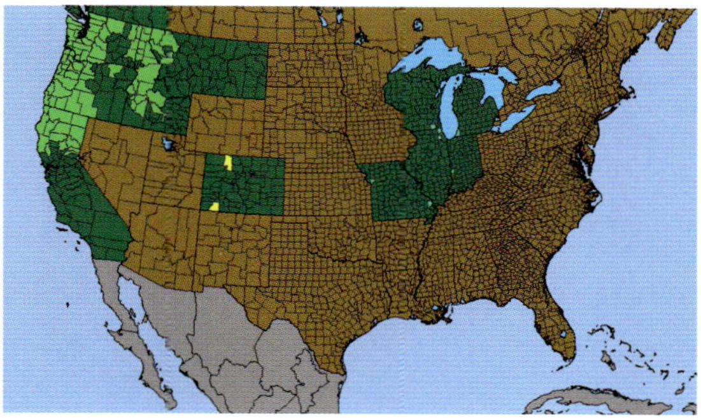

- Deciduous shrub; 3 to 6 feet.
- Mid- to late-summer pink flowers.
- Sun to part shade; wet to moist soil.
- VHPV: Pollinated by native bees, butterflies, other insects. Host to moth and butterfly caterpillars.
- Deer resistant.

Almost every description of our native spireas includes a variation of the phrase "dense clusters" of flowers. Although native spireas produce flowers in spikes rather than the flat flower clusters of Japanese spirea, these fast-growing plants send up many prolifically blooming flower stems. These species differ mostly in their native range and their bloom color, with *Spiraea tomentosa* and *S. douglasii* throwing up a range of pink blossoms and *S. alba* blooming in whites and creams. The spireas featured here are widely available, but there are others to choose from—keep an eye out for them at native nurseries.

More great native choices: *Ceanothus* spp. (page 20), *Clethra alnifolia* (page 73), *Itea virginica* (page 73), *Rhododendron periclymenoides* (page 86)

INSTEAD OF THESE:

Viburnum opulus
EUROPEAN CRANBERRY BUSH

Viburnum plicatum
SNOWBALL BUSH

Viburnum sieboldii
SIEBOLD'S VIBURNUM

Viburnum dilatatum
LINDEN VIBURNUM

Asian and European viburnums have become garden regulars for their showy white flower clusters—large spheres or abundant flat custers of bright white blooms—and for the plants' adaptability to a variety of growing conditions. Among the nonnative viburnums available in the United States, the ones listed here have all become invasive in some areas. Others are sterile or of little value to local ecosystems. There are plenty of native alternatives that offer equal beauty and more benefits.

PLANT THESE:

Viburnum prunifolium

BLACK-HAW VIBURNUM

AL, AR, CT, DC, DE, GA, IA, IL, IN, KS, KY, LA, MD, MI, MO, MS, NC, NJ, NY, OH, OK, PA, SC, TN, TX, VA, WI, WV

Cephalanthus occidentalis

BUTTONBUSH

AL, AR, AZ, CA, CT, DC, DE, FL, GA, IA, IL, IN, KS, KY, LA, MA, MD, ME, MI, MN, MO, MS, NC, NE, NH, NJ, NY, OH, OK, PA, RI, SC, TN, TX, VA, VT, WI, WV

Holodiscus discolor

OCEAN SPRAY, CREAM BUSH, MOUNTAIN SPRAY

AZ, CA, CO, ID, MT, NV, OR, UT, WA

Viburnum prunifolium

BLACK-HAW VIBURNUM

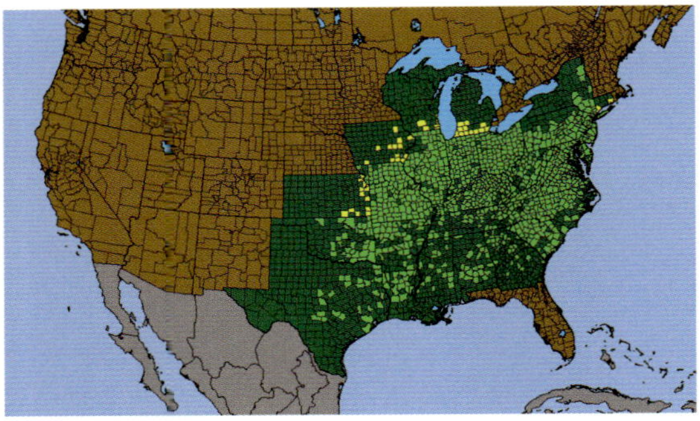

- Deciduous shrub; 5 to 12 feet.
- Mid-spring white flowers followed by purple fruit. Red to purple fall color.
- Sun to shade; moist soil.
- Workhorse. VHPV: Pollinated by native bees, moths, butterflies, other insects. Host to moth caterpillars.

Among native viburnums, *Viburnum prunifolium* has one of the broadest ranges. It can grow as a single- or multistemmed trunk, with prolific white flowers in spring followed by bunches of edible dark blue fruit whose small olive-shaped drupes add to a vivid fall foliage display. Although one plant will produce fruit, fruiting is improved with two or more plants. Other native viburnums (such as *V. dentatum*, *V. lentago*, and *V. nudum*) are native to a similar area and may work well depending on your specific growing conditions.

Cephalanthus occidentalis

BUTTONBUSH

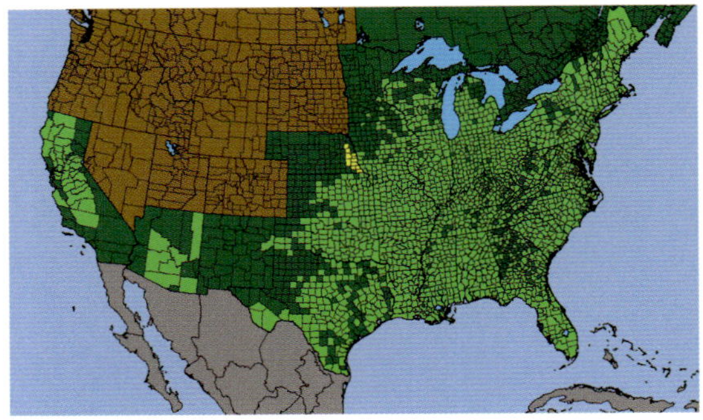

- Deciduous shrub; 6 to 12 feet.
- Summer white flowers followed by red fruits.
- Sun to part shade; wet to moist soil.
- Workhorse. VHPV: Pollinated by native bees, butterflies (including monarchs), other insects, hummingbirds. Host to moth caterpillars.
- Deer resistant.

The unique spherical flower clusters of *Cephalanthus occidentalis*, surrounded by protruding pistils, make this plant a garden conversation piece. The blooms resemble satellites or pincushions more than the buttons they're named for. Round, ruby-red fruits follow the white summer blooms and may persist through winter if birds don't eat them. The plant's twisting branches provide additional winter interest. *C. occidentalis* needs consistently moist soil and is a great plant for a rain garden or wet area.

Holodiscus discolor

OCEAN SPRAY, CREAM BUSH, MOUNTAIN SPRAY

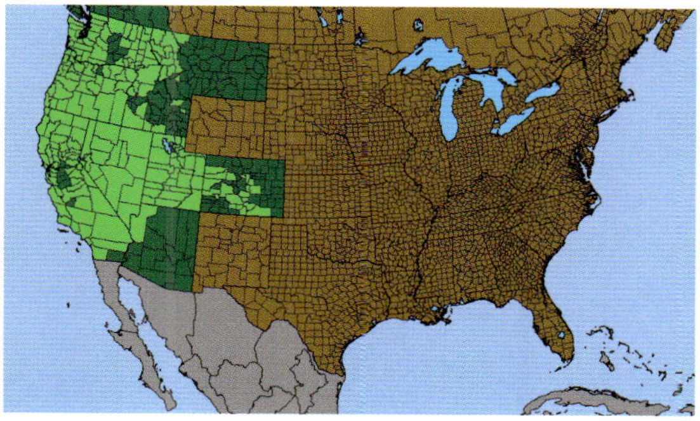

- Deciduous shrub; 3 to 12 feet.
- Mid- to late-summer white flowers.
- Sun to part shade; moist to dry soil.
- Workhorse. VHPV: Pollinated by native bees, butterflies, other insects. Host to moth and butterfly caterpillars.

Delicate, fragrant, foamy-looking cream flowers cover *Holodiscus discolor* during its blooming season, which may extend from spring through summer. Deeply lobed foliage and exfoliating bark—which may be red, gray, or brown as it matures—add to this plant's attractions.

More great native choices: *Hydrangea arborescens* (page 30), *Sambucus canadensis* (page 54)

INSTEAD OF THIS:

Alcea rosea

HOLLYHOCKS

Hollyhocks tower over the high-summer garden, valued for their height that lets them hold their own at the back of the border as well as for their variety of bloom colors. These Far East natives grow in full sun in Zones 3 to 9. Technically biennial, hollyhocks may persist as short-lived perennials in the northern part of their range or grow as annuals in the southern. They are prone to hollyhock rust, a fungal disease that appears as orange spots on leaves, which then drop prematurely. There a number of reliably perennial natives that are as spectacular as they are stately to plant instead.

PLANT THESE:

Vernonia noveboracensis

NEW YORK IRONWEED

AL, CT, DC, DE, FL, GA, KY, MA, MD, NC, NH, NJ, NY, OH, PA, RI, SC, TN, VA, WV

Vernonia fasciculata

COMMON IRONWEED

AR, CO, IA, IL, IN, KS, KY, MI, MN, MO, MS, ND, NE, OH, OK, SD, TX, WI

Vernonia missurica

MISSOURI IRONWEED

AL, AR, FL, IA, IL, IN, KS, KY, LA, MI, MO, MS, NE, OH, OK, TN, TX

Eryngium yuccifolium

RATTLESNAKE MASTER

AL, AR, FL, GA, IA, IL, IN, KS, KY, LA, MD, MI, MN, MO, MS, NC, NE, NJ, OH, OK, SC, TN, TX, VA, WI, WV

Chamaenerion angustifolium

(syn. *Chamerion angustifolium*)

FIREWEED, WILLOW HERB

AZ, CA, CO, CT, DC, DE, IA, ID, IL, IN, MA, MD, ME, MI, MN, MT, NC, ND, NE, NH, NJ, NV, NY, OR, PA, RI, SD, TN, WA, UT, VA, VT, WI, WV, WY

Monarda fistulosa

WILD BERGAMOT, BEE BALM

Throughout the contiguous US, except CA, FL, NV

Vernonia noveboracensis

NEW YORK IRONWEED

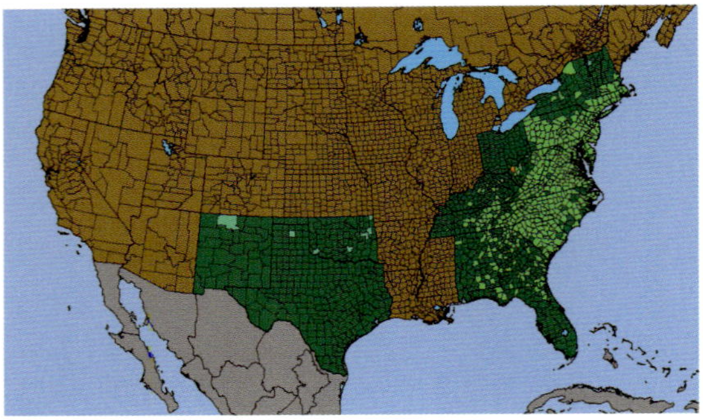

- Herbaceous perennial; 3 to 7 feet.
- Mid- to late-summer purple flowers.
- Sun to part shade; wet to moist soil.
- Workhorse. VHPV: Pollinated by native bees, butterflies, other insects. Host to moth caterpillars.

Vernonia fasciculata

COMMON IRONWEED

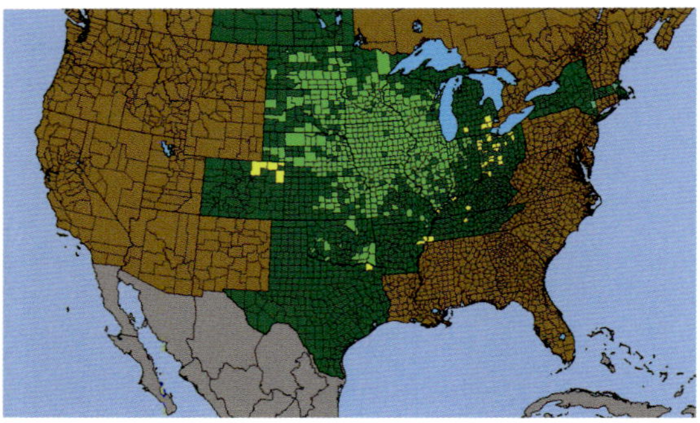

- Herbaceous perennial; 3 to 7 feet.
- Mid- to late-summer purple flowers.
- Sun; wet to dry soil.
- Workhorse. VHPV: Pollinated by native bees, moths, butterflies (including monarchs), other insects, hummingbirds. Host to moth and butterfly caterpillars.
- Deer resistant.

Vernonia missurica

MISSOURI IRONWEED

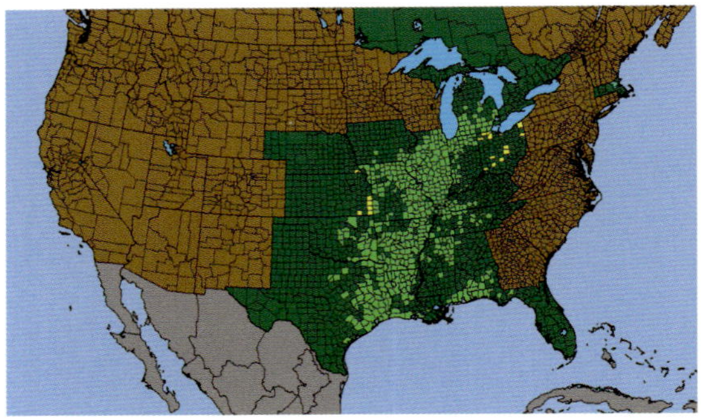

- Herbaceous perennial; 4 to 6 feet.
- Mid- to late-summer purple flowers.
- Sun; moist soil.
- Workhorse. VHPV: Feeds adult native bees, moths, butterflies, hummingbirds. Host to moth caterpillars.
- Deer resistant.

There are nearly two dozen locally native *Vernonia* species, but the differences among them, except for their range, are subtle. All are tall; some a little less so. All have benefits to pollinators, but some have a very high value, and others mainly provide nectar to adult insects. All are workhorse plants, easily established and maintained. The common name, ironweed, is said to reflect the sturdy strength of the plant's root system. The terminal clusters of deep purple flowers announce a vernonia's presence from a great distance. Roughly speaking, there's a local vernonia for every garden east of the Rockies; these choices represent some of the most widely available, so if your county isn't shown here, it's still worth checking at your nursery.

Eryngium yuccifolium

RATTLESNAKE MASTER

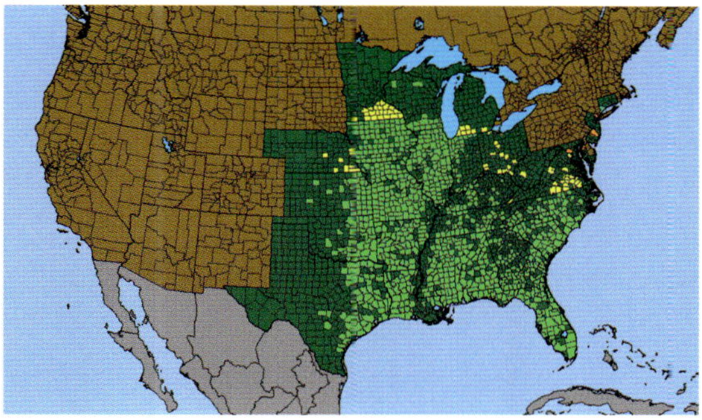

- Herbaceous perennial; 5 to 6 feet.
- Mid- to late-summer white flowers.
- Sun to part shade; wet to dry soil.
- Workhorse. VHPV: Pollinated by native bees, moths, butterflies (including monarchs), other insects.

Rising from its basal rosette of stiff, yucca-like leaves, *Eryngium yuccifolium* has a tall, spiky, architectural appearance unlike any other North American perennial. In bloom, its clusters of 1-inch, globe-shaped greenish white flowers surrounded by spiky bracts are held in loose clusters above the stems.

Chamaenerion angustifolium

(syn. *Chamerion angustifolium*)

FIREWEED, WILLOW HERB

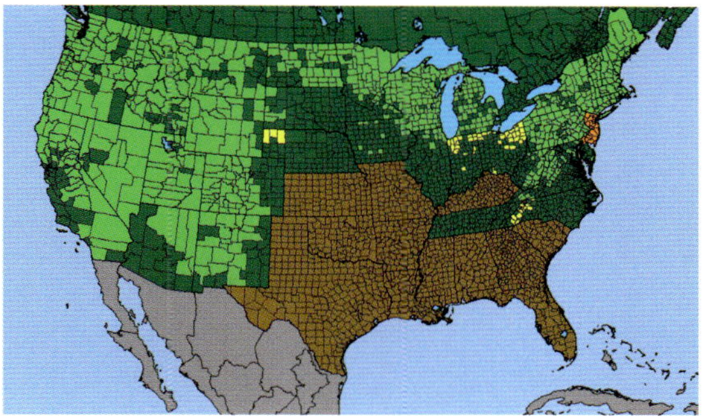

- Herbaceous perennial; 5 to 6 feet.
- Mid- to late-summer pink to purple flowers.
- Full sun; moist soil.
- Workhorse. VHPV: Pollinated by native bees, moths, other insects, hummingbirds. Host to moth caterpillars.

If you're inclined to think pink, consider *Chamaenerion angustifolium*. Its abundant tall spikes of delicate magenta flowers are a pollinator magnet. *Chamaenerion* will quickly fill a bare area—it takes its common name from its ability to do just that after a fire. But growing among most other perennials, it will typically bow out and let them take over, so it's most long-lived where it has room—but not too much—to do its own thing.

Monarda fistulosa

WILD BERGAMOT, BEE BALM

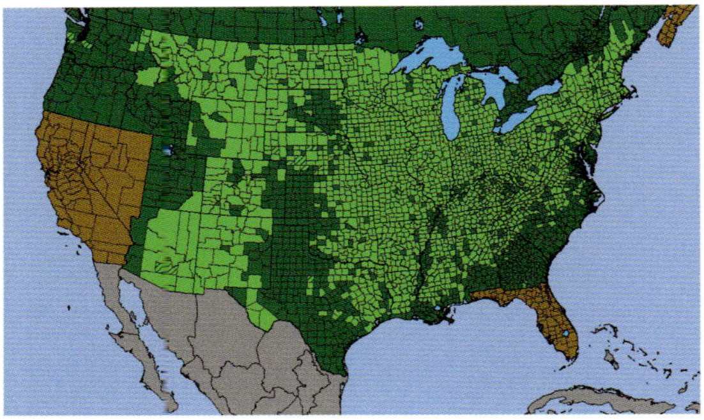

- Herbaceous perennial; 2 to 4 feet.
- Mid- to late-summer pink flowers.
- Sun to part shade; moist to dry soil. Drought tolerant.
- Workhorse. VHPV: Pollinated by native bees, moths, butterflies (including monarchs), hummingbirds. Host to moth caterpillars.
- Deer resistant.

Among plants in the genus *Monarda*, *M. fistulosa* has the largest native range, but many others—*M. bradburiana*, *M. citriodora*, *M. didyma*, and *M. punctata*—will do similar work in their smaller native ranges. All have high to very high pollinator value. The pleasant, notably minty scent of these plants deters deer and other browsers. (In my Maine garden, where monardas traveled freely, they seemed to provide protection for nearby shrubs that usually draw deer and groundhogs.) *M. fistulosa* blooms profusely in shades ranging from pale pink to lavender, managing to look at once both glamorous and cheerful. However, all monardas are subject to powdery mildew; good air circulation will help prevent it.

INSTEAD OF THIS:

Anemone × hybrida

JAPANESE ANEMONE

The typically white or pink blooms of Japanese anemone rise well above its foliage and provide a bit of color to a late-summer or early-fall garden. This late-summer bloomer is adaptable to a variety of soil types in sun or shade, preferring afternoon shade in the warmest part of its range. Once anemone is settled, it can be an aggressive spreader, though it's not officially invasive in any region of the United States.

PLANT THESE:

Chelone glabra

WHITE TURTLEHEAD

AL, AR, CT, DC, DE, GA, IA, IL, IN, KY, MA, MD, ME, MI, MN, MO, MS, NC, NH, NJ, NY, OH, PA, RI, SC, TN, VA, VT, WI, WV

Veronicastrum virginicum

CULVER'S ROOT

AL, AR, CT, DC, DE, FL, GA, IA, IL, IN, KS, KY, LA, MA, MD, MI, MN, MO, MS, NC, ND, NE, NJ, NY, OH, OK, PA, SC, SD, TN, TX, VA, VT, WI, WV

Chelone glabra

WHITE TURTLEHEAD

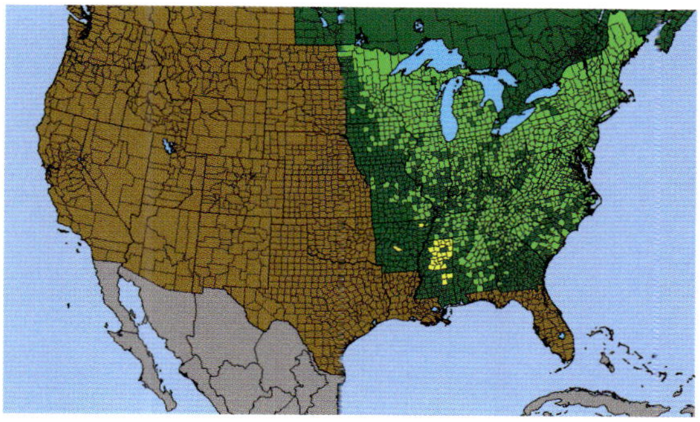

- Herbaceous perennial; 2 to 3 feet.
- Midsummer to early-fall white flowers.
- Sun to shade; wet soil.
- Workhorse. VHPV: Pollinated by native bees, moths, butterflies, hummingbirds. Host to moth and butterfly caterpillars.

Chelone glabra will tolerate a variety of light conditions but prefers to grow in reliably damp soil—in the wild, it's often found along wet roadside culverts. Its compact clusters of flowers give the plant a neat, almost formal look compared to many other fall native bloomers. The unique flower shape gives the plant its common name as well as its Latin genus name: *Chelone* means "tortoise" in Greek.

Veronicastrum virginicum

CULVER'S ROOT

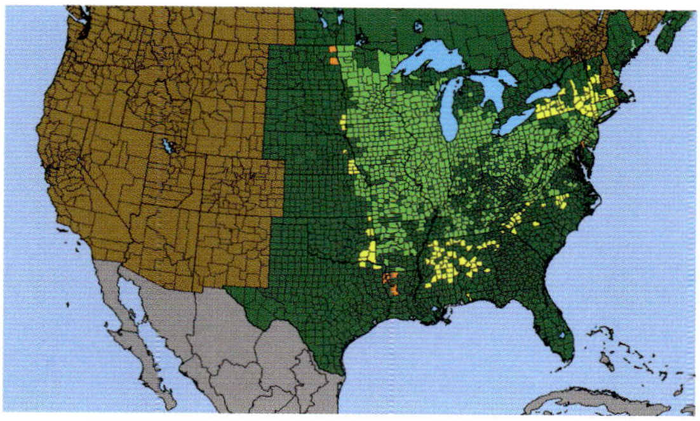

- Herbaceous perennial; 3 to 5 feet.
- Summer white flowers.
- Sun to part shade; wet to dry acidic soil.
- Workhorse. VHPV: Pollinated by native bees, moths, butterflies, other insects, hummingbirds. Host to moth caterpillars.

Veronicastrum virginicum produces long, fluffy plumes of flowers that tend to sway in the breeze and lean toward the light, especially as they reach the limits of their height. Although *V. virginicum* looks great in groups, its long, candlelike inflorescences make it a key accent plant, which suits its tendency to pop up here and there in a garden (but not aggressively). In my late-summer garden, the veronicastrums are always pleasantly humming with pollinators.

More great native choices:
Symphyotrichum spp. (pages 103, 147), *Solidago* spp. (pages 112–113)

INSTEAD OF THESE:

Aster × frikartii
FRIKART'S ASTER

Aster tatarica
TATARIAN ASTER

Asters have long been a mainstay of the fall garden. The European hybrid *Aster × frikartii* has been popular for a prolonged bloom time starting in summer and lasting for several weeks. Frikart's aster grows 2 to 3 feet in full sun, requiring partial shade in the South, where it is often treated as an annual.

Tatarian aster can grow from 3 to 10 feet and has an exceptionally long bloom time. Tatarian aster has escaped cultivation and has been called a garden bully, if not invasive.

There are at least eighty native *Symphyotrichum* (formerly *Aster*) species in North America, and many nurseries will carry twenty or more species. (You'll also find native asters, such as white wood aster and big-leaved aster, in the *Eurybia* genus.) These three have an especially broad range and are widely available.

PLANT THESE:

Symphyotrichum novae-angliae
NEW ENGLAND ASTER

AL, AR, CO, CT, DC, DE, GA, IA, IL, IN, KS, KY, MA, MD, ME, MI, MN, MO, MS, NC, ND, NE, NH, NJ, NM, NY, OH, OK, PA, RI, SC, SD, TN, VA, VT, WI, WV, WY

Symphyotrichum oblongifolium
AROMATIC ASTER

AL, AR, CO, DC, IA, IL, IN, KS, KY, MD, MN, MO, MS, MT, NC, ND, NE, NJ, NM, OH, OK, PA, SD, TN, TX, VA, WI, WV, WY

Symphyotrichum eatonii
EATON'S ASTER

AZ, CA, CO, ID, MT, NM, NV, OR, UT, WA, WY

Symphyotrichum novae-angliae

NEW ENGLAND ASTER

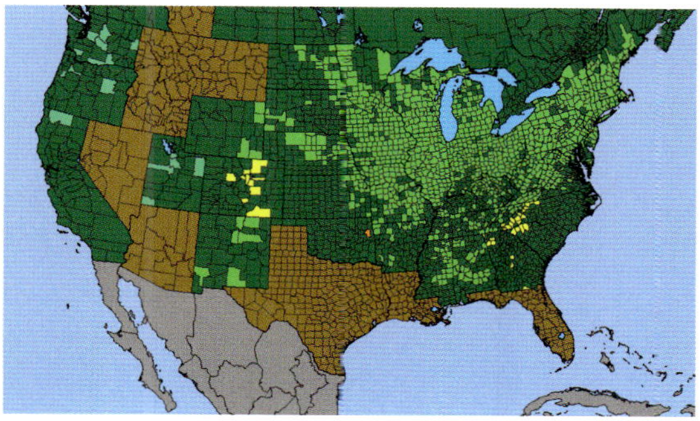

- Herbaceous perennial; 2½ to 3½ feet.
- Late-summer to fall pink to purple flowers.
- Sun; wet to moist soil.
- Workhorse. VHPV: Pollinated by native bees, moths, butterflies (including monarchs), other insects. Host to moth and butterfly caterpillars.

Symphyotrichum oblongifolium

AROMATIC ASTER

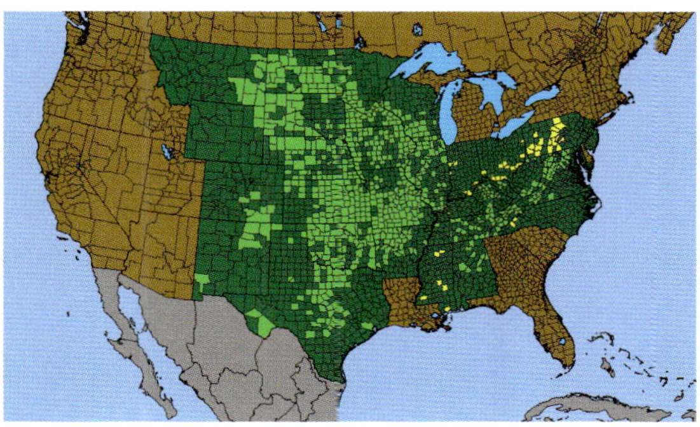

- Herbaceous perennial; 2 to 3 feet.
- Late-summer purple blooms.
- Sun; dry soil.
- Workhorse. HPV: Pollinated by native bees, moths, butterflies (including monarchs), other insects.

Symphyotrichum eatonii

EATON'S ASTER

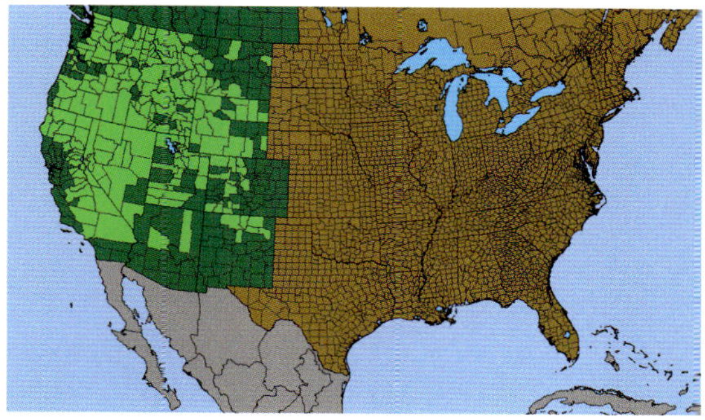

- Herbaceous perennial; 2 to 3 feet.
- Late-summer white, pink blooms.
- Sun, moist soil.
- Workhorse. HPV: Pollinated by native bees, moths, butterflies (including monarchs), other insects.

Various *Symphyotrichum* species will bloom from midsummer to late fall, in shades of white, blue, and purple and in combinations of sun or shade and wet to dry soil. They are generally long-lived plants that play well with their neighbors, including goldenrods, whose yellow blooms offer a classic complement to purple asters, as Robin Wall Kimmerer notes in *Braiding Sweetgrass*. These late bloomers are a key source of pollinator food and shelter long after most others have faded away. Late in the season, the casual beauty and relaxed form of native asters mark a perfect end to summer's garden party.

INSTEAD OF THESE:

Astilbe species

FALSE SPIREA

Astilbes are valued for their rugged durability and the late-summer color of their flowering plumes in shades of white to deep reds and purples; they thrive in shade gardens and are hardy in all but the hottest regions, growing around 2 feet tall in part shade to shade in moist soil. They are not drought tolerant.

PLANT THESE:

Aruncus dioicus

GOATSBEARD, BRIDE'S FEATHERS

AL, AR, CA, DC, GA, IA, IL, IN, KY, MD, MO, MS, NC, NJ, OH, OK, OR, PA, SC, TN, VA, WA, WV

Achillea millefolium

YARROW

Throughout the contiguous US

Verbena hastata

BLUE VERBENA/VERVAIN, SWAMP VERBENA

Throughout the contiguous US, except LA, SC

Aruncus dioicus

GOATSBEARD, BRIDE'S FEATHERS

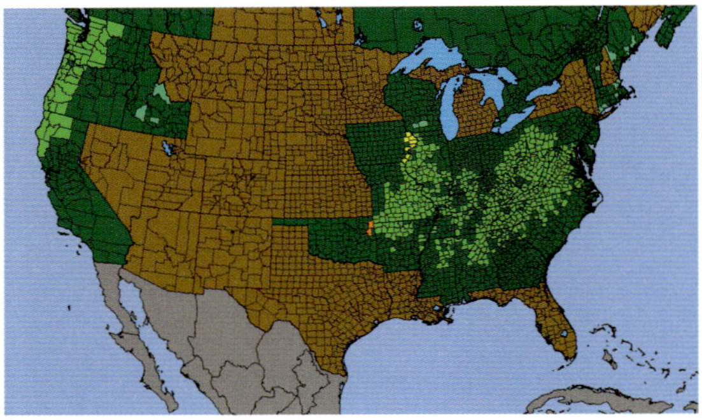

- Herbaceous perennial; 3 to 6 feet.
- Late-spring to summer white flowers.
- Sun to shade; wet to moist acidic soil.
- Workhorse. VHPV: Pollinated by native bees, moths, butterflies, other insects, hummingbirds. Host to moth and butterfly caterpillars.
- Deer resistant.

The feathery plumes of *Aruncus dioicus* make a glamorous addition to any garden. Including the spires of small white flowers sitting atop long stems, *A. dioicus* easily reaches heights of 4 to 6 feet, but it has an airy, open nature that makes it a good garden neighbor. Goatsbeard is long lasting when given enough water; in dry conditions, the flowers are fragile. *A. dioicus* is dioecious; both male and female plants have flowers. The male flowers are showier, but the female plants produce ornamental seed heads.

Achillea millefolium

YARROW

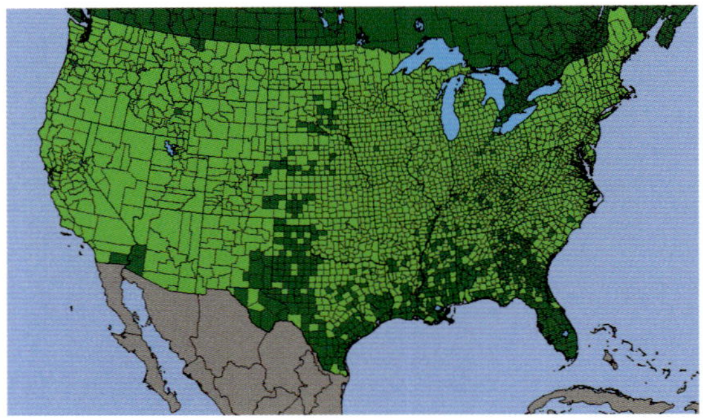

- Herbaceous perennial; 1 to 3 feet.
- Spring to fall white flowers.
- Sun to part shade; moist to dry soil. Drought tolerant.
- Workhorse. VHPV: Pollinated by native bees, moths, butterflies, other insects, hummingbirds. Host to butterfly caterpillars.

Achillea millefolium's broad bloom time reflects its enormous native range; in temperate gardens, it's a summer-into-fall bloomer, with flat, clustered heads of small white flowers occasionally tending to pink rising above soft, fernlike foliage. There are introduced yarrows and subspecies of the native, and they often interbreed, but the true native achillea is predominantly white, so that's the one to add to your native plant garden.

Verbena hastata

BLUE VERBENA/VERVAIN, SWAMP VERBENA

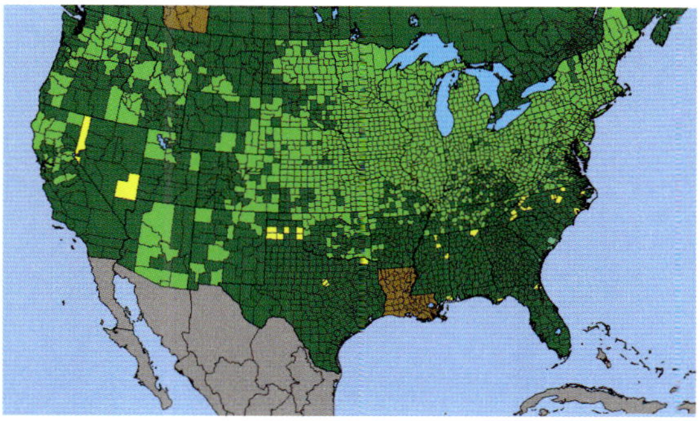

- Herbaceous perennial; 2 to 5 feet.
- Late-spring to early-summer blue flowers.
- Full sun to part shade. Wet to moist soil.
- Workhorse. VHPV: Pollinated by native bees, moths, butterflies, other insects, hummingbirds.

Verbena hastata throws up many slender spikes of tiny, bright violet-blue flowers from a single stem, putting on a display that can last several weeks. This verbena is usually considered a short-lived perennial, but I've seen it classified as biennial that produces new stems from rhizomes. Either way, all those blooms contribute to a freely self-sowing habit. Although this verbena does well in wet soil, it's also typically happy in average garden soil.

More great native choices: *Veronicastrum virginicum* (page 101), *Symphyotrichum* spp. (pages 103, 147)

INSTEAD OF THIS:

Convallaria majalis

LILY OF THE VALLEY

The delicate bell flowers and sweet scent of *Convallaria majalis* confirm the arrival of high spring. Lilies of the valley thrive in shady, cool, moist areas. They spread via rhizomes and have been valued as lush ground covers, but this import from Europe and Asia has escaped cultivation to take over woodlands and crowd out the locals and is now classified as invasive.

PLANT THESE:

Mertensia virginica

VIRGINIA BLUEBELLS

AL, AR, DC, DE, GA, IA, IL, IN, KS, KY, MD, MI, MN, MO, MS, NC, NJ, NY, OH, PA, TN, VA, WI, WV

Maianthemum stellatum

STARRY FALSE LILY OF THE VALLEY

AR, AZ, CA, CO, CT, DC, IA, ID, IL, IN, KS, KY, MA, MD, ME, MI, MN, MO, MT, ND, NE, NH, NJ, NM, NV, NY, OH, OK, OR, PA, RI, SD, TN, UT, VA, VT, WA, WI, WV, WY

Mertensia virginica

VIRGINIA BLUEBELLS

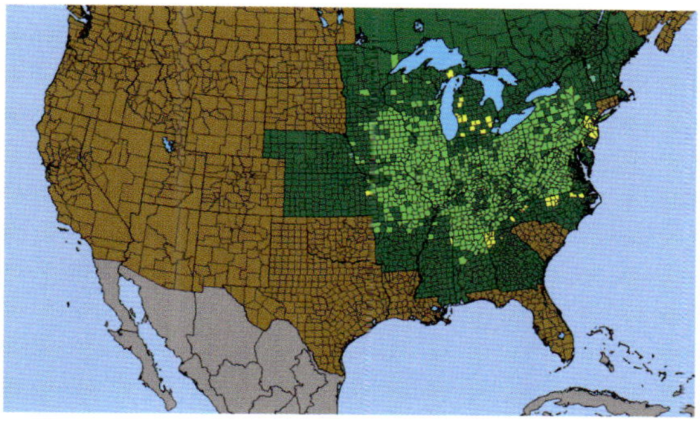

- Herbaceous perennial; 1 to 1½ feet.
- Early- to mid-spring pink, blue, and purple flowers.
- Part shade to shade; wet to moist soil.
- Workhorse. VHPV: Pollinated by native bees, moths, butterflies, hummingbirds. Host to moth caterpillars.

These spring beauties are breathtaking given the space to colonize freely, but they're equally beautiful in the garden, where they will bloom for several weeks before going fully dormant by midsummer. *Mertensia virginica* spreads by underground rhizomes, forming clumps that will appear year after year, but not so aggressively that they crowd out other plants.

Maianthemum stellatum

STARRY FALSE LILY OF THE VALLEY

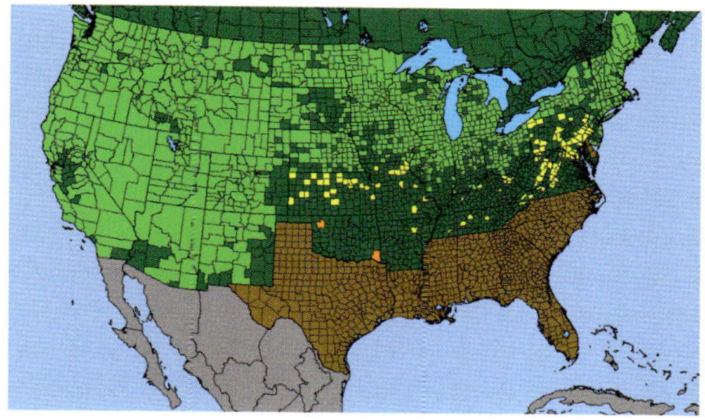

- Herbaceous perennial; 8 to 18 inches.
- Spring white flowers followed by clusters of red to purple berries.
- Part shade to shade; moist soil.
- Workhorse. Pollinated by native bees, other insects. Host to moth caterpillars.

The common name says it all: In its range *Maianthemum stellatum*, or starry false lily of the valley, provides a beauty very similar to its introduced namesake. Small white star-shaped flowers, lightly fragrant, hang along a short stem.

INSTEAD OF THESE:

Zinnia elegans, Chrysanthemum, and other late-season bloomers

While many of a traditional garden's later bloomers are not hardy perennials, they offer color when other plants are already retreating into dormancy. Annuals like zinnias don't do much for the garden until they make their fall appearance; chrysanthemums are often bought and treated like annuals, which must be purchased and planted each season. And all these plants are typically so manipulated by human intervention that their benefits to pollinators, birds, and other wildlife are minimal.

PLANT THESE:

Solidago multiradiata

ROCKY MOUNTAIN GOLDENROD

AZ, CA, CO, ID, MT, NM, NV, OR, UT, WA, WY

Solidago velutina

THREENERVE GOLDENROD, WESTERN GOLDENROD, CALIFORNIA GOLDENROD

AZ, CA, CO, ID, MT, NM, NV, OK, SD, TX, UT, WY

Solidago odora

SWEET GOLDENROD, ANISE-SCENTED GOLDENROD

AL, AR, CT, DC, DE, FL, GA, KY, LA, MA, MD, MO, MS, NC, NH, NJ, NY, OH, OK, PA, RI, SC, TN, TX, VA, VT, WV

Solidago flexicaulis

ZIGZAG GOLDENROD

AL, AR, CT, DC, DE, GA, IA, IL, IN, KS, KY, LA, MA, MD, ME, MI, MN, MO, MS, NC, ND, NE, NH, NJ, NY, OH, PA, RI, SC, SD, TN, VA, VT, WI, WV

Solidago rigida

(syn. *Oligoneuron rigidum*)

STIFF GOLDENROD

AL, AR, CO, CT, DC, GA, IA, IL, IN, KS, KY, LA, MA, MD, MI, MN, MO, MS, MT, NC, ND, NE, NJ, NM, NY, OH, OK, PA, RI, SC, SD, TN, TX, VA, WI, WV, WY

Solidago multiradiata

ROCKY MOUNTAIN GOLDENROD

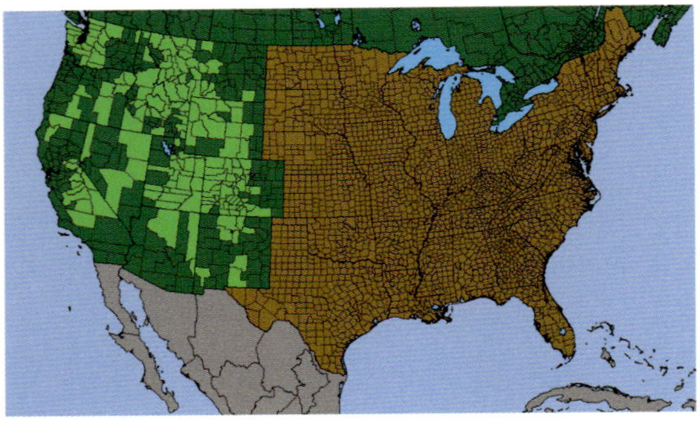

- Herbaceous perennial; 1 to 2 feet.
- Summer to fall yellow flowers.
- Sun to part shade; moist to dry alkaline soil.
- Workhorse. VHPV: Pollinated by native bees, butterflies, other insects. Host to butterfly caterpillars.

Solidago velutina

THREENERVE GOLDENROD, WESTERN GOLDENROD, CALIFORNIA GOLDENROD

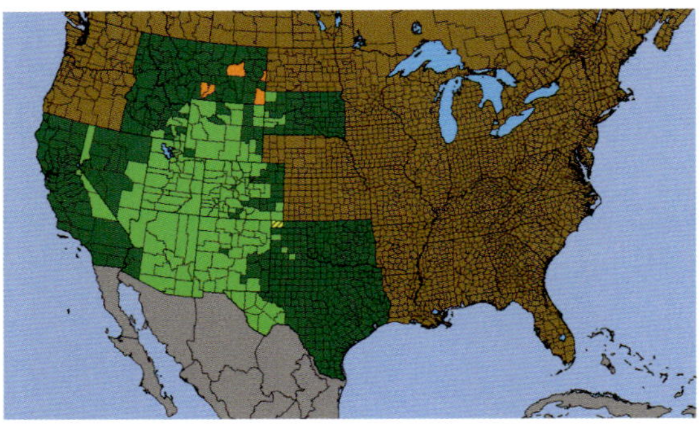

- Herbaceous perennial; 2 to 3 feet.
- Spring to summer yellow flowers.
- Sun to part shade; dry soil.
- HPV: Pollinated by native bees, butterflies, other insects.

Solidago flexicaulis

ZIGZAG GOLDENROD

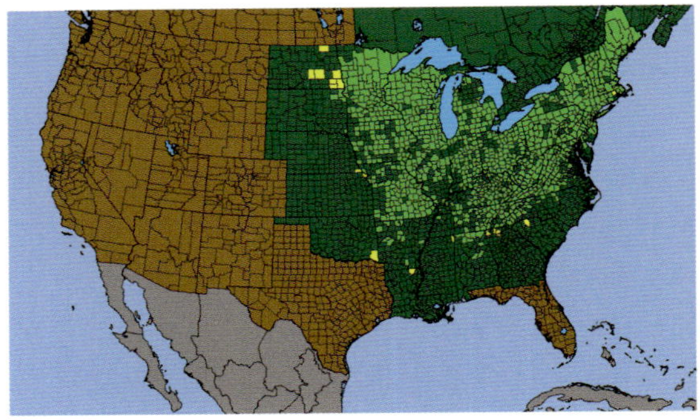

- Herbaceous perennial; 1 to 3 feet.
- Late-summer to fall yellow flowers.
- Sun to part shade; moist to dry acidic soil.
- Workhorse. VHPV: Provides food to native bees, moths, butterflies (including monarchs), other insects. Host to moth caterpillars.
- Deer resistant.

Solidago odora

SWEET GOLDENROD, ANISE-SCENTED GOLDENROD

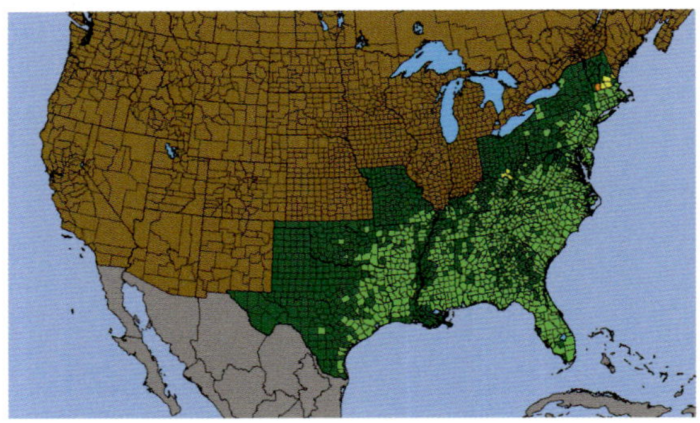

- Herbaceous perennial; 2 to 4 feet.
- Late-summer to fall yellow flowers.
- Sun to part shade; moist to dry acidic soil.
- VHPV: Pollinated by native bees, moths, butterflies (including monarchs), other insects. Host to moth caterpillars.

Solidago rigida

(syn. *Oligoneuron rigidum*)

STIFF GOLDENROD

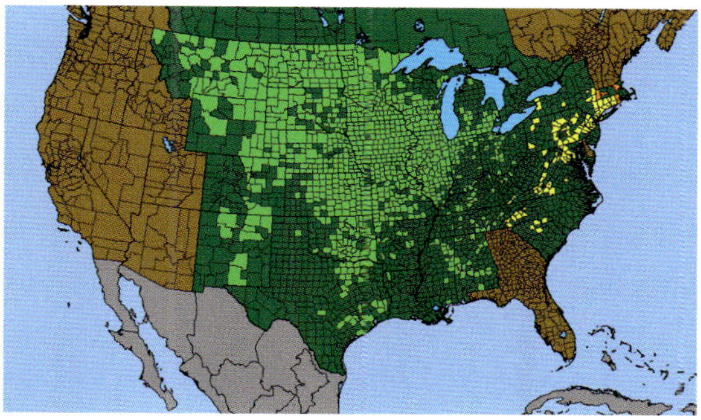

- Herbaceous perennial; 1 to 5 feet.
- Late-summer to fall yellow flowers.
- Sun to part shade; dry soil.
- Workhorse. VHPV: Pollinated by native bees, moths, butterflies (including monarchs). Host to moth caterpillars.

Of all the perennials in North America, the *Solidago* genus supports the most pollinators—and there's at least one species of *Solidago* native to virtually every county in the contiguous United States. These examples only begin to suggest the breadth of species available to extend bloom times from midsummer well into fall in some cases. They offer vibrant late-season blooms, providing essential nectar for pollinators and seeds for birds at a critical time.

Most solidagos are characterized by their lance-shaped leaves and spikes of bright yellow flowers. Of the solidagos represented here, the leaves of *S. flexicaulis* have a distinctive zigzag pattern, while *S. velutina*'s leaves are velvety. *S. multiradiata* has a clumping habit with flowers that are shorter but wider than more typical solidagos. *S. rigida* features clustered, flat-topped flowers rather than the more usual spike. *S. odora*'s leaves have a distinct anise scent. Other species are white flowered, or salt tolerant, suited to wet or dry gardens, sun or shade. In short, if you're looking for a way to introduce the perennial most broadly beneficial to wildlife into your garden, there is likely a locally native solidago out there for you.

The many members of the broad *Solidago* genus falsely get a bad rap for being allergenic and badly behaved in the garden. It's *Ambrosia artemisiifolia* (ragweed) that causes fall allergies—solidago pollen is too big to be the culprit. Some solidagos are aggressive spreaders and best avoided in the home garden, but the ones featured here are well behaved enough to be good garden neighbors, as are many other species.

NOTE: *Solidago* is not the only genus to contain the flowers we call goldenrods. Other goldenrod species, which you'll find listed as *Euthamia* and *Oligoneuron*, may make great selections for native gardens, too.

More great native choices: *Veronicastrum virginicum* (page 101), *Symphyotrichum* spp. (pages 103, 147)

INSTEAD OF THESE:

Dianthus species

PINKS, SWEET WILLIAM

Dianthus, commonly known as pinks and native to Europe, Asia, and South Africa, are planted for their spring and summer carpet of flowers in shades of red, pink, and white and for their strong spicy fragrance. Dianthus grow in full sun across the contiguous United States, in well-drained neutral soil. A number of native plants fill the same roles with higher benefits for local ecosystems.

PLANT THESE:

Phlox paniculata

GARDEN PHLOX, FALL PHLOX, PERENNIAL PHLOX

AL, AR, DC, GA, IL, IN, KS, KY, MD, MO, MS, NC, NJ, OH, OK, PA, SC, TN, VA, WV

Phlox pilosa

DOWNY PHLOX, PRAIRIE PHLOX, FRAGRANT PHLOX

AL, AR, CT, DC, DE, FL, GA, IA, IL, IN, KS, KY, LA, MD, MI, MN, MO, MS, NC, ND, NE, NJ, NY, OH, OK, PA, SC, SD, TN, TX, VA, WI, WV

Phlox subulata

CREEPING PHLOX, MOSS PHLOX, MOSS PINK

DE, IL, KY, MD, NC, NJ, NY, OH, PA, TN, UT, VA, WV

Geum triflorum

PRAIRIE SMOKE, PURPLE AVENS

AZ, CA, CO, IA, ID, IL, MI, MN, MO, MT, ND, NM, NV, NY, OR, SD, UT, WA, WI, WY

Phlox paniculata

GARDEN PHLOX, FALL PHLOX, PERENNIAL PHLOX

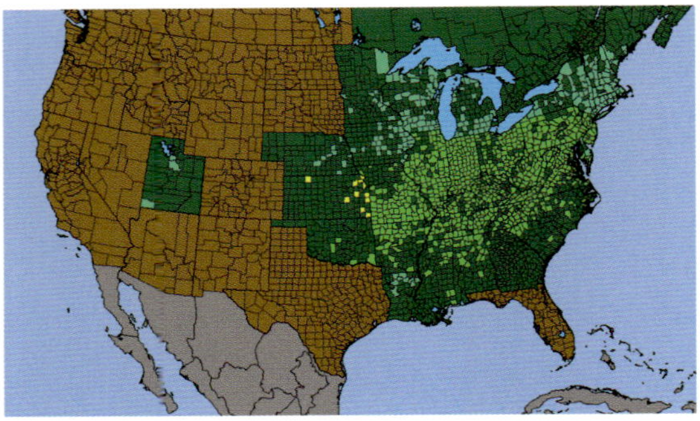

- Herbaceous perennial; 2 to 6 feet.
- Summer pink, purple, or white flowers.
- Sun; moist to dry soil.
- Workhorse. Feeds butterflies.

Phlox pilosa

DOWNY PHLOX, PRAIRIE PHLOX, FRAGRANT PHLOX

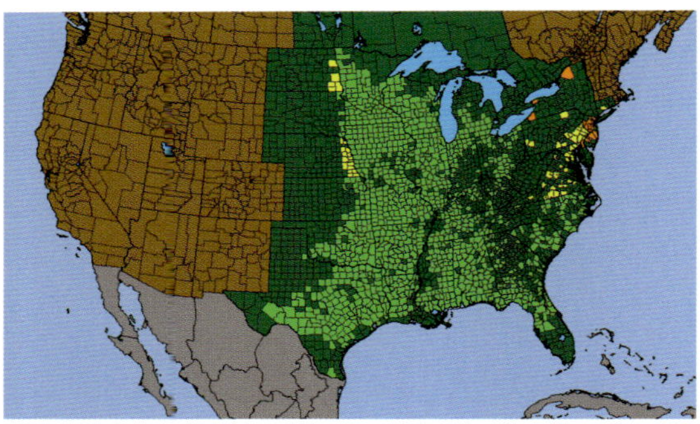

- Herbaceous perennial; 1 to 2 feet.
- Spring to summer pink flowers.
- Full sun to part shade; moist to dry acidic soil.
- Workhorse. VHPV: Pollinated by native bees, moths, butterflies, other insects, hummingbirds. Host to moth caterpillars.

Here's a pair of old-fashioned garden classics that happen to be North American natives. These two phlox are more the height of pinks' tall cousin, carnation, no longer much grown in home gardens. They both have pink to lavender blooms (rarely white) that top each stem in an abundant terminal cluster and a strong fragrance. In the wild, *Phlox paniculata* has naturalized beyond its native range.

NOTE: Watch out for the near lookalike invasive (*Hesperis matronalis*, dame's rocket), which is distinguished by its four-petaled flower where phlox has five; it can quickly take over and displace native species.

Phlox subulata

CREEPING PHLOX, MOSS PHLOX, MOSS PINK

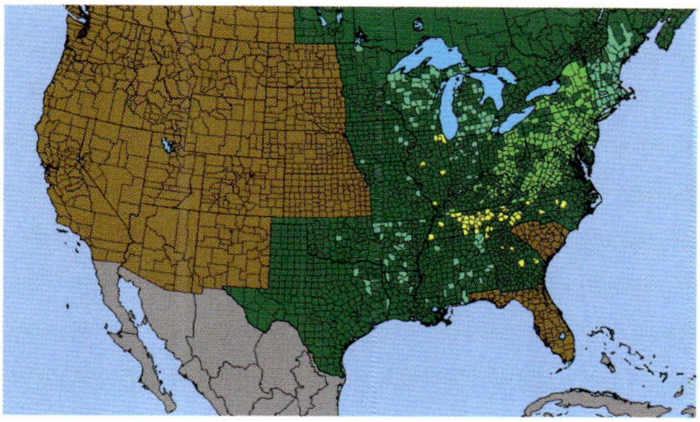

- Herbaceous perennial; 4 to 6 inches.
- Early-spring pink, purple, or white flowers.
- Sun to part shade; moist to dry soil. Drought and salt tolerant.
- Workhorse. Feeds butterflies.
- Deer resistant.

With a spreading, mat-forming habit, fragrant *Phlox subulata* is a widely available native plant that's an ideal substitute for dianthus. Blooming profusely in spring, it may continue to flower lightly until fall, but its dense, cushiony, mosslike foliage is attractive, too. *P. subulata* prefers moist soil but tolerates occasionally dry soil as well.

Geum triflorum

PRAIRIE SMOKE, PURPLE AVENS

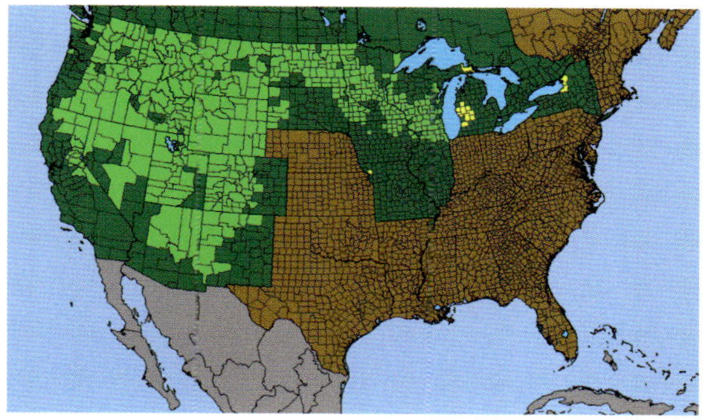

- Herbaceous perennial; semi-evergreen; 6 to 18 inches.
- Spring to early-summer pink flowers. Orange to red fall foliage.
- Sun to shade; moist to dry soil. Drought tolerant.
- Workhorse. Pollinated by native bees. Host to butterfly caterpillars.

The common name prairie smoke comes from the plant's fruit, which appears as smokelike tendrils on flowers that turn upward after they are pollinated and their reddish pink bloom has finished. The cheerful conical seed heads that follow the fruit add late-season interest, as does the colorful fall foliage.

Another great native choice: *Aquilegia* spp. (page 120)

INSTEAD OF THIS:

Lamprocapnos spectabilis
ASIAN BLEEDING HEART

Lamprocapnos spectabilis, an old-fashioned garden standard, takes its common name from its heart-shaped pink-and-white flowers, which hang in a row beneath arching stems. Bleeding heart grows 2 to 3 feet tall in well-drained moist soil in partial to full shade in virtually every area of the contiguous United States. Bleeding heart doesn't tolerate full sun, standing water, or completely dry soil, and it goes dormant in full summer, leaving behind a blank spot in the garden. A number of North American natives are equally distinctive and far less finicky.

PLANT THESE:

Aquilegia canadensis
WILD COLUMBINE, CANADIAN COLUMBINE, RED COLUMBINE

AL, AR, CT, DC, DE, FL, GA, IA, IL, IN, KS, KY, MA, MD, ME, MI, MN, MO, MS, NC, ND, NE, NH, NJ, NY, OH, OK, PA, RI, SC, SD, TN, TX, VA, VT, WI, WV

Aquilegia coerulea
(syn. *Aquilegia caerulea*)
COLORADO COLUMBINE, COLORADO BLUE COLUMBINE

CO, ID, MT, NM, SD, UT, WY

Aquilegia formosa

WESTERN COLUMBINE, RED COLUMBINE

AZ, CA, ID, MT, NV, OR, UT, WA, WY

Polygonatum biflorum

SMOOTH SOLOMON'S SEAL, GREAT SOLOMON'S SEAL

AL, AR, AZ, CO, CT, DC, DE, FL, GA, IA, IL, IN, KS, KY, LA, MA, MD, ME, MI, MN, MO, MS, NC, ND, NE, NH, NJ, NM, NY, OH, OK, PA, RI, SC, SD, TN, TX, VA, VT, WI, WV, WY

Dicentra formosa

WESTERN BLEEDING HEART, PACIFIC BLEEDING HEART

CA, OR, WA

Aquilegia canadensis

WILD COLUMBINE, CANADIAN COLUMBINE, RED COLUMBINE

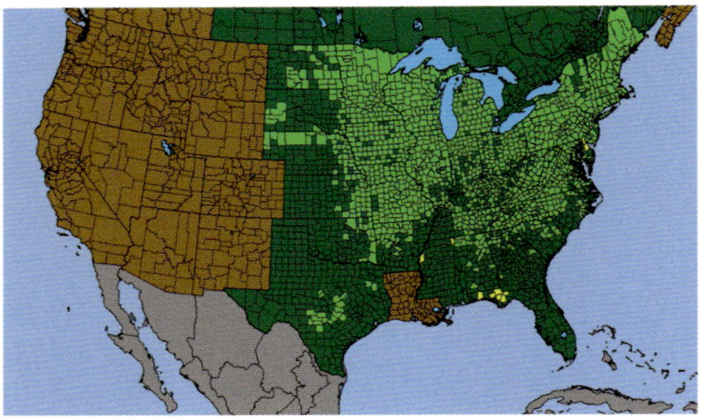

- Herbaceous perennial; 1 to 2½ feet.
- Late-spring to early-summer red-and-yellow flowers.
- Sun to part shade. Wet to dry soils.
- Workhorse. VHPV: Pollinated by native bees, moths, butterflies, hummingbirds. Host to moth and butterfly caterpillars.

Aquilegia coerulea

(syn. *Aquilegia caerulea*)

COLORADO COLUMBINE, COLORADO BLUE COLUMBINE

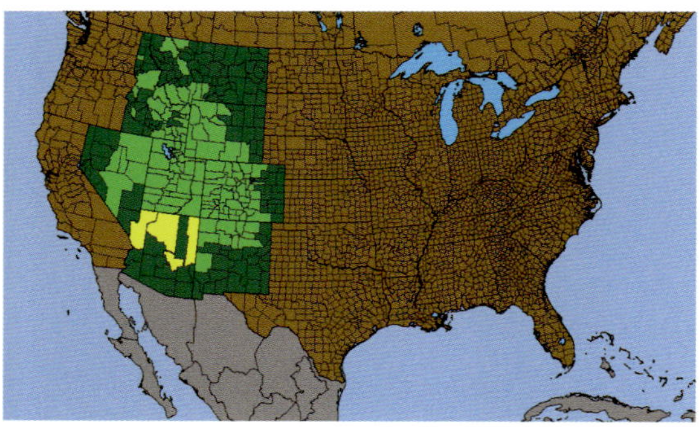

- Herbaceous perennial; 1 to 3 feet.
- Late-spring to early-summer blue-and-white flowers.
- Sun to part shade; moist soil.
- Workhorse. VHPV: Feeds moths, butterflies, hummingbirds.

Aquilegia formosa

WESTERN COLUMBINE, RED COLUMBINE

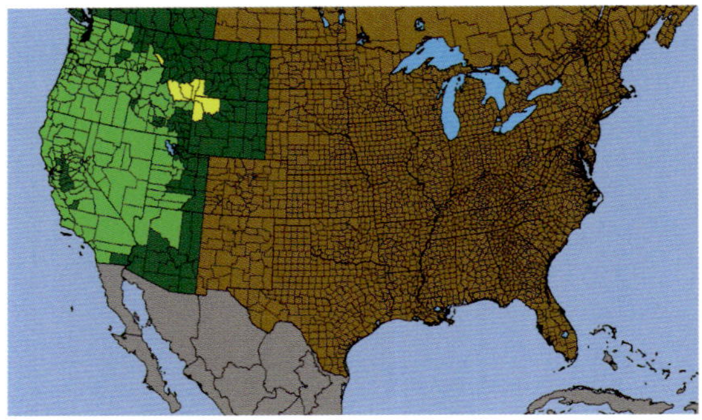

- Herbaceous perennial; 1 to 3 feet.
- Summer red-and-yellow flowers.
- Sun to shade; moist soil.
- HPV: Pollinated by native bees, moths, hummingbirds.

Aquilegias have their own two-toned beauty, with sepals and petals in contrasting colors suspended from delicate stems. The nectar found in the long spurs is especially appealing to hummingbirds. Aquilegias are not long-lived, but they self-sow freely and will pop up cheerfully, but not aggressively, around the garden. The ones featured here are among the most widely available of many native varieties. While there are many hybrid varieties, they may not have the same nutritional value as natives, especially those with doubled or quadrupled flowers or no spurs.

Polygonatum biflorum

SMOOTH SOLOMON'S SEAL, GREAT SOLOMON'S SEAL

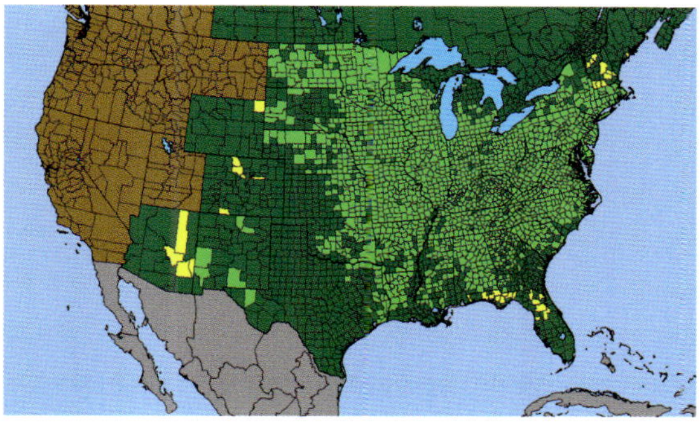

- Herbaceous perennial; 8 to 24 inches.
- Late-spring to early-summer white flowers followed by blue-black berries. Yellow fall foliage.
- Part shade to shade; moist to dry soil.
- HPV: Pollinated by native bees, other insects, hummingbirds. Berries feed birds, small mammals.

The bell-shaped blossoms of *Polygonatum biflorum* hang in pairs from arching stems, typically 2 to 3 feet but sometimes longer. These white flowers with green recurving tips hang beneath long, pointed, deeply veined leaves. The flowers are followed by small, dark round berries loved by birds and small mammals. *P. biflorum* colonizes politely into attractive drifts where garden space permits without crowding out established neighbors.

Dicentra formosa

WESTERN BLEEDING HEART, PACIFIC BLEEDING HEART

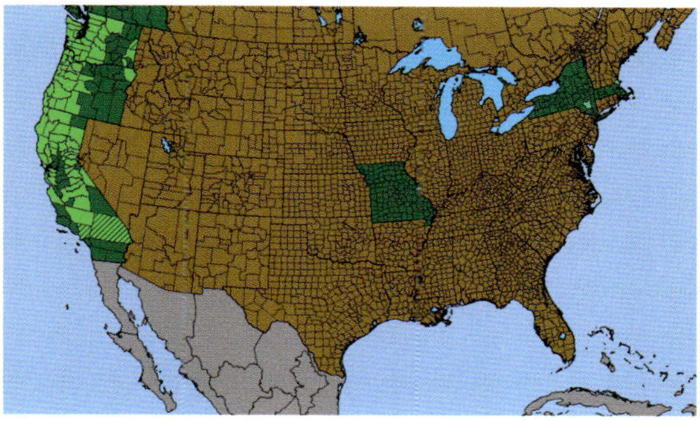

- Herbaceous perennial; 1 to 2 feet.
- Spring to summer pink flowers.
- Sun to shade; moist soil.
- HPV: Pollinated by native bees, hummingbirds. Host to moth and butterfly caterpillars.

The small, heart-shaped flowers of *Dicentra formosa* range from light pink to pale lavender, appearing in clusters on arched stems 1 to 2 feet long, over soft, blue-green fernlike foliage. Like other *Dicentra* species, this one tends to go dormant by midsummer.

INSTEAD OF THIS:

Digitalis purpurea

FOXGLOVE

The spires of tubular foxglove flowers add vertical punctuation to the late-spring or early-summer border. Foxgloves grow 3 to 5 feet tall in well-drained soil in full sun to part shade. Among the many cultivars are biennials and short-lived perennials. By contrast, the natives that make the best subsitutes for foxglove are among the most durable perennials.

PLANT THESE:

Penstemon digitalis

FOXGLOVE BEARDTONGUE

AL, AR, DC, DE, IA, IL, IN, KS, KY, LA, MD, MI, MO, MS, NC, NE, NJ, OH, OK, PA, SC, TN, TX, VA, WV

Penstemon gracilis

LILAC PENSTEMON, SLENDER BEARDTONGUE

CO, IA, IL, MI, MN, MT, ND, NE, NM, SD, WI, WY

Penstemon speciosus

ROYAL PENSTEMON

CA, ID, NV, OR, UT, WA

Baptisia tinctoria

YELLOW WILD INDIGO

CT, DC, DE, GA, IA, IL, IN, KY, MA, MD, ME, MI, NC, NH, NJ, NY, OH, PA, RI, SC, TN, VA, VT, WI, WV

Baptisia alba

WILD WHITE INDIGO, WHITE BAPTISIA

AL, AR, FL, GA, IA, IL, IN, KS, KY, LA, MA, MI, MN, MO, MS, NC, NE, OH, OK, SC, TN, TX, VA, WI

Baptisia australis

BLUE FALSE INDIGO, BLUE WILD INDIGO

AR, DC, GA, IA, IL, IN, KS, KY, MA, MD, MO, NC, NE, NJ, OH, OK, PA, TN, TX, VA, WV

Penstemon digitalis

FOXGLOVE BEARDTONGUE

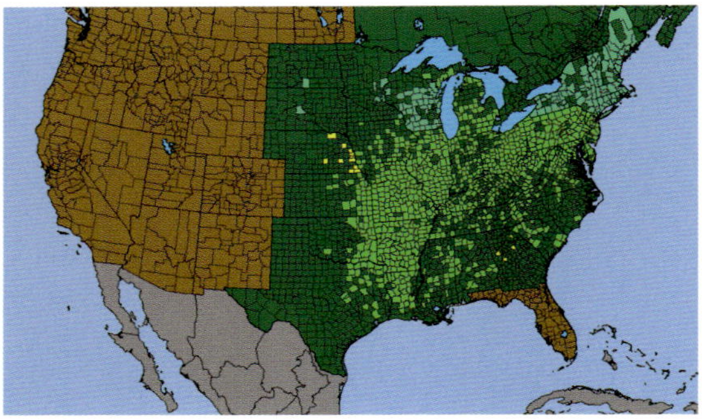

- Herbaceous perennial; 2 to 4 feet.
- Summer white or pink tubular flowers. Red fall foliage.
- Sun to part shade; wet to dry acidic soil.
- Workhorse. VHPV: Pollinated by native bees, moths, butterflies, other insects, hummingbirds. Host to moth caterpillars.

Penstemon gracilis

LILAC PENSTEMON, SLENDER BEARDTONGUE

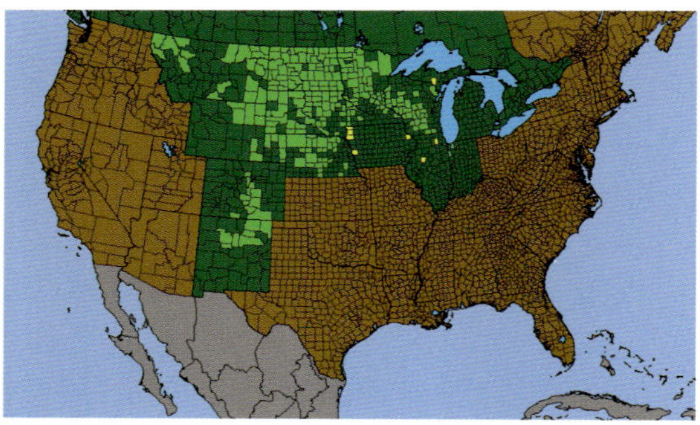

- Herbaceous perennial; 1 to 2 feet.
- Spring to summer purple flowers.
- Sun to part shade; moist to dry soil. Drought tolerant.
- Workhorse. Pollinated by native bees, hummingbirds.

Penstemon speciosus

ROYAL PENSTEMON

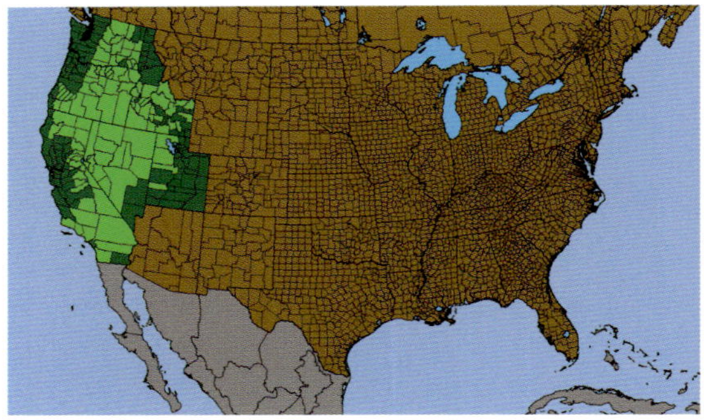

- Herbaceous perennial; 1 to 3 feet.
- Late-spring to summer blue to purple flowers.
- Full sun; dry soil. Drought tolerant.
- HPV: Pollinated by native bees, butterflies, hummingbirds. Host to butterfly caterpillars.

These three varieties represent just a sampling of the penstemons widely available across the United States. All told, there are nearly three hundred species, ranging from subshrubs (short, woody-stemmed perennials) with dark purple summer flowers growing in the West to tall, graceful early-spring bloomers with lavender blossoms elsewhere. Among the penstemons are varieties suitable to a broad range of conditions. All feature dramatic tubular flowers that attract long-tongued pollinators. A local native plant nursery may be the best place to discover the full range of penstemons native to your ecoregion.

Baptisia tinctoria

YELLOW WILD INDIGO

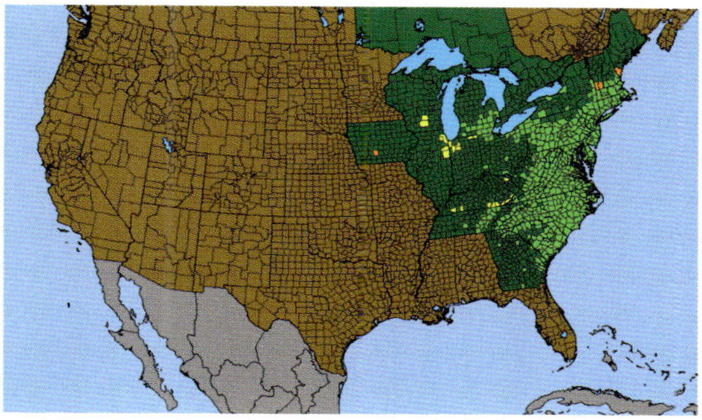

- Herbaceous perennial; 3 to 4 feet.
- Late-spring to summer yellow flowers.
- Full sun to part shade; dry acidic soil. Drought tolerant.
- HPV: Pollinated by native bees, butterflies. Host to moth and butterfly caterpillars.

Baptisia alba

WILD WHITE INDIGO, WHITE BAPTISIA

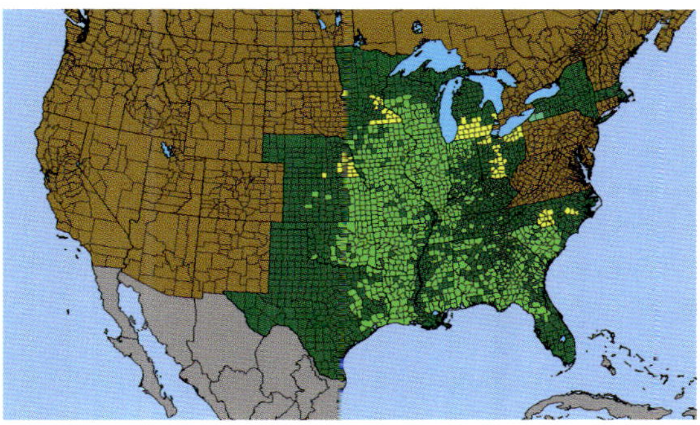

- Herbaceous perennial; 2½ to 5 feet.
- Spring to summer white flowers.
- Sun to part shade; moist to dry acidic soil. Drought tolerant.
- Workhorse. HPV: Pollinated by native bees, butterflies. Host to moth and butterfly caterpillars.

Baptisia australis

BLUE FALSE INDIGO, BLUE WILD INDIGO

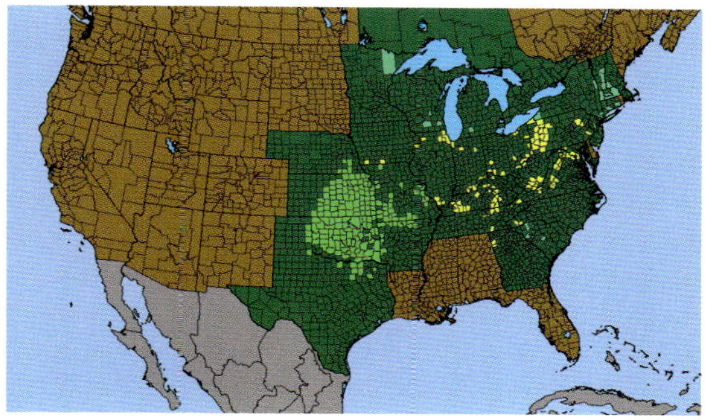

- Herbaceous perennial; 2 to 4 feet.
- Spring to early-summer blue to purple flowers.
- Full sun; moist to dry acidic soil. Drought tolerant.
- Workhorse. HPV: Pollinated by native bees, butterflies. Host to moth and butterfly caterpillars.

All these baptisias have a shrubby growth habit, throwing flowers up profusely from many stems of pealike foliage. The flowers of *Baptisia australis* and *B. alba* are held up in spikes, while *B. tinctoria*'s flowers have a more relaxed form. Ornamental large, black seedpods appear in fall. With deep and extensive root systems, baptisias have a reputation for being difficult to transplant but I've found that if care is taken with the roots, these plants will tolerate moving.

INSTEAD OF THIS:

Helleborus × hybridus

HELLEBORE, LENTEN ROSE

The blooms of the evergreen hellebores appear as early as late November in the South and break through snow and ice in late winter farther north. After their bloom period, these shade-tolerant perennials are background plants. Frayed, crisp, or ragged leaves can sometimes overstay their welcome, requiring cutting back in spring. Hellebores are listed as an invasive species in North Carolina, and observers have reported that they've escaped garden populations and entered woodlands in other areas of the country as well.

PLANT THESE:

Heuchera americana

ALUMROOT, CORAL BELLS

AL, AR, CT, DC, DE, GA, IL, IN, KY, LA, MD, MI, MO, MS, NC, NE, NJ, NY, OH, OK, PA, SC, TN, VA, WV

Heuchera richardsonii

RICHARDSON'S ALUMROOT, PRAIRIE ALUMROOT

CO, IA, IL, IN, KS, MI, MN, MO, MT, ND, NE, OK, SD, WI, WY

Heuchera parvifolia

SMALL-FLOWERED ALUMROOT, CORAL BELLS

AZ, CO, ID, MT, NM, NV, OR, SD, UT, WY

Heuchera micrantha

CREVICE ALUMROOT, CORAL BELLS

CA, ID, OR, WA

Tiarella species

FOAMFLOWER

AL, CA, CT, DC, DE, GA, ID, KY, MA, MD, ME, MI, MN, MS, MT, NC, NH, NJ, NY, OH, OR, PA, RI, SC, TN, VA, VT, WA, WI, WV

Heuchera americana

ALUMROOT, CORAL BELLS

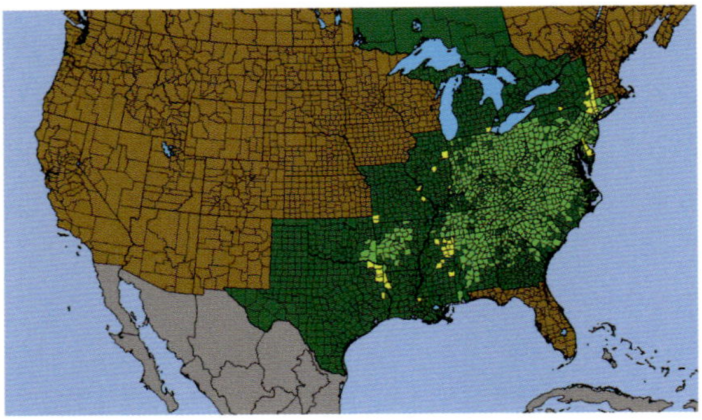

- Herbaceous perennial; 1½ to 3 feet.
- Spring to summer white to yellow flowers.
- Sun to shade; moist to dry acidic soil.
- Workhorse. HPV: Pollinated by native bees, moths, hummingbirds. Host to moth caterpillars.

Heuchera parvifolia

SMALL-FLOWERED ALUMROOT, CORAL BELLS

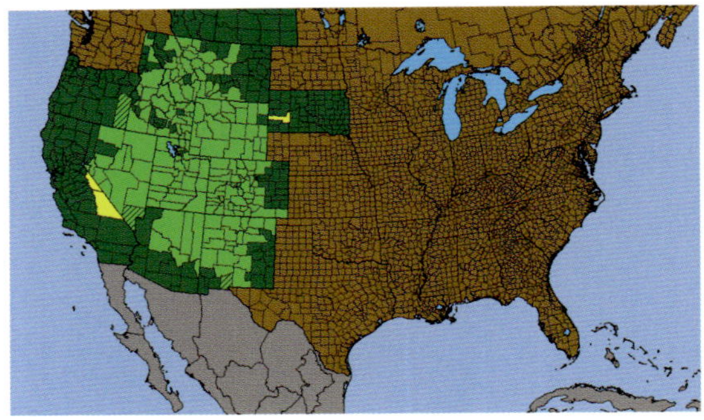

- Herbaceous perennial; 6 to 18 inches.
- Late-spring to early-summer white flowers on slender stems.
- Part shade; dry soil.
- HPV: Pollinated by native bees, moths, hummingbirds.

Heuchera richardsonii

RICHARDSON'S ALUMROOT, PRAIRIE ALUMROOT

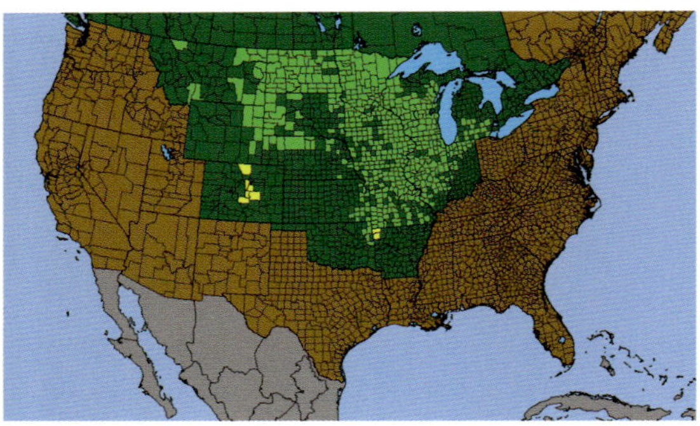

- Herbaceous perennial; 1 to 3 feet.
- Spring to summer white, pink, green, or purple flowers.
- Sun to part shade; moist to dry soil.
- Workhorse. HPV: Pollinated by native bees, butterflies, hummingbirds.

Heuchera micrantha

CREVICE ALUMROOT, CORAL BELLS

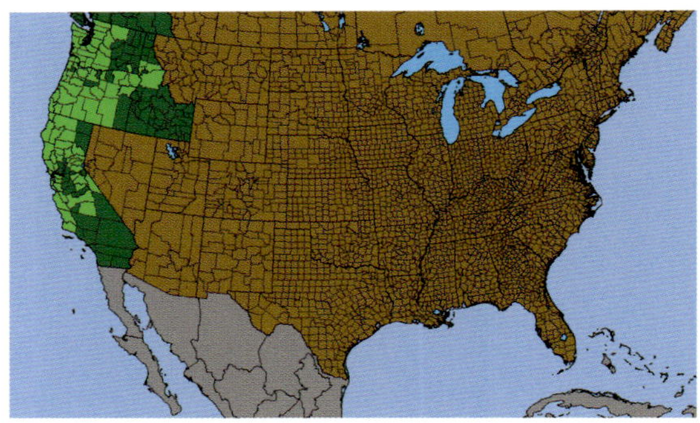

- Herbaceous perennial; 1 to 2 feet.
- Summer greenish white flowers.
- Part shade to shade; moist to dry soil.
- HPV: Pollinated by native bees, moths, hummingbirds.

Getting to know the various *Heuchera* species is a little like attending a cousins' reunion: Across remarkable differences, the family resemblance shines through, chiefly through the lobed leaves, sometimes rounded, sometimes pointed, and the stalks of small, bell-shaped flowers, sometimes insignificant, sometimes showy. All are valuable as ground cover plants, with beautiful yet durable foliage. Some heuchera varieties have naturally occurring red leaves, but there are also numerous cultivated varieties with foliage ranging from peach to burgundy. Because these manipulated colors can reduce plants' value to pollinators, look for straight species.

Tiarella species

FOAMFLOWER

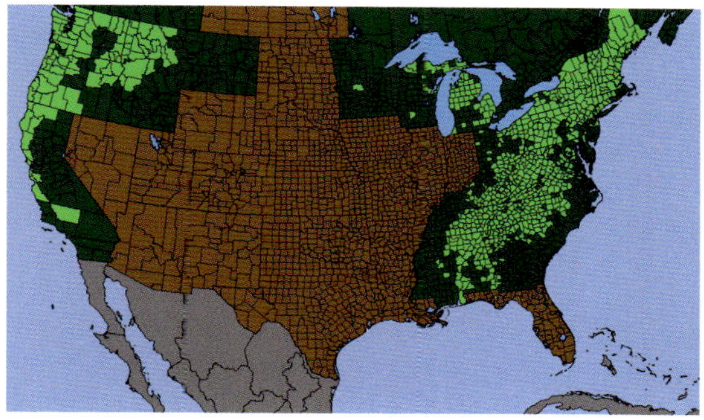

- Herbaceous perennial; 6 to 12 inches.
- Late-spring to early-summer white to pink flowers.
- Part shade to shade; moist acidic soil.
- HPV: Pollinated by native bees, moths, butterflies, other insects.

Tiarella has recently been reclassified, from two species with several subspecies into six distinct species. Many sources still use the old classification. All *Tiarella* species are similar in their growth requirements and appearance. Stalks of tiny flowers form a fluffy mass that gives these plants the common name foamflower. The flowers sit above lobed leaves, which vary across species from rounded to heart-shaped or deeply cut. Some species produce stolons, or runners, that grow across a garden's surface. Further slight variations appear in the *Tiarella* species in the east, which now include *T. austrina*, *T. cordifolia*, *T. nautila*, *T. stolonifera*, and *T. wherryi*. The most widely available are *T. cordifolia*, *T. stolonifera*, and *T. wherryi*. The single western species is *T. trifoliata*. In cooler areas, *Tiarella* will tolerate some morning sun but prefers shady conditions

INSTEAD OF THESE:

Hemerocallis species

DAYLILIES

Daylilies are popular for their vibrant trumpet-shaped blooms—in a wide range of yellows, oranges, and reds—and for their ease of care. Adaptable to various soil types, they thrive in well-drained soil and prefer full sun to partial shade in all but the hottest climates. Anyone who has ever visited the garden one day to find a plant covered in buds, only to see it picked clean the next morning, knows that daylilies are the cotton candy of the deer world.

PLANT THESE:

Lilium michiganense

MICHIGAN LILY

AL, AR, IA, IL, IN, KS, KY, MI, MN, MO, MS, NE, NY, OH, OK, SD, TN, WI

Lilium philadelphicum

WOOD LILY

AR, CO, CT, DC, DE, GA, IA, IL, IN, KY, MA, MD, ME, MI, MN, MT, NC, ND, NE, NH, NJ, NM, NY, OH, PA, RI, SD, TN, TX, VA, VT, WI, WV, WY

Lilium columbianum

COLUMBIA(N) LILY, OREGON LILY, WILD TIGER LILY

CA, ID, OR, WA

Rudbeckia hirta

BLACK-EYED SUSAN

Throughout the contiguous US, except AZ, CA, ID, MT, NV, OR, UT, WA

Rudbeckia fulgida

ORANGE CONEFLOWER

AL, AR, DC, DE, FL, GA, IL, IN, KY, MA, MD, MI, MO, MS, NC, NJ, OH, OK, PA, SC, TN, TX, VA, WI, WV

Rudbeckia triloba

BROWN-EYED SUSAN

AL, AR, DC, FL, GA, IA, IL, IN, KS, KY, LA, MD, MI, MN, MO, MS, NC, NJ, NY, OH, OK, PA, RI, SC, TN, TX, VA, WI, WV

Asclepias tuberosa

BUTTERFLY MILKWEED

AL, AR, AZ, CO, CT, DC, DE, FL, GA, IA, IL, IN, KS, KY, LA, MA, MD, ME, MI, MN, MO, MS, NC, NE, NH, NJ, NM, NY, OH, OK, PA, RI, SC, SD, TN, TX, UT, VA, VT, WI, WV

Helenium autumnale

COMMON SNEEZEWEED

Throughout the contiguous US, except ME, NH

Lilium michiganense

MICHIGAN LILY

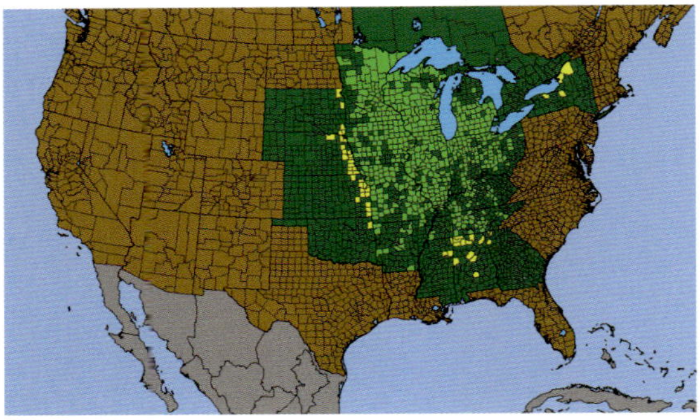

- Herbaceous perennial; 2 to 6 feet.
- Midsummer orange flowers.
- Sun to part shade; wet to moist soil.
- Pollinated by native bees, butterflies, hummingbirds.

Lilium philadelphicum

WOOD LILY

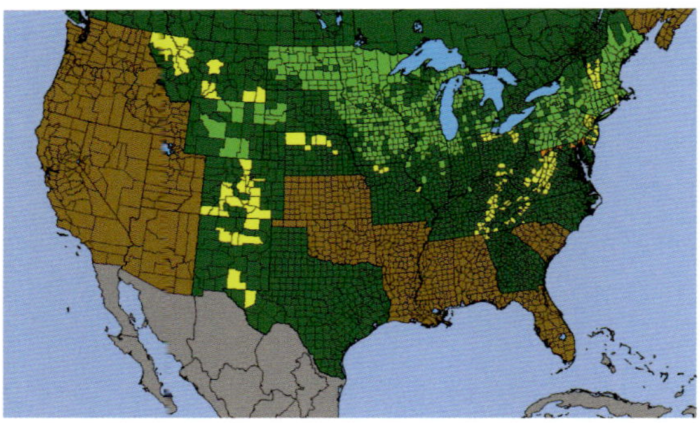

- Herbaceous perennial; 2 to 5 feet.
- Mid- to late-summer orange flowers.
- Sun to shade; moist to dry soil.
- Feeds moths, butterflies, hummingbirds.

Lilium columbianum

COLUMBIA(N) LILY, OREGON LILY, WILD TIGER LILY

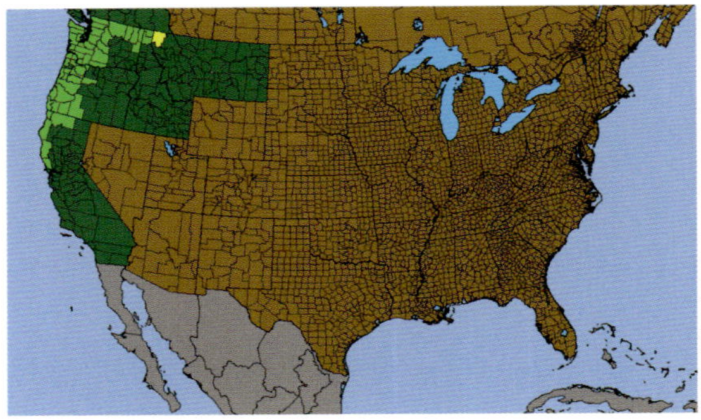

- Herbaceous perennial; 2 to 7 feet.
- Summer orange flowers.
- Part shade; dry soil.
- Pollinated by native bees, butterflies, hummingbirds.

The petals of both *Lilium michiganense* and *L. columbianum* hang down from their stems and are strongly recurved; the flowers of *L. philadelphicum* face upward. All are vibrant in color, ranging from a deep orange to reddish orange. These are among the most widely commercially available of the North American native lilies. Their form can vary across their native range, so for the most benefit to wildlife, it's ideal to buy them from a reputable local nursery with a known source. All these lilies have been over-collected from their wild habitats and in some places are becoming uncommon. Deer graze them eagerly, so in high-deer-pressure areas, another choice might be wiser.

Rudbeckia hirta
BLACK-EYED SUSAN

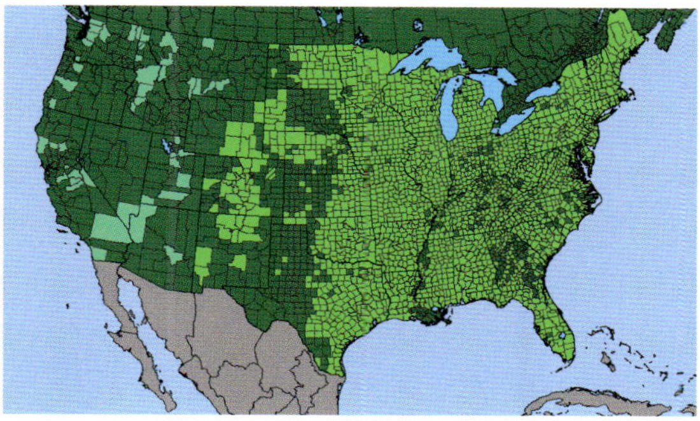

- Herbaceous perennial; 1 to 2½ feet.
- Summer yellow flowers.
- Sun to part shade; moist to dry soil.
- Workhorse. VHPV: Pollinated by native bees, moths, butterflies, other insects. Host to moth and butterfly caterpillars.
- Deer resistant.

Rudbeckia triloba
BROWN-EYED SUSAN

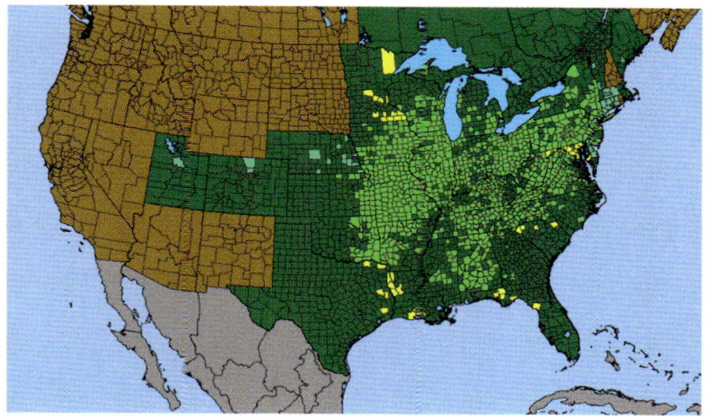

- Herbaceous perennial; 1 to 5 feet.
- Late-summer to early-fall yellow flowers.
- Full sun to part shade; moist to dry soil. Drought tolerant.
- Workhorse. VHPV: Pollinated by native bees, moths, butterflies, other insects. Seeds feed birds.

Rudbeckia fulgida
ORANGE CONEFLOWER

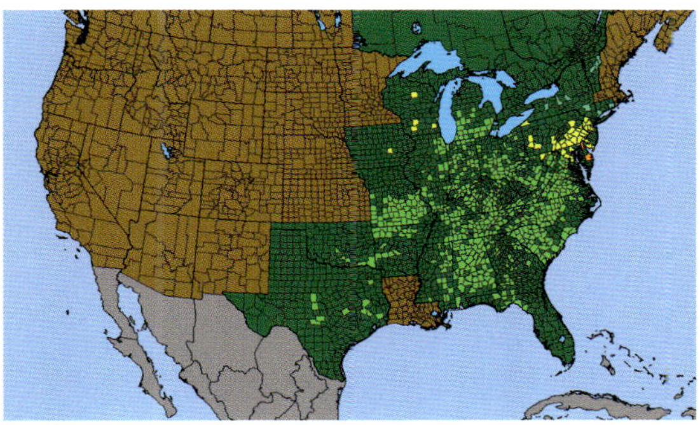

- Herbaceous perennial; 2 to 3 feet.
- Late-summer to early-fall yellow flowers.
- Sun to part shade; wet to moist soil.
- Workhorse. Pollinated by native bees, butterflies. Seeds feed birds.

All the rudbeckias listed here (and others) will fill the garden with bright yellow cheer in summer, sometimes into fall. They are vigorous growers that need plenty of garden companions to keep them from filling every empty spot with their seedlings. While they are relatively short-lived, they're a workhorse species because they multiply persistently. Their dark centers are filled with seeds all winter and are an important food source for birds. As its map suggests, *R. hirta* has naturalized coast to coast, well beyond its original native range.

Asclepias tuberosa

BUTTERFLY MILKWEED

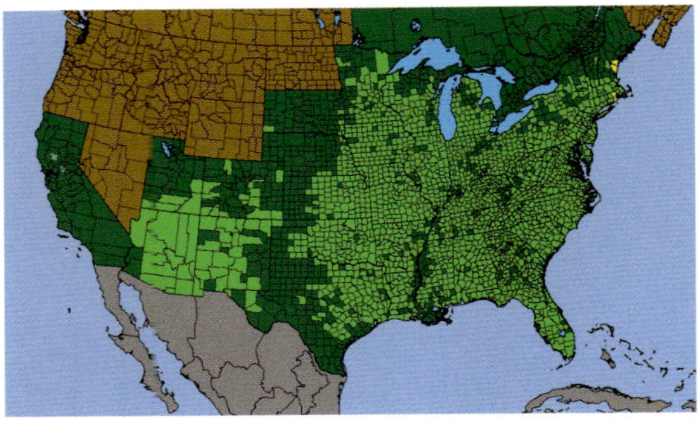

- Herbaceous perennial; 1 to 3 feet.
- Summer bright orange flowers.
- Sun to part shade; dry soil. Drought tolerant.
- VHPV: Pollinated by native bees, butterflies (including monarchs), other insects, hummingbirds. Host to moth and butterfly caterpillars, including monarchs.
- Deer resistant.

The broad, flat flower clusters of *Asclepias tuberosa* deliver a bright pop of midsummer orange like no other plant in the garden. It's a butterfly magnet and a monarch host plant, like all milkweeds. It won't tolerate wet soil and can take a while to settle in a spot and establish its taproot, but once it does, it's long-lived. It has an ornamental seedpod that extends its seasonal interest, something else it has in common with other milkweeds.

Helenium autumnale

COMMON SNEEZEWEED

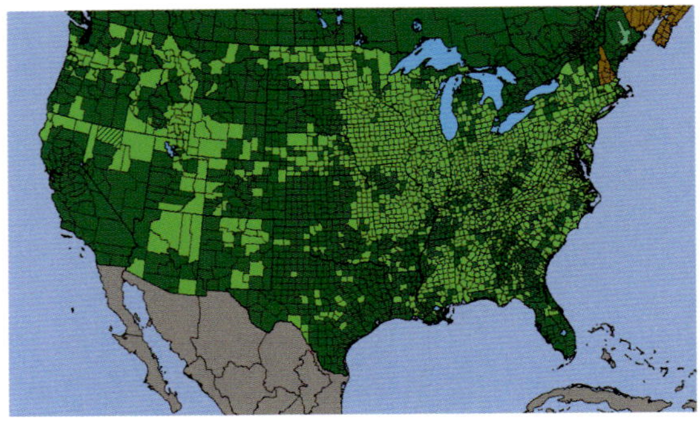

- Herbaceous perennial; 2 to 4 feet.
- Fall yellow flowers.
- Sun to part shade; wet to moist soil.
- Workhorse. VHPV: Pollinated by native bees, moths, butterflies, other insects. Host to moth caterpillars.

When other perennials are in retreat, *Helenium* is jumping into the garden foreground with large, bright yellow flowers on stems that vault above most of their neighbors. The daisylike petals surround an almost spherical center. The round seed heads mature and persist as a novel garden feature and source of late-autumn and winter food for birds.

More great native choices: *Solidago* spp. (pages 112–113)

INSTEAD OF THESE:

Hosta species

PLANTAIN LILY

Pulmonaria species

LUNGWORT

Both these plants have claimed their place as stalwarts for shady landscapes. Hostas are widely recognized for their varied leaf and flower forms and adaptability. They prefer moist, well-drained soil in partial to full shade. Their diverse array of leaf shapes and colors bring texture and visual interest to gardens, but at a cost: Slugs love their leaves and deer their blooms, and gardeners go to elaborate lengths to keep both critters at bay.

Pulmonaria fills shady or semi-shady gardens spots with upward-facing, sometimes spotted leaves that stay neat all season beneath abundant small blooms in shades of pink, purple, and blue. That neatness is unfortunately evidence that pulmonaria does not usually attract or feed native fauna.

PLANT THESE:

Athyrium filix-femina var. *angustum* (syn. *A. angustum*)

NORTHERN LADY FERN

AR, CO, CT, DC, DE, IA, IL, IN, KY, MA, MD, ME, MI, MN, MO, NC, ND, NE, NH, NJ, NY, OH, PA, RI, SD, TN, VA, VT, WI, WV

Athyrium asplenioides

SOUTHERN LADY FERN

AL, AR, CT, DC, DE, FL, GA, IL, IN, KS, LA, MA, MD, MO, MS, NC, NJ, NY, OH, OK, PA, RI, SC, TN, TX, VA, WV

Athyrium cyclosorum

WESTERN LADY FERN

AZ, CA, CO, ID, MI, MN, MT, ND, NE, NM, NV, OR, SD, UT, WA, WY

Polemonium reptans

JACOB'S LADDER

AL, AR, DC, DE, GA, IA, IL, IN, KS, KY, MD, MI, MN, MO, MS, NC, NJ, NY, OH, OK, PA, SD, TN, VA, WI, WV

Athyrium filix-femina var. *angustum* (syn. *A. angustum*)

NORTHERN LADY FERN

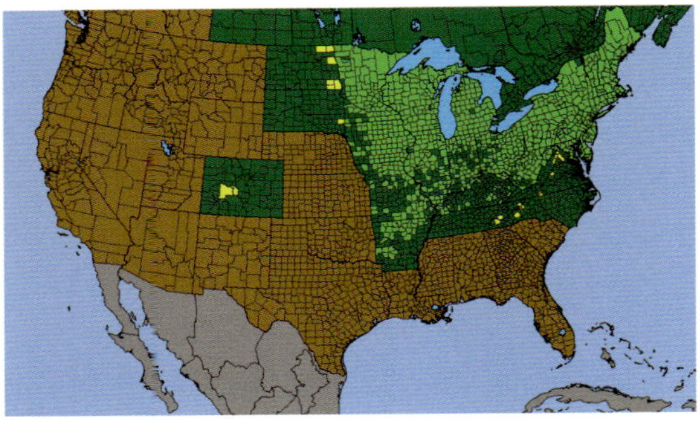

- Herbaceous perennial; 1 to 3 feet.
- Part shade to shade; wet to moist soil.
- Workhorse. Host to moth caterpillars.

Athyrium asplenioides

SOUTHERN LADY FERN

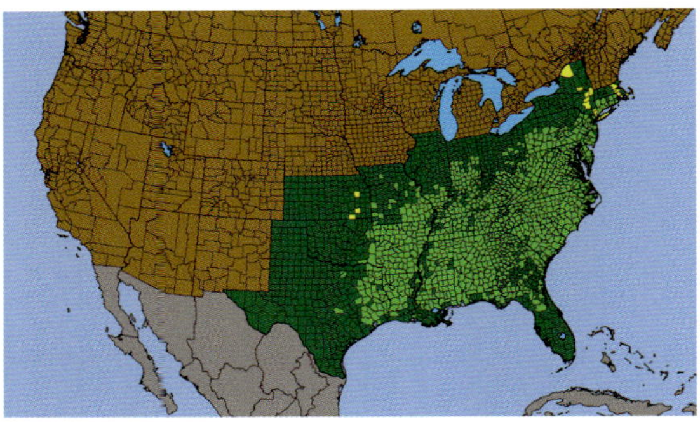

- Herbaceous perennial; 1 to 3 feet.
- Partial to full shade; moist soil.
- Provides habitat for insects, including moths and butterflies.

Athyrium cyclosorum

WESTERN LADY FERN

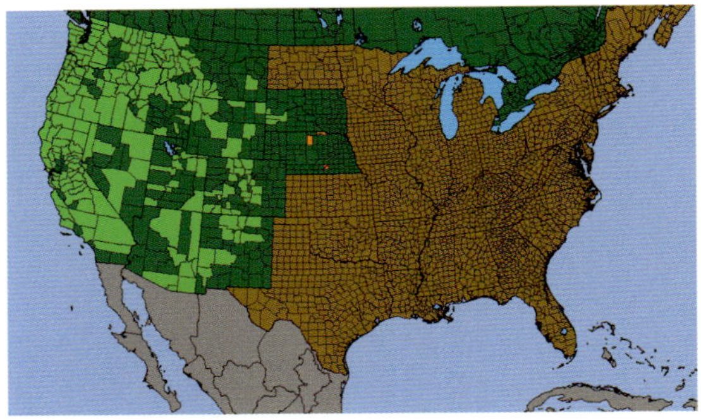

- Herbaceous perennial; 6 to 12 inches.
- Partial to full shade; moist soil.
- Provides habitat for moths, butterflies, other insects.

These local varieties of *Athyrium*, sometimes regarded as variations of a single plant across a large native range, illustrate how broadly useful ferns can be for filling shady spots, from wet to dry in all kinds of soil. Other native ferns to consider include eastern and western *Polystichum* species (including the semi-evergreen Christmas fern), *Osmunda* species (native to the eastern half of the country), and the tough, drought-tolerant, broadly native *Dryopteris* species.

Polemonium reptans

JACOB'S LADDER

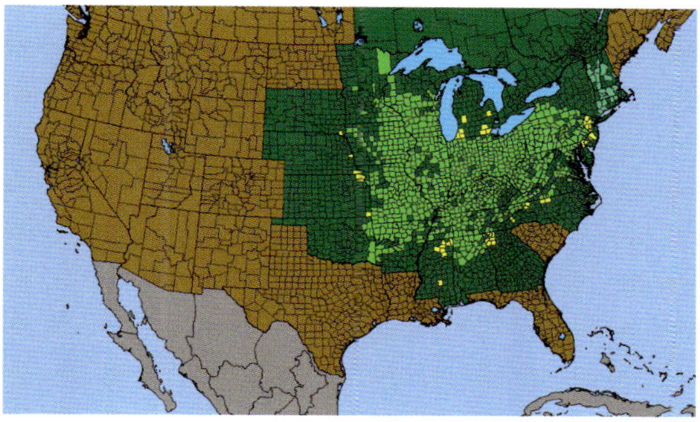

- Herbaceous perennial; 1 to 1½ feet.
- Late-spring to early-summer blue to purple flowers.
- Part shade to shade; moist to dry soil.
- Workhorse. VHPV: Pollinated by native bees, moths, butterflies, other insects. Host to moth caterpillars.

It's the compound leaves of *Polemonium reptans* that are said to give it the common name Jacob's ladder, but you could make an argument in favor of its flowers, which rise on their own stalks to float above the foliage. While polemoniums may go dormant in a drought, their bright green foliage is otherwise reliably cheerful and tidy throughout the growing season.

More great native choices: *Polygonatum biflorum* (page 121), *Heuchera* spp. (pages 128–129), *Tiarella* spp. (page 129), *Asarum* spp. (page 187)

INSTEAD OF THESE:

Iris germanica

BEARDED IRIS

Iris pallida

SWEET IRIS

Iris pseudacorus

YELLOW FLAG IRIS

Iris sibirica

SIBERIAN IRIS

Irises are among the formal beauties of the garden, with their straight, swordlike foliage and symmetrical intricate blooms. Irises are adaptable; they prefer full sun and grow across most of the contiguous United States, but will tolerate partial shade, blooming from early to late summer. *I. pseudacorus* is listed as invasive in several states, but due to the fact that they multiply via rhizomes, all these introduced irises have escaped cultivation (bearded iris across a notably wide area), displacing native plants.

PLANT THESE:

Iris missouriensis

ROCKY MOUNTAIN IRIS, WESTERN BLUE FLAG

AZ, CA, CO, ID, MT, ND, NE, NM, NV, OR, SD, UT, WA, WY

Iris versicolor

BLUE FLAG

CT, DC, DE, MA, MD, ME, MI, MN, NE, NH, NJ, NY, OH, PA, RI, VA, VT, WI

Iris virginica

VIRGINIA IRIS, GREAT BLUE FLAG, SOUTHERN BLUE FLAG

AL, AR, DC, FL, GA, IA, IL, IN, KS, KY, LA, MD, MI, MN, MO, MS, NC, NE, NY, OH, OK, PA, SC, TN, TX, VA, WI, WV

Lobelia cardinalis

CARDINAL FLOWER

AL, AR, AZ, CA, CO, CT, DC, DE, FL, GA, IA, IL, IN, KS, KY, LA, MA, MD, ME, MI, MN, MO, MS, NC, NE, NH, NJ, NM, NV, NY, OH, OK, PA, RI, SC, TN, TX, UT, VA, VT, WI, WV

Lobelia siphilitica

GREAT BLUE LOBELIA

AL, AR, CO, CT, DC, DE, GA, IA, IL, IN, KS, KY, LA, MA, MD, ME, MI, MN, MO, MS, NC, ND, NE, NH, NJ, NY, OH, OK, PA, SC, SD, TN, TX, VA, VT, WI, WV, WY

Iris missouriensis

ROCKY MOUNTAIN IRIS, WESTERN BLUE FLAG

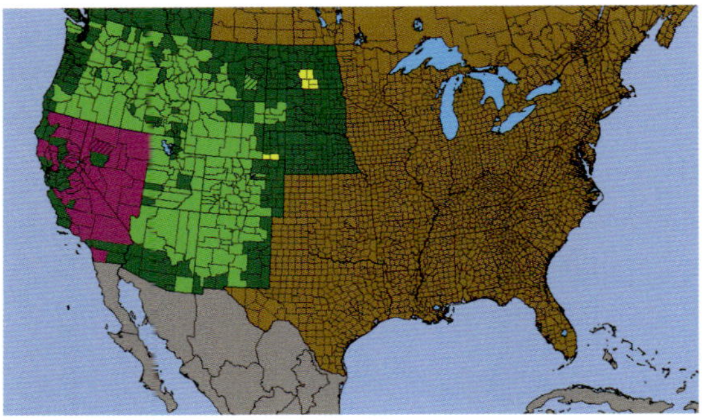

- Herbaceous perennial; 1 to 2 feet.
- Late-spring to early-summer blue to purple flowers.
- Sun to part shade; wet to moist soil.
- Workhorse. HPV: Pollinated by native bees, butterflies, hummingbirds. Host to moth caterpillars.
- Deer resistant.

Iris versicolor

BLUE FLAG

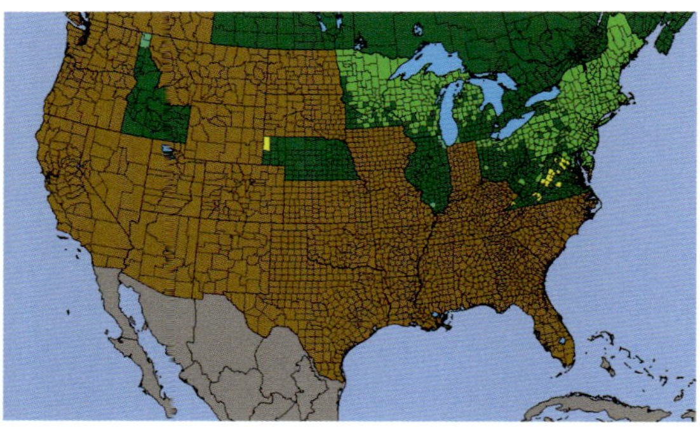

- Herbaceous perennial; 2 to 3 feet.
- Late-spring to early-summer blue flowers.
- Sun to part shade; wet to moist soil.
- VHPV: Pollinated by native bees, butterflies, other insects. Host to moth caterpillars.
- Deer resistant.

Iris virginica

VIRGINIA IRIS, GREAT BLUE FLAG, SOUTHERN BLUE FLAG

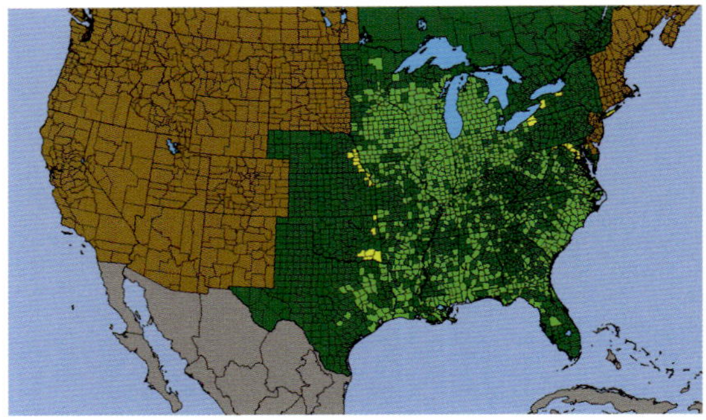

- Herbaceous perennial; 2 to 3 feet.
- Late-spring to early-summer blue to purple flowers.
- Sun to part shade; wet to moist soil.
- HPV: Feeds native bees, butterflies, other insects, hummingbirds.
- Deer resistant.

Luckily for gardeners who love the formal beauty and old-fashioned feel of irises, there are widely native and dependably glamorous species across all regions, with swordlike foliage and pale to deep blue or purple flowers, splashed with yellow. Although irises will thrive when constantly wet and are often found in rain gardens, they will grow in a typical garden setting in moist soil. Irises do best with regular division. As the pink color in the range map of *Iris missouriensis* shows, even native plants can become invasive outside their original range, displacing plants that coevolved with and support locally native wildlife, another great argument for planting local, not just North American, natives.

Lobelia cardinalis

CARDINAL FLOWER

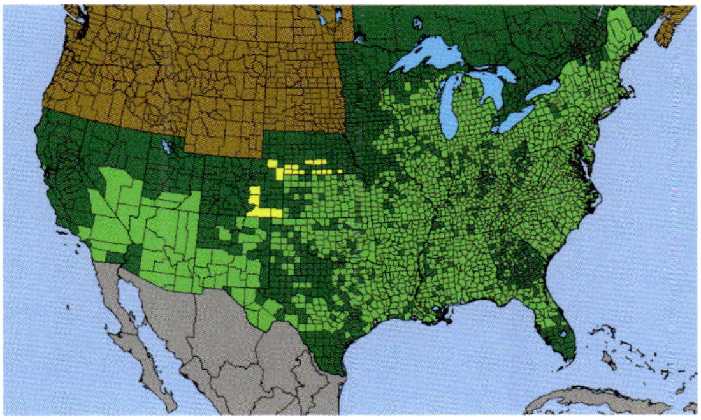

- Herbaceous perennial; 2 to 5 feet.
- Summer to early-fall red flowers.
- Sun to shade; wet to moist soil.
- HPV: Pollinated by native bees, butterflies, hummingbirds.

The vivid red tubular flowers hanging along the length of *Lobelia cardinalis*'s tall spikes are a hummingbird favorite. This short-lived perennial reseeds freely where it's happy, which means where the soil is constantly moist.

Lobelia siphilitica

GREAT BLUE LOBELIA

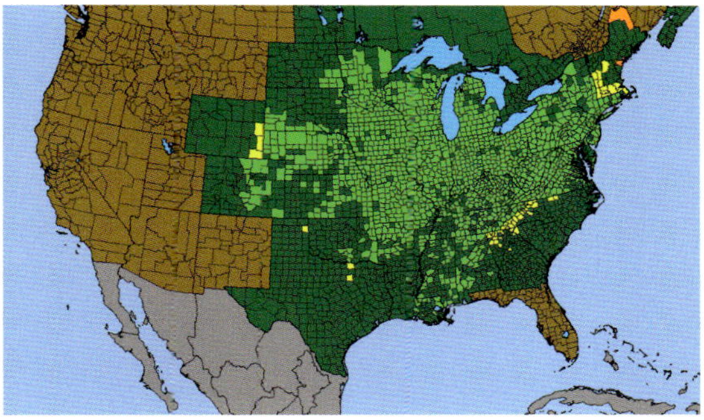

- Herbaceous perennial; 2 to 5 feet.
- Summer to early-fall clear blue flowers.
- Sun to part shade; wet to moist soil.
- HPV: Pollinated by native bees, moths, butterflies (including monarchs), other insects, hummingbirds. Host to moth caterpillars.

The cheerful lavender blue relation of *Lobelia cardinalis* prefers similar conditions, though I've found in my own New England garden that *L. siphilitica* will tolerate drier soil, is longer lived and self-sows prolifically. Although it does sometimes get very tall, particularly where naturalized in fields and meadows, in garden settings it's usually closer to 2 or 2½ feet. Occasionally a blue parent plant will produce white offspring, which make charming accents.

INSTEAD OF THESE:

Leucanthemum × superbum

SHASTA DAISY

Leucanthemum vulgare

OXEYE DAISY

Daisies have been ubiquitous in American fields and childhood memories for so long that it can be surprising to learn they are not native flowers. Both *Leucanthemum × superbum* and *L. vulgare* are recognized by their classic white, upward-facing, many-petaled blooms on stems from 1 to 3 feet high. Shasta daisies grow in Zones 4 to 9, in full sun to part shade and well-drained soil, blooming from mid- to late summer, sometimes into early fall. *L. vulgare*, the classic field daisy, which grows in Zones 3 to 8, has become invasive and is banned for sale in several western states.

PLANT THESE:

Echinacea pallida

PALE PURPLE CONEFLOWER

AR, IA, IL, IN, KS, LA, MO, NE, OK, SC, TX, WI

Echinacea purpurea

PURPLE CONEFLOWER, EASTERN PURPLE CONEFLOWER

AL, AR, FL, GA, IA, IL, IN, KS, KY, LA, MI, MO, MS, NC, OH, OK, TN, TX

Echinacea angustifolia

NARROWLEAF CONEFLOWER

AR, CO, DC, IA, IN, KS, LA, MN, MO, MT, ND, NE, NM, OK, SD, TX, WY

Gaillardia pulchella

BLANKETFLOWER

AR, AZ, CO, LA, NE, NM, OK, TX

Symphyotrichum lanceolatum

WHITE PANICLE ASTER

Throughout the contiguous US

Echinacea pallida

PALE PURPLE CONEFLOWER

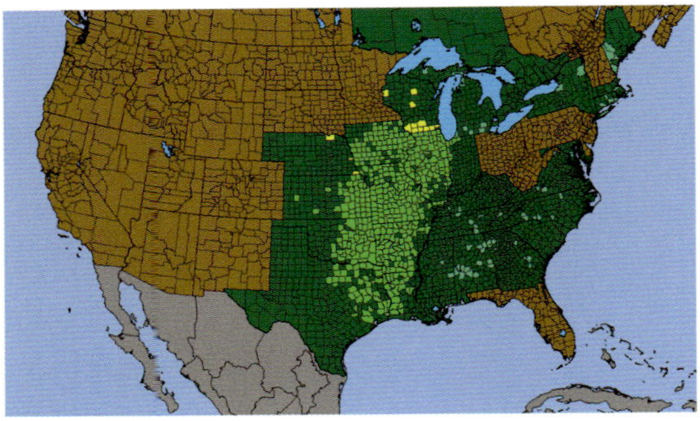

- Herbaceous perennial; 1½ to 3 feet.
- Spring to summer pale pink to purple flowers.
- Sun; moist to dry soil.
- Workhorse. VHPV: Pollinated by native bees, moths, butterflies (including monarchs), other insects, hummingbirds. Host to moth caterpillars.

Echinacea purpurea

PURPLE CONEFLOWER, EASTERN PURPLE CONEFLOWER

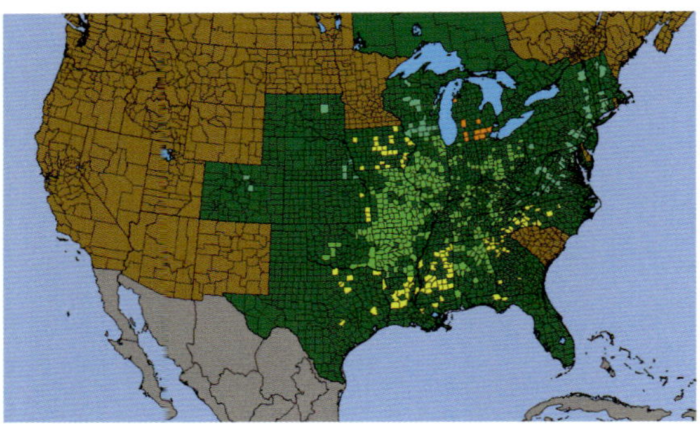

- Herbaceous perennial; 2 to 4 feet.
- Spring to summer pink to purple flowers.
- Sun to part shade; dry soil.
- Workhorse. VHPV: Pollinated by native bees, moths, butterflies (including monarchs), other insects, hummingbirds. Host to moth caterpillars.
- Deer resistant.

Echinacea angustifolia

NARROWLEAF CONEFLOWER

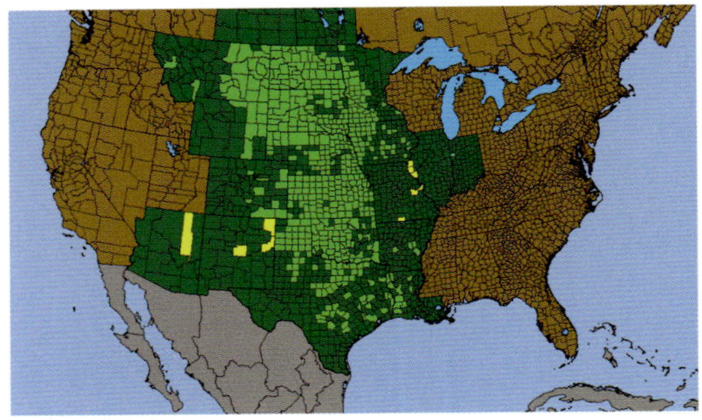

- Herbaceous perennial; 1 to 3 feet.
- Spring to summer pink to purple flowers.
- Sun to part shade; dry soil.
- Workhorse. VHPV: Pollinated by native bees, moths, butterflies (including monarchs).
- Deer resistant.

All these *Echinacea* species feature pleasantly drooping daisylike flowers in shades of pink or pale purple with a prominent central cone for seeds. They all have strong upright stems but do best among many plant neighbors. Planted too far apart, they may lean or fall over. Birds love the seeds in winter. Echinaceas are abundantly self-sowing, another reason to plant equally assertive natives, such as *Rudbeckia* and *Symphyotrichum* species (see box, opposite) or meadow grasses, nearby.

Gaillardia pulchella

BLANKETFLOWER

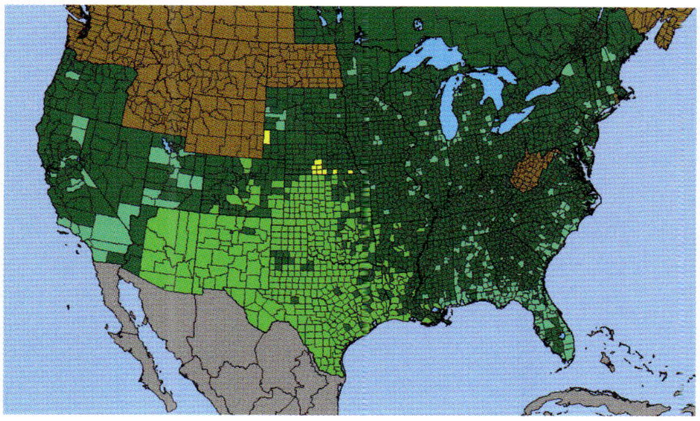

- Herbaceous perennial; 1 to 2 feet.
- Spring to summer red-and-yellow flowers.
- Sun to part shade; moist to dry soil. Drought tolerant.
- Workhorse. VHPV: Pollinated by native bees, butterflies (including monarchs), other insects. Host to moth and butterfly caterpillars.

Gaillardia pulchella adds a sunny pop like no other native to the summer garden, with its multicolored blooms made of up wide, three-toothed, daisylike petals, which vary in appearance across the many naturally occurring varieties of this plant. In the southern part of its native range, *G. pulchella* blooms as early as January. Farther north and in the areas where it has naturalized, blooms extend into summer months. Gaillardias are short-lived perennials that maintain their place in the garden with a freely self-sowing habit.

Symphyotrichum lanceolatum

WHITE PANICLE ASTER

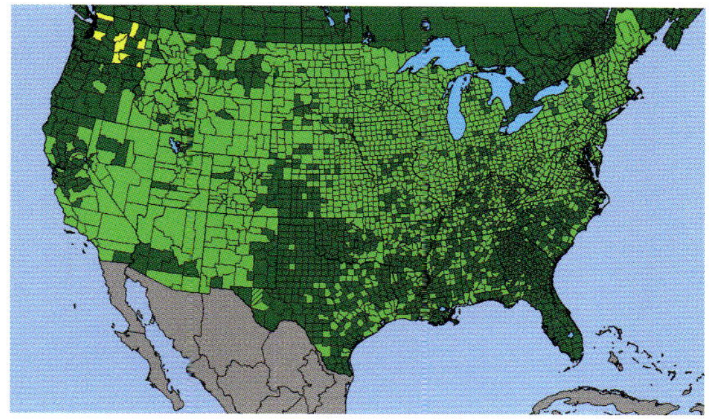

- Herbaceous perennial; 2 to 5 feet.
- Late-summer to fall white flowers.
- Sun to part shade; wet to moist soil.
- VHPV: Pollinated by native bees, moths, butterflies (including monarchs), other insects. Host to butterfly caterpillars.
- Deer resistant.

The wide-ranging *Symphyotrichum lanceolatum* is one of the many *Symphyotrichum* (aster) species that make good substitutes for Shasta daisies, if white flowers are wanted. There are white *Symphyotrichum* species native to many eco-regions and widely available; they vary in flower and leaf size, some with a bushy shape and others more upright.

More great native choices: Other *Symphyotrichum* spp. (page 103), *Rudbeckia* spp. (page 133)

INSTEAD OF THESE:

Perovskia species

RUSSIAN SAGE

Nepeta cataria

CATMINT

Tall, semi-woody Russian sage blossoms in the heat of high summer, in a shrubby form. Its primary value in the garden is the long bloom period of its tall purple-blue flowers, aromatic silvery gray foliage that discourages deer browsing, and its drought resistance. *Perovskia* grows 2½ to 3 feet tall (with some cultivars shorter) in poor, dry soil.

Similarly shrubby, *Nepeta cataria* also grows 2 to 3 feet, in sunny sites in poor, dry soil, without *Perovskia*'s woody habit. Its foliage has a strong, minty scent that cats love. *Nepeta* is now considered invasive in many US states.

PLANT THESE:

Liatris scariosa

LARGE BLAZING STAR, SAVANNA BLAZING STAR

AL, AR, CT, DE, GA, IL, IN, MA, MD, ME, MI, MO, NC, NH, NJ, NY, OH, PA, RI, SC, TN, VA, WI, WV

Liatris punctata

DOTTED BLAZING STAR, DOTTED GAYFEATHER

AR, CO, IA, KS, LA, MN, MO, MT, ND, NE, NM, OK, SD, TN, TX, WI, WY

Verbena stricta

HOARY VERBENA, WOOLY VERBENA

AR, CO, IA, IL, IN, KS, KY, MI, MN, MO, MS, MT, ND, NE, OH, OK, SD, TN, TX, WI, WY

Linum lewisii

WILD BLUE FLAX, PRAIRIE FLAX

AR, AZ, CA, CO, IA, ID, KS, LA, MI, MN, MO, MT, ND, NE, NM, NV, OK, OR, SD, TX, UT, WA, WY

Liatris scariosa

LARGE BLAZING STAR, SAVANNA BLAZING STAR

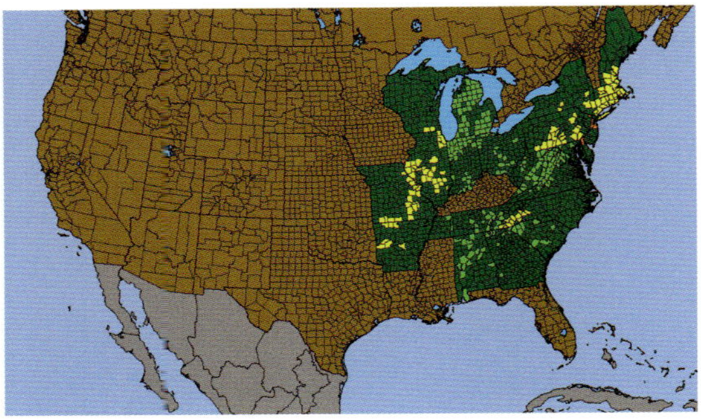

- Herbaceous perennial; 1½ to 2 feet.
- Late-summer purple flowers.
- Sun; dry soil. Drought tolerant.
- Workhorse. VHPV: Pollinated by native bees, butterflies (including monarchs). Host to moth caterpillars.

Of the many commercially available species of *Liatris*, these two both grow well in dry soil and together cover a broad native range. The single rosy purple spikes of *L. punctata* appear in clusters, with flowers covering a third to a half of its stem. The taller pink to purple spikes of *L. scariosa* hold their thistlelike flowers somewhat farther from the stem.

Liatris punctata

DOTTED BLAZING STAR, DOTTED GAYFEATHER

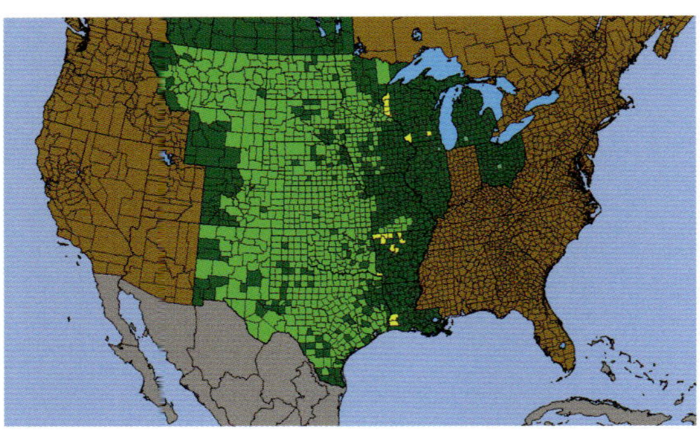

- Herbaceous perennial; 1½ to 2½ feet.
- Late-summer pink to purple flowers.
- Sun; dry soil. Drought tolerant.
- Workhorse. VHPV: Pollinated by native bees, butterflies (including monarchs), hummingbirds. Host to moth caterpillars.

Verbena stricta

HOARY VERBENA, WOOLY VERBENA

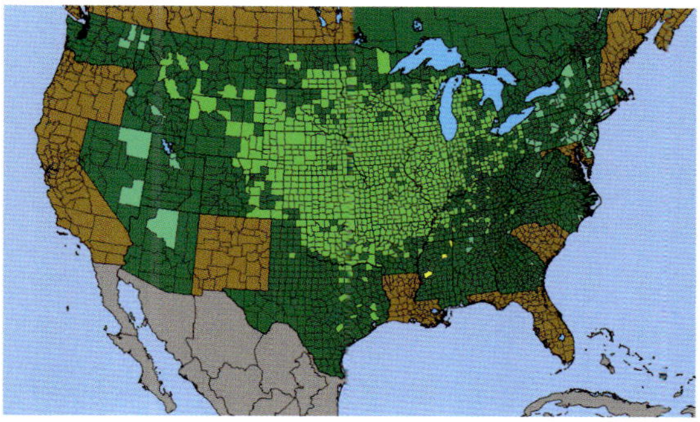

- Herbaceous perennial; 1 to 4 feet.
- Summer to early-fall lavender to purple flowers.
- Sun; dry soil. Drought tolerant.
- Workhorse. VHPV: Pollinated by native bees, moths, butterflies (including monarchs), other insects, hummingbirds. Host to moth caterpillars.
- Deer resistant.

Like other verbenas, this one features long-lived blooms on a short-lived plant. Flowers bloom in a ring, gradually circling from midway up to the spiky top of the stem. This plant seeds freely and germinates readily to maintain its place in the garden. It will quickly give up in the presence of very competitive companions, though.

Linum lewisii

WILD BLUE FLAX, PRAIRIE FLAX

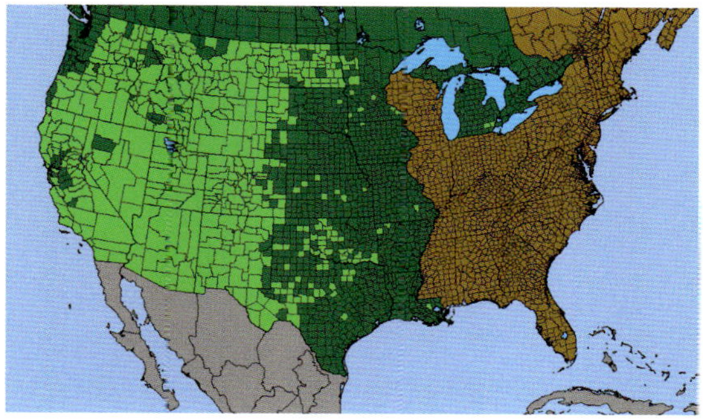

- Herbaceous perennial 1½ to 2 feet.
- Spring to summer pale blue flowers.
- Sun; dry soil. Drought tolerant.
- Workhorse. Pollinated by native bees, butterflies, other insects.

Blue flowers bloom gradually but profusely up the delicate-looking stems of *Linum lewisii*, with the topmost blooms finally appearing like a blue cloud that floats above the foliage. A massed display is especially stunning.

NOTE: Many wildflower seed companies offer *Linum perenne*, which is the European species and not native to the United States.

More great native choices: *Monarda* spp. (pages 98, 179), *Salvia* spp. (page 154)

INSTEAD OF THESE:

Salvia nemorosa

MEADOW SAGE

Saliva × superba

WOODLAND SAGE

Salvia × sylvestris

BLUE SAGE

Introduced salvias, native to Europe, Asia, and Africa, are known for their adaptability, easy care, and profuse blooms. *Salvia aethiopis* (Mediterranean sage), no longer commonly sold in the United States, is the one species listed as invasive, but other commonly grown salvias have escaped gardens and established wild populations that displace native plants. While introduced salvias have a reputation for attracting pollinators, the best nutrition for pollinators comes from the plants with which they coevolved. And salvias, like other widely available garden plants, have been hybridized and altered into many new cultivated varieties whose value to the pollinators that visit them is uncertain. Low-value plants that draw pollinators away from those with more nutritionally rich food sources may be harmful to these pollinator populations.

PLANT THESE:

Salvia lyrata

LYRELEAF SAGE

AL, AR, CT, DC, DE, FL, GA, IL, IN, KS, KY, LA, MD, MO, MS, NC, NJ, NY, OH, OK, PA, SC, TN, TX, VA, WV

Salvia azurea

AZURE SAGE

AL, AR, CT, FL, GA, IA, KS, LA, MA, MO, MS, NC, NE, NH, OK, SC, TX

Salvia dorrii

PURPLE SAGE

AZ, CA, ID, NV, OR, UT, WA

Delphinium carolinianum

CAROLINA LARKSPUR, PRAIRIE LARKSPUR, BLUE LARKSPUR

AL, AR, CO, FL, GA, IA, IL, KS, KY, LA, MN, MO, MS, ND, NE, NM, OK, SC, SD, TN, TX, WI

Salvia lyrata

LYRELEAF SAGE

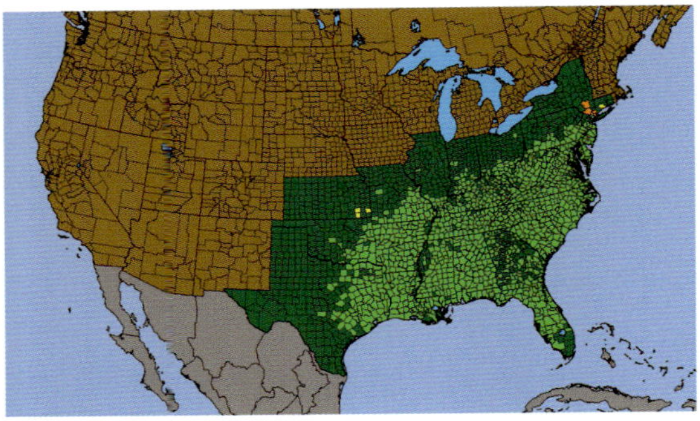

- Herbaceous perennial; 1 to 2 feet.
- Spring to summer blue flowers.
- Sun to part shade; wet to dry soil.
- Workhorse. VHPV: Pollinated by native bees, butterflies (including monarchs), other insects, hummingbirds.
- Deer resistant.

Salvia azurea

AZURE SAGE

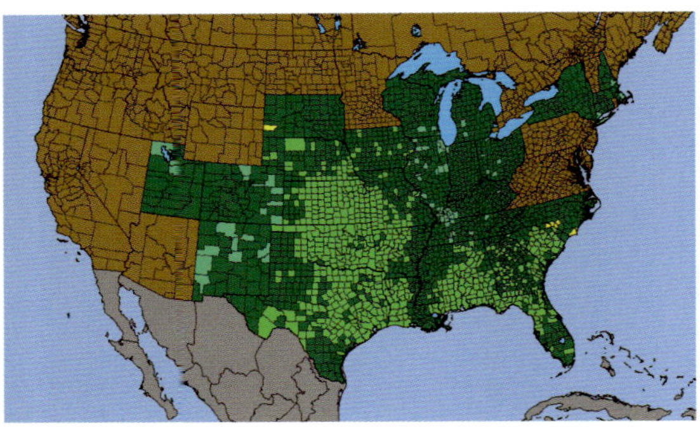

- Herbaceous perennial; 2 to 5 feet.
- Summer blue flowers.
- Part shade; dry soil.
- Workhorse. VHPV: Pollinated by native bees, butterflies (including monarchs), other insects, hummingbirds. Host to moth caterpillars.
- Deer resistant.

Salvia dorrii

PURPLE SAGE

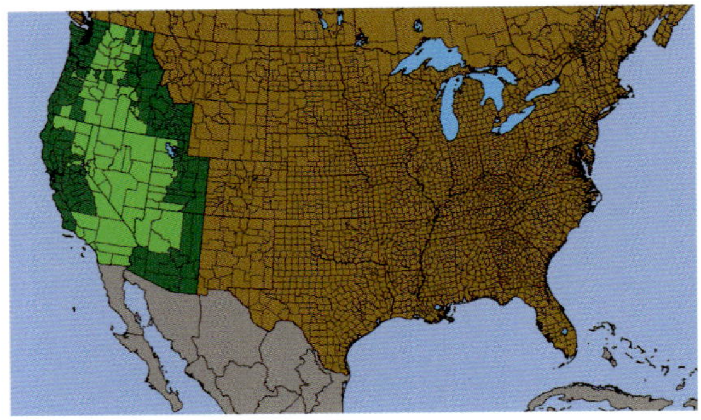

- Deciduous shrub; 2½ to 4 feet.
- Spring blue flowers.
- Sun; dry soil.
- Workhorse. HPV: Pollinated by native bees, hummingbirds.
- Deer resistant.

The native salvias are an enormous group of annual and perennial plants with a variety of forms, from herbaceous plants to shrubs. The examples here include some of the most widely native and commercially available. Sages are mostly sun lovers, with some varieties tolerating or preferring some shade. All thrive in dry soil and have aromatic leaves that discourage browsing by mammals.

Delphinium carolinianum

CAROLINA LARKSPUR, PRAIRIE LARKSPUR, BLUE LARKSPUR

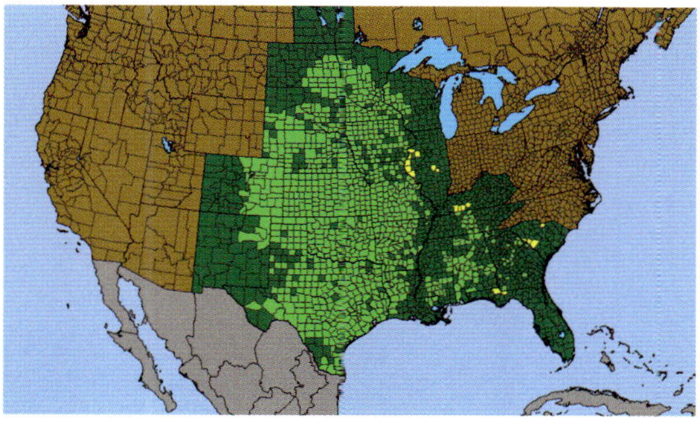

- Herbaceous perennial; 1 to 4 feet.
- Summer white to blue flowers.
- Sun to part shade; moist to dry soil.
- HPV: Pollinated by native bees, moths, butterflies, hummingbirds.
- Deer resistant.

Delicate, spurred flowers ranging from white to blue (most often pale blue) brighten the length of stems up to 4 feet tall, blooming in early to midsummer. *Delphinium carolinianum*'s native range extends farther north than our native salvias, making it an especially good choice where no native salvia can be grown.

More great native choices: *Monarda* spp. (pages 98, 179), *Liatris* spp. (page 150), *Verbena stricta* (page 151)

INSTEAD OF THESE:

Pennisetum species

FOUNTAIN GRASS

Annual and perennial varieties of fountain grass are grown for their tall, arching foliage and plumelike flower heads. Many species are grown as annuals in cool areas, but along the West Coast and in the Southwest where they are hardier, some pennisetums have been identified as invasive. Many reliably perennial sun-loving native grass species will offer equal beauty with more benefits to the garden and local ecology.

PLANT THESE:

Schizachyrium scoparium

LITTLE BLUESTEM

Throughout the contiguous US, except CA, NV, OR

Deschampsia cespitosa

TUFTED HAIRGRASS

AZ, CA, CO, CT, ID, IL, IN, KY, MA, MD, ME, MI, MN, MT, NC, ND, NH, NJ, NM, NV, NY, OH, OR, PA, RI, SD, UT, VA, VT, WA, WI, WV, WY

Schizachyrium scoparium

LITTLE BLUESTEM

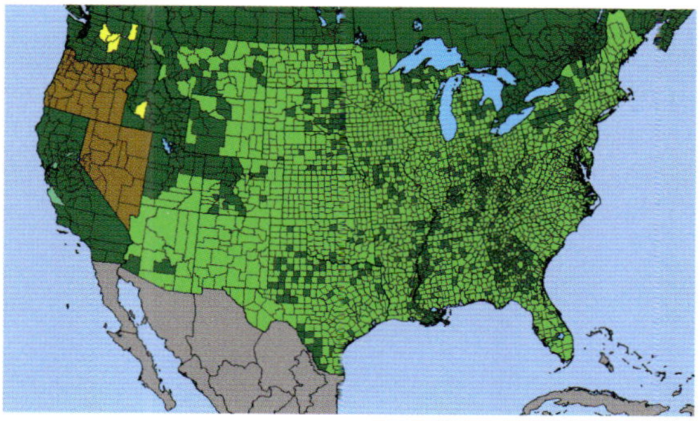

- Herbaceous grass; 2 to 4 feet.
- Late-summer to fall white to pink seed heads. Bronze fall foliage.
- Sun to part shade; moist to dry soil.
- Workhorse. HPV: Feeds butterflies. Host to moth and butterfly caterpillars.
- Deer resistant.

This widely native bunchgrass is one of the most versatile for gardens, with a clumping habit, blue-green color on new spring growth, and red fall foliage that fades to a beige on stems that persist throughout winter. In addition to hosting a number of moth and butterflies species, the fuzzy seed heads of bluestem draw birds from their fall appearance through winter. Little bluestem is adaptable to a variety of soils but does not thrive in very wet conditions.

Deschampsia cespitosa

TUFTED HAIRGRASS

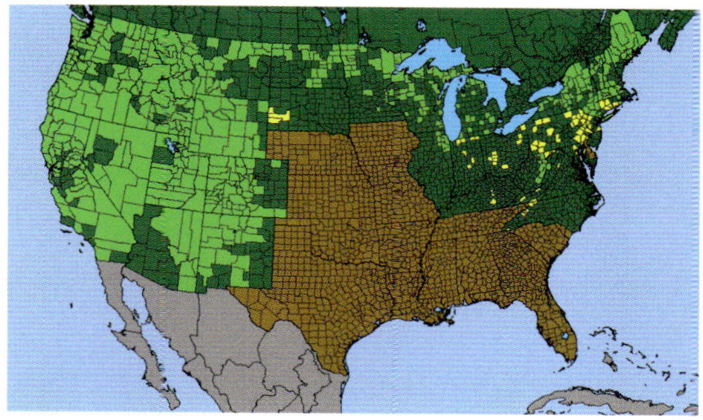

- Semi-evergreen herbaceous grass; 2 to 5 feet.
- Summer purple foliage; fall white seed heads.
- Sun to part shade; wet to moist alkaline soil.
- Workhorse. Host to butterfly caterpillars.
- Deer resistant.

One of the shorter native grasses, *Deschampsia cespitosa* has exceptionally long inflorescences, typically 2 to 3 feet but sometimes reaching up to 5 feet tall. The upright panicle emerges purplish but bleaches to an ornamental white, persisting to late fall. The basal foliage tends to be evergreen.

INSTEAD OF THESE:

Miscanthus sinensis
CHINESE SILVERGRASS

Cortaderia selloana
PAMPAS GRASS

Calamagrostis × *acutiflora* 'Karl Foerster'
FEATHER REED GRASS

Chinese silvergrass and pampas are both clump-forming grasses grown in warm regions for their architectural structure in full-sun gardens. Both reach up to 7 feet in full sun. Unfortunately, both have also jumped garden boundaries to form large invasive clumps in fields and along roadsides, displacing native plants.

Feather reed grass, a hybrid of European and Asian natives, is valued as a cool-season ornamental grass for full sun that grows most strongly early in the season, before warm-season grasses have awakened. But the 4- to 6-foot-tall seed plumes are sterile, meaning this plant, while not invasive, is of no nutritional value to pollinators or birds.

PLANT THESE:

Muhlenbergia capillaris

PINK MUHLY, HAIRAWN MUHLY

AL, AR, CT, DC, DE, FL, GA, IL, IN, KS, KY, LA, MA, MD, MO, MS, NC, NJ, NY, OH, OK, PA, SC, TN, TX, VA, WV

Sporobolus heterolepis

PRAIRIE DROPSEED

AR, CO, CT, GA, IA, IL, IN, KS, KY, MA, MD, MI, MN, MO, MT, NC, ND, NE, NM, NY, OH, OK, PA, SD, TN, VA, WI, WY

Sporobolus airoides

ALKALI SACATON, ZACATE ALCALINO

AR, AZ, CA, CO, ID, KS, MO, MT, ND, NE, NM, NV, OK, OR, SD, TX, UT, WA, WY

Muhlenbergia capillaris

PINK MUHLY, HAIRAWN MUHLY

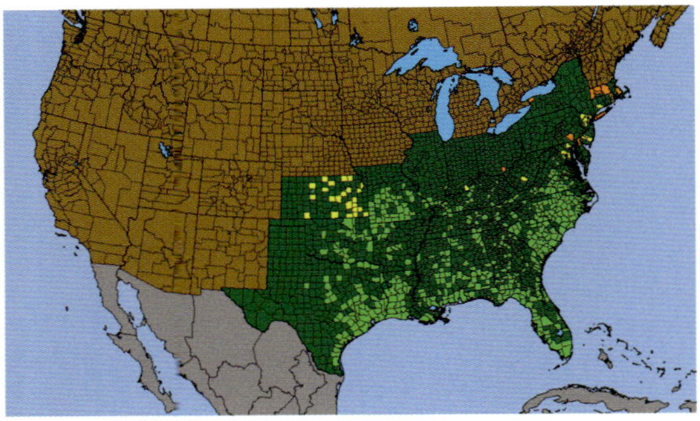

- Perennial grass; 1½ to 3 feet.
- Red fall flowers followed by pink seed heads. Yellow fall foliage.
- Sun to part shade; moist to dry soil. Drought and salt tolerant.
- Workhorse.
- Deer resistant.

In bloom, *Muhlenbergia capillaris* may rise as high as 5 feet tall, with its many-branched bunches of red seed heads accounting for half the plant's height. In fall, soft purplish pink seed heads light the fading landscape and can be seen from great distances.

Sporobolus heterolepis

PRAIRIE DROPSEED

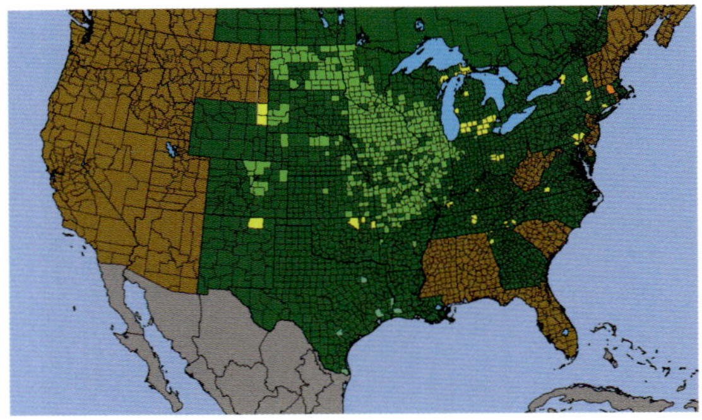

- Perennial grass; 1½ to 4 feet.
- Late-summer yellow flowers. Yellow fall foliage.
- Sun; moist to dry soil.
- Workhorse. Host to butterfly caterpillars.

This bright green, finely textured grass has a bunching habit that makes it a polite and especially useful foliage plant in garden settings. In bloom, airy panicles rise to 3 or 4 feet, after which the foliage fades to a golden hue. The scent of the foliage when brushed is said to resemble cilantro.

Sporobolus airoides

ALKALI SACATON, ZACATE ALCALINO

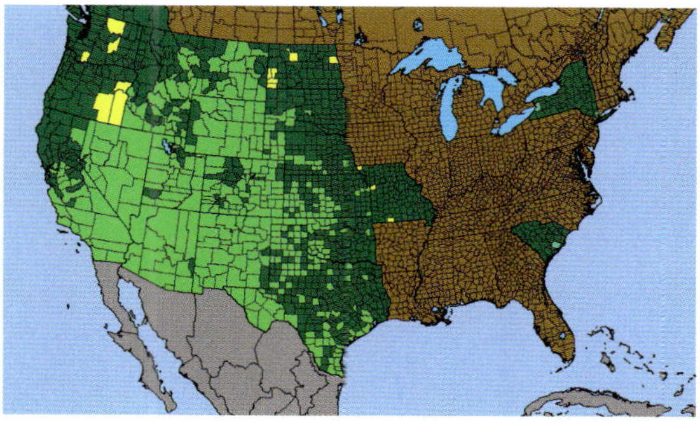

- Perennial grass; 1 to 5 feet.
- Summer yellow flowers followed by red seed heads. Yellow fall foliage.
- Sun to part shade; wet to dry alkaline soil. Drought tolerant.
- Workhorse. Host to moth caterpillars.

Airy, open flowering panicles float far above the foliage of *Sporobolus airoides* in summer, followed by decorative fall seed heads. This highly adaptable plant is shorter in very dry locations and closer to its maximum height where more moisture is present.

More great native choices: *Andropogon gerardi* (page 63), *Sorghastrum nutans* (page 63)

CHAPTER FOUR

The Hellstrip

One of the key benefits of a native garden is that it connects wildlife corridors, extending the availability of food and habitat resources that are so important for sustaining pollinator communities and seasonal migration. Hellstrips or boulevard gardens—those narrow strips of land between the sidewalk and the street—can play a key part in creating these corridors.

But they often present challenging conditions: limited space, compacted soil, and exposure to road salt. In addition, safety and local regulations may require that plants stay low for visibility where driveways meet the street and allow room for utility structures, pedestrian passage, and traffic sight lines. Choosing the right plants for these areas has to factor all of this into account. Many of the plant options highlighted in earlier sections of this book will work well in hellstrip gardens, particularly drought- and salt-tolerant varieties whose mature height doesn't exceed more than 3 feet or so. This section highlights additional plants that are especially good in plantings that border streets.

INSTEAD OF THESE:

Rosa rugosa

RUGOSA ROSE, BEACH ROSE

Buxus sempervirens

BOXWOOD

Euonymus japonicus

JAPANESE EUONYMUS

While many shrubs are used in hellstrip plantings, these favorites represent the low-profile, easily maintained, salt- and pollution-resistant plants that are most popular for streetside gardens that must often endure heavy car and foot traffic, overspray of road salt, or being buried under winter snow.

PLANT THIS:

Rhus aromatica

FRAGRANT SUMAC, AROMATIC SUMAC

Throughout the contiguous US, except DE, MA, ME, NH, NJ, RI, WA

Rhus aromatica

FRAGRANT SUMAC, AROMATIC SUMAC

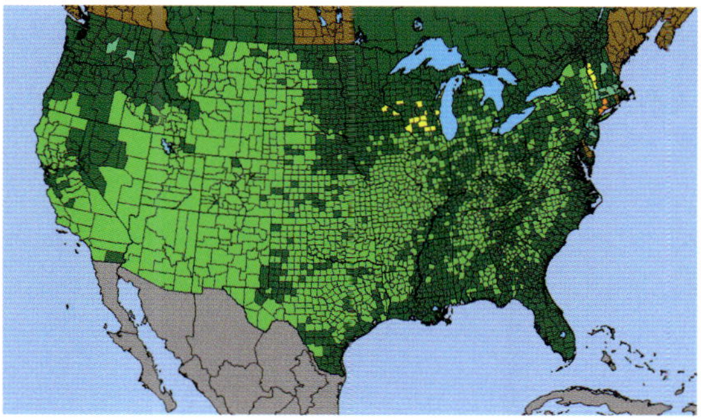

- Deciduous shrub; 3 to 6 feet.
- Spring yellow flowers followed by red berries. Yellow, red, and orange fall foliage.
- Sun to shade; moist to dry soil. Drought and salt tolerant.
- Workhorse. VHPV: Pollinated by native bees, moths, butterflies (including monarchs), other insects. Host to butterfly caterpillars.
- Deer resistant.

Rhus aromatica takes its name from the strong scent of both its flowers and its crushed leaves, which some find pleasantly lemony or resinous but others describe as unpleasant. Although fragrant sumac can reach a mature height of up to 6 feet, it grows less than 12 inches a year and is easily pruned in early spring to stay the right height in a curbside garden, where its rugged nature makes it a good fit. A cultivated variety, 'Grow-Lo', reaches only 1 to 2 feet and, like other native plants bred *only* for a shorter mature height (without manipulation of foliage or flowers), is thought to maintain the straight species' benefits to wildlife. *R. aromatica*'s edible berries, with a classic sour sumac flavor, persist in winter until birds have found them all.

More great native choices: *Ilex* spp. (pages 20, 34), *Hypericum prolificum* (page 25), *Ceanothus* spp. (page 31), *Diervilla lonicera* (page 47), *Morella* spp. (page 52), *Rosa* spp. (pages 65–67), *Itea virginica* (page 73), *Amorpha canescens* (page 75)

INSTEAD OF THIS:

Alchemilla mollis

LADY'S MANTLE

Alchemilla mollis is a hellstrip mainstay because of its large, lobed, velvety leaves; springtime sprays of chartreuse flowers; and low profile. In bloom, the plants stand about 18 inches tall. This plant prefers part shade, balking at excessive heat and humidity, and doesn't tolerate dry soil. The foliage can get ragged by summer's end and require pruning of spent leaves for rejuvenation.

PLANT THESE:

Packera aurea

GOLDEN GROUNDSEL, GOLDEN RAGWORT

AL, AR, CT, DC, DE, FL, GA, IA, IL, IN, KY, MA, MD, ME, MI, MN, MO, NC, NH, NJ, NY, OH, OK, PA, RI, SC, TN, VA, VT, WI, WV

Packera obovata

GOLDEN GROUNDSEL, ROUNDLEAF GROUNDSEL, ROUNDLEAF RAGWORT

AL, AR, CT, DC, FL, GA, IL, IN, KS, KY, LA, MA, MD, ME, MI, MO, MS, NC, NH, NJ, NM, NY, OH, OK, PA, RI, SC, TN, TX, VA, VT, WV

Packera plattensis

PRAIRIE GROUNDSEL, PRAIRIE RAGWORT

AR, AZ, CO, IA, IL, IN, KS, LA, MI, MN, MO, MS, MT, NC, ND, NE, NM, OK, SD, TX, VT, WI, WV, WY

Coreopsis lanceolata

LANCELEAF COREOPSIS, LANCELEAF TICKSEED

AL, AR, FL, GA, IL, IN, KS, KY, LA, MD, MI, MO, MS, NC, OH, OK, SC, TN, TX, UT, VA, WI, WV

Packera aurea

GOLDEN GROUNDSEL, GOLDEN RAGWORT

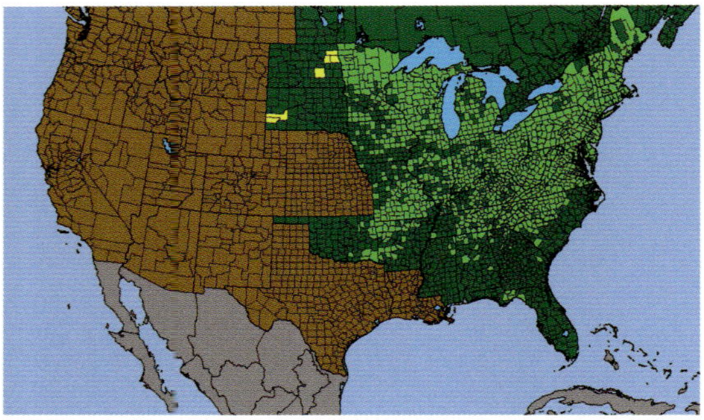

- Herbaceous perennial; 1 to 2 feet.
- Early- to mid-spring yellow flowers.
- Sun to part shade; wet to moist acidic soil.
- Workhorse. VHPV: Pollinated by native bees, moths, butterflies, other insects. Host to moth caterpillars.
- Deer resistant.

Packera obovata

GOLDEN GROUNDSEL, ROUNDLEAF GROUNDSEL, ROUNDLEAF RAGWORT

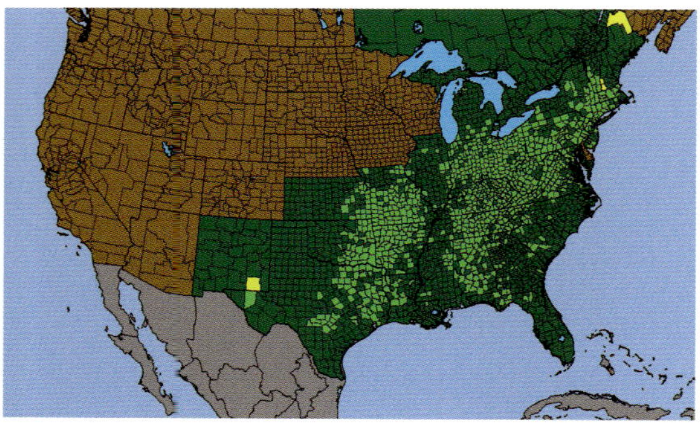

- Herbaceous perennial; 1 to 2 feet.
- Early- to mid-spring yellow flowers.
- Sun to part shade; moist to dry soil.
- VHPV: Pollinated by native bees, moths, butterflies, other insects. Host to moth caterpillars.
- Deer resistant.

Packera plattensis

PRAIRIE GROUNDSEL, PRAIRIE RAGWORT

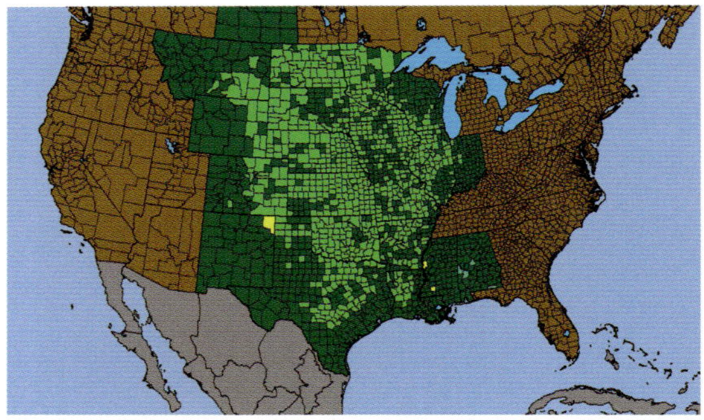

- Herbaceous perennial; 1 to 3 feet.
- Spring to summer yellow flowers.
- Sun to shade; dry alkaline soil.
- HPV: Pollinated by native bees, moths, butterflies, other insects.
- Deer resistant.

With differences among their native ranges, cultural requirements, and leaf shape, what all *Packera* species have in common is their cheerful yellow, daisylike flowers rising on straight stems above attractive basal foliage. The leaves of *P. obovata* and *P. plattensis* are more oval; those of *P. aurea* are heart-shaped. All will spread via rhizomes to form a ground cover, *P. plattensis* less aggressively than the other two noted here. Deer will not touch packeras.

Coreopsis lanceolata

LANCELEAF COREOPSIS, LANCELEAF TICKSEED

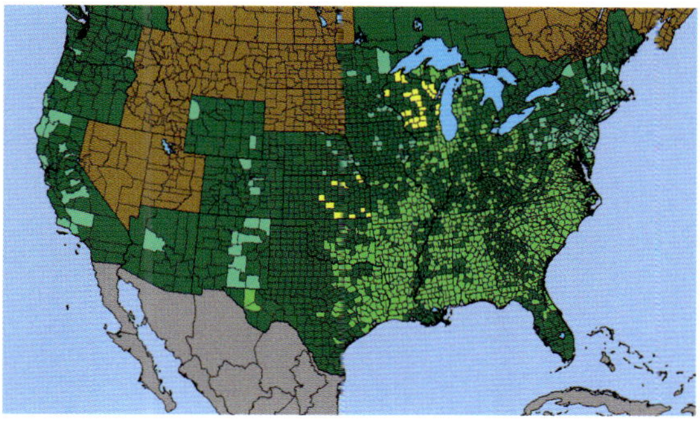

- Herbaceous perennial: 1 to 3 feet.
- Spring to summer yellow flowers.
- Sun to shade; moist to dry soil.
- Workhorse/pollinator: Pollinated by native bees, moths, butterflies, other insects.
- Deer resistant.

Like many other short-lived perennials, *Coreopsis lanceolata* throws up an abundance of blooms: bright yellow daisylike flowers with deeply lobed petals around an equally bright yellow center. This coreopsis is often described as not reliably long-lived but freely self-sowing. *C. lanceolata* is the mostly widely native perennial coreopsis, but many others are native to smaller areas, especially in the East, and readily available. An annual coreopsis, *C. tinctoria*, is native to the Great Plains and Pacific Northwest.

Another great native choice: *Heuchera* spp. (pages 128–129)

INSTEAD OF THESE:

Liriope muscari and *L. spicata*

LILYTURF

Festuca ovina glauca

BLUE FESCUE

A number of low, non-native grasses and grasslike plants have been introduced to American gardens as edgers and fillers. Lilyturfs are tough evergreen or semi-evergreen plants that have been among the most popular, valued for their sturdy foliage, late-season short spikes of small purple flowers, and tendency to spread and fill in nearby empty spaces in full sun to shade. Unfortunately, that spreading tendency, particularly the rhizomes of *L. spicata*, have contributed to this plant becoming invasive, especially in the Southeast. In the North, while the foliage stays evergreen, lilyturfs can get ragged enough that they require laborious cutting back each spring to encourage fresh new growth.

Festuca ovina glauca is a cool-season European native commonly used for its semi-evergreen nature, clumping growth habit, and blue color in full sun. While blue fescue and some other popular introduced grasses may not be invasive, there are native grasses and grasslike plants that offer greater benefits to the local ecosystem.

PLANT THESE:

Carex albicans

WHITETINGE SEDGE

AL, AR, CT, DC, DE, FL, GA, IA, IL, IN, KS, KY, LA, MA, MD, ME, MI, MN, MO, MS, NC, NE, NH, NJ, NY, OH, OK, PA, RI, SC, TN, TX, VA, VT, WI, WV

Carex brevior

PLAINS OVAL SEDGE, SHORTBEAK SEDGE

AL, AR, AZ, CO, CT, DC, DE, GA, IA, ID, IL, IN, KS, KY, MA, MD, ME, MI, MN, MO, MS, MT, NC, ND, NE, NH, NJ, NM, NY, OH, OK, OR, PA, RI, SD, TN, TX, VA, VT, WA, WI, WV, WY

Carex blanda

EASTERN WOODLAND SEDGE

AL, AR, CT, DC, DE, FL, GA, IA, IL, IN, KS, KY, LA, MA, MD, ME, MI, MN, MO, MS, NC, ND, NE, NH, NJ, NY, OH, OK, PA, RI, SC, SD, TN, TX, VA, VT, WI, WV, WY

Sisyrinchium species

BLUE-EYED GRASS

Throughout the contiguous US

Carex albicans

WHITETINGE SEDGE

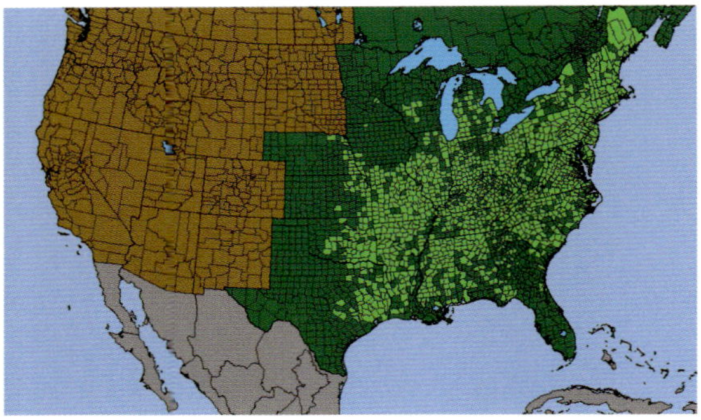

- Grasslike perennial; 1 to 1½ feet.
- Part shade to shade; moist to dry soil.

Carex blanda

EASTERN WOODLAND SEDGE

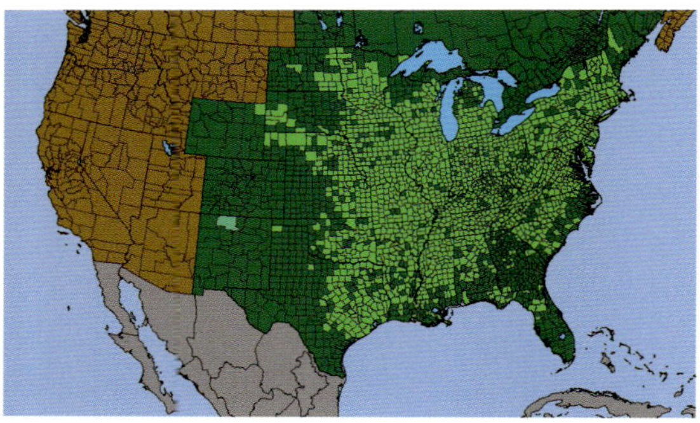

- Grasslike evergreen perennial; 1 to 2 feet.
- Sun to shade; moist to dry soil.
- Deer resistant.

Carex brevior

PLAINS OVAL SEDGE, SHORTBEAK SEDGE

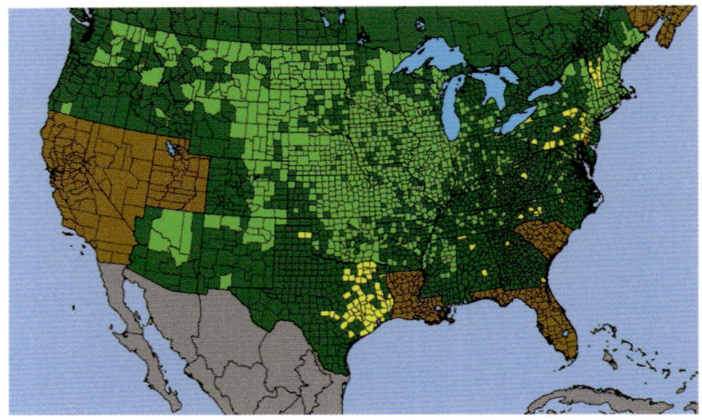

- Grasslike perennial; 1 to 2 feet.
- Sun to shade; wet to dry soil. Drought tolerant.
- Deer resistant.

Carexes, or sedges, are native to every state and almost every county of the United States. These three represent some of the most widely native among commercially available species. *Carex blanda* has fine, arching, white-tinged leaves and will form a dense ground cover, but nearby companion plants will keep it from taking over. *C. brevior* is highly adaptable, and its fall seed spikes extend its seasonal interest. If you look locally, you will find other carexes native to your ecoregion that are evergreen or deciduous, sun lovers and shade lovers (or both), ones that thrive in moist or dry soils, and wide-leaved and narrow-leaved varieties. While these sedges are not of significant food value to pollinators, they play a key role in providing habitat and cover for small mammals, birds, and insects.

Sisyrinchium species

BLUE-EYED GRASS

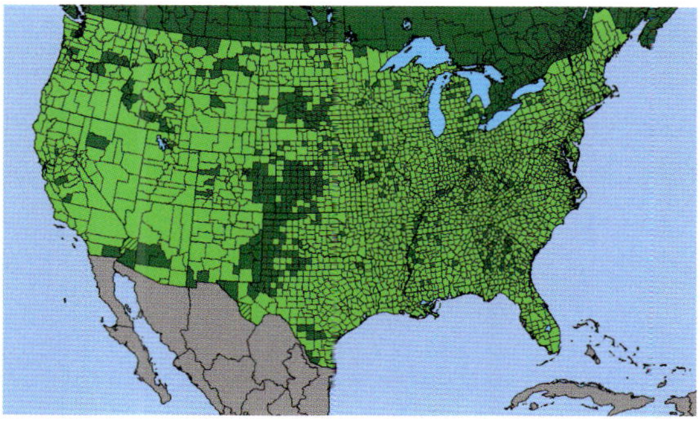

> **More great native choices:** *Deschampsia cespitosa* (page 157), *Schizachyrium scoparium* (page 157)

- Herbaceous perennial; 6 to 18 inches.
- Late-spring to early-summer blue to violet flowers.
- Sun to part shade; wet to moist soil.
- Workhorse. HPV: Pollinated by native bees, butterflies, other insects.
- Deer resistant.

A number of commercially available, local species of *Sisyrinchium* are very similar in appearance. Generally speaking, these include *S. angustifolium* in the East, *S. campestre* in the Midwest, *S. montanum* in the Mountain West and across the North coast to coast, *S. idahoense* in the Pacific Northwest, and *S. bellum* on the West Coast. (There are many more *Sisyrinchium* species in the wild.) The blue-eyed grasses are not truly grasses but members of the lily family, with dainty star-shaped blue blooms with yellow centers and grasslike foliage. (*S. californicum* has yellow flowers.) Sisyrinchiums self-sow readily, and the species hybridize freely where they are found together.

INSTEAD OF THIS:

Hylotelephium 'Herbstfreude'

(syn. *Sedum* 'Herbstfreude')

'AUTUMN JOY' SEDUM, 'AUTUMN JOY' STONECROP

As a succulent, this Eurasian sedum cultivar has distinct fleshy leaves. It grows in a variety of climates in full sun and is often used in areas where lean soil can be dry or compacted. The cultivar name comes from the way its clusters of tiny pink flowers gradually turn a coppery color as autumn arrives, when other garden blooms have faded.

PLANT THESE:

Sedum lanceolatum

SPEARLEAF STONECROP

AZ, CA, CO, ID, MT, NE, NM, NV, OR, SD, UT, WA, WY

Sedum ternatum

WILD STONECROP, WOODLAND STONECROP

AL, AR, DC, DE, GA, IA, IL, IN, KY, MD, MO, MS, NC, NJ, OH, PA, SC, TN, VA, WV

Sedum lanceolatum
SPEARLEAF STONECROP

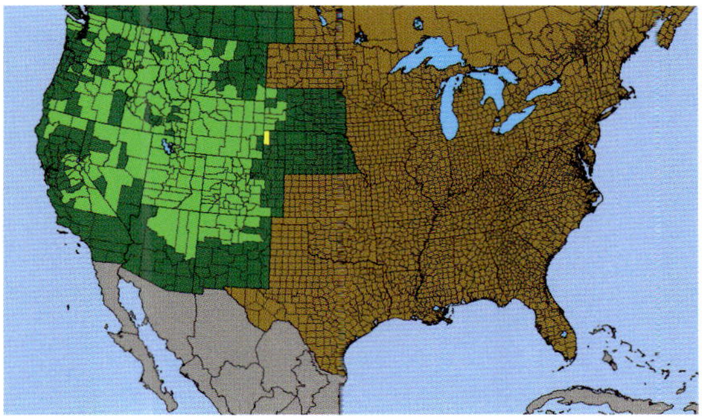

- Herbaceous perennial; 4 to 6 inches.
- Spring to fall yellow flowers.
- Sun; dry soil. Drought tolerant.
- HPV: Pollinated by native bees, butterflies, other insects. Host to butterfly caterpillars.
- Deer resistant.

Sedum ternatum
WILD STONECROP, WOODLAND STONECROP

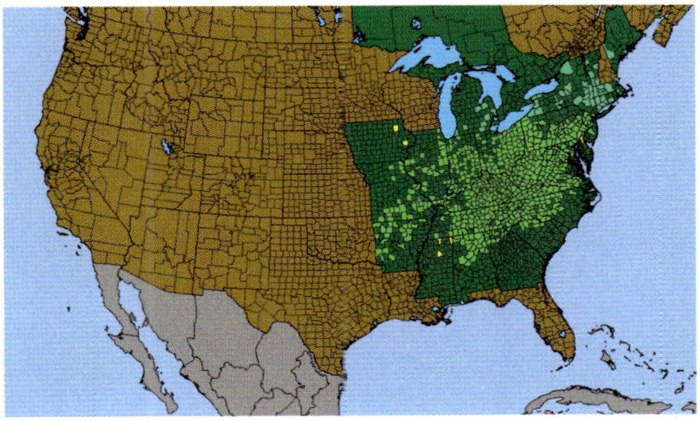

- Herbaceous perennial; 4 to 8 inches.
- Spring to early-summer white flowers.
- Part shade; moist soil.
- Workhorse. HPV: Pollinated by native bees, butterflies, other insects.
- Deer resistant.

These native sedums are inexplicably lesser-known than the introduced sedum 'Autumn Joy' and others. Both are charming yet tough ground cover plants with succulent foliage and attractive star-shaped flowers on stalks somewhat shorter than the usual introduced plants. They are especially excellent choices where low-maintenance, drought-tolerant plants are wanted.

INSTEAD OF THESE:

Veronica species
SPEEDWELL

Lavandula species
LAVENDER

Both of these low-profile plants are rugged and long-lived and can be used to fill a dry, difficult spot with summer color. *Veronica* is a genus of more than two hundred European and Asian plants commonly known as speedwell. They grow in a variety of forms, but the ones typically chosen for hellstrip gardens grow around a foot tall and send up taller spikes of blue, purple, or sometimes pink or white flowers.

Lavender can be difficult to grow and not reliably hardy in American gardens, but it has found a place near the curb because of its preference for hot, dry, sunny spots in the landscape—as well as for its fragrant blue-gray foliage and purple flowers. Though it has a scent like no other garden plant, there are fragrant natives that can hold their own in similar spots.

PLANT THESE:

Geranium maculatum

WILD GERANIUM, SPOTTED GERANIUM, CRANESBILL

AL, AR, CT, DC, DE, FL, GA, IA, IL, IN, KS, KY, LA, MA, MD, ME, MI, MN, MO, MS, NC, ND, NH, NJ, NY, OH, OK, PA, RI, SC, SD, TN, VA, VT, WI, WV

Monarda punctata

SPOTTED BEE BALM, HORSEMINT

AL, AR, AZ, CT, DC, DE, FL, GA, IA, IL, IN, KS, KY, LA, MD, MI, MN, MO, MS, NC, NJ, NM, NY, OH, OK, PA, SC, TN, TX, VA, VT, WI

Geranium richardsonii

RICHARD'S GERANIUM

AZ, CA, CO, ID, MT, NM, NV, OR, SD, UT, WA, WY

Pycnanthemum muticum

CLUSTERED MOUNTAIN MINT

AL, AR, CT, DC, DE, FL, GA, IL, KY, LA, MA, MD, ME, MI, MO, MS, NC, NH, NJ, NY, OH, PA, RI, SC, TN, TX, VA, VT, WV

Geranium maculatum

WILD GERANIUM, SPOTTED GERANIUM, CRANESBILL

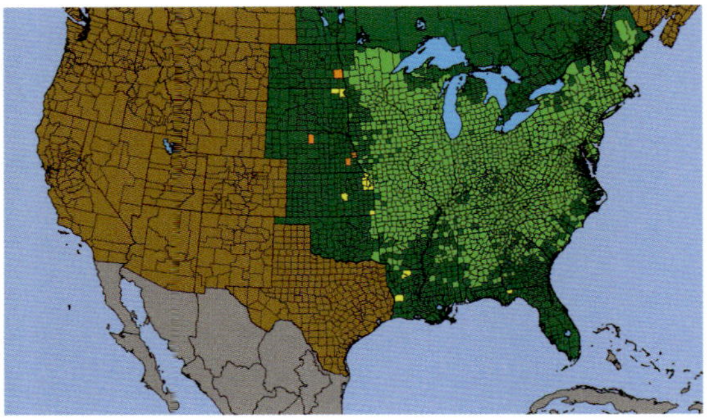

These eastern and western species of geranium are very similar in appearance, with long, straight delicate stems holding bright, upward-facing pink to purple flowers above deeply lobed leaves. Geraniums typically bloom lightly across a long season; the mounding habit of their distinct, deeply lobed, almost star-shaped foliage adds to their interest. The common name cranesbill comes from the plant's tall, slender seedpod.

- Herbaceous perennial; 1 to 2½ feet.
- Spring to early-summer pale to deep pink flowers.
- Part shade to shade; moist to dry acidic soil.
- Workhorse. VHPV: Food for native bees, moths, butterflies, other insects. Host to moth caterpillars.
- Deer resistant.

Geranium richardsonii

RICHARD'S GERANIUM

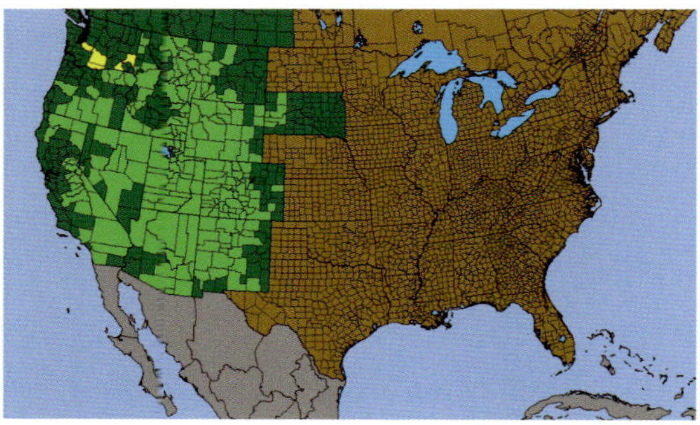

- Herbaceous perennial; 2 to 3 feet.
- Late-spring to early-summer pink to lavender-pink flowers.
- Part shade; moist to dry soil.
- Pollinated by native bees, butterflies, other insects

Monarda punctata

SPOTTED BEE BALM, HORSEMINT

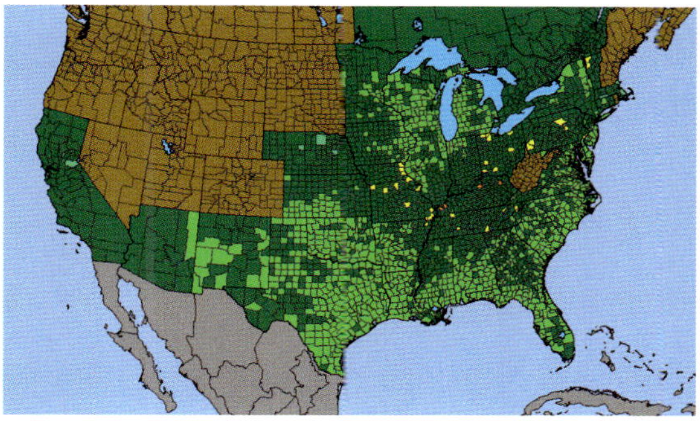

- Herbaceous perennial; 1 to 2½ feet.
- Mid- to late-summer pink flowers with unusually ornamental purple, white, and green bracts.
- Sun, part shade; moist to dry soil.
- Workhorse. VHPV: Pollinated by native bees, moths, butterflies (including monarchs), other insects, hummingbirds.
- Deer resistant.

Monarda punctata is aromatic, like all monardas, with an herbal smell often compared to oregano, but its flowers, with prominent bracts, have a beauty all their own. This species tolerates heat and drought better than others. It's sometimes described as aggressive, but it's short-lived and can be kept in checked by planting with assertive neighbors—such as asclepias, echinaceas, rudbeckias, and some ferns—that will hold their own against nearby competition.

Pycnanthemum muticum

CLUSTERED MOUNTAIN MINT

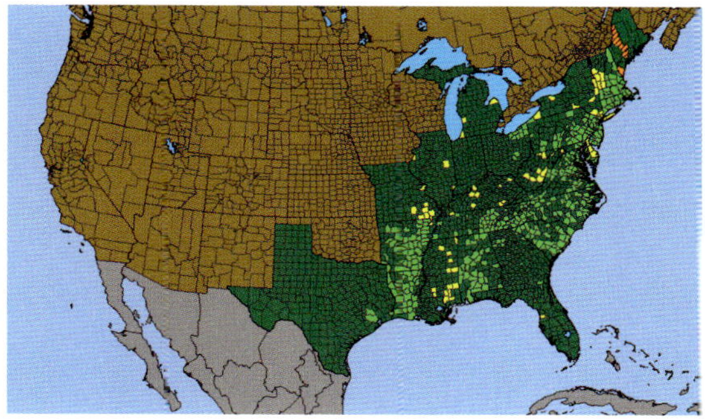

- Herbaceous perennial; 1½ to 3 feet.
- Mid- to late-summer white to pink flowers.
- Sun to part shade; wet to dry soil.
- HPV: Pollinated by native bees, butterflies, other insects.
- Deer resistant.

This fragrant beauty holds its small pink flowers above pale green spade-shaped leaves. It's less aggressive than some other mints but does best with other strong growers. Root pruning at the beginning or end of the growing season will also help check its spread. A number of other aromatic *Pycnanthemum* species are native to the eastern half of the country and one to California (*P. californicum*), but not all are as showy as this one.

More great native choices:
Symphyotrichum oblongifolium (page 103), *Verbena* spp. (pages 107, 151), *Phlox* spp. (pages 116–117), *Geum triflorum* (page 117), *Polemonium reptans* (page 139), *Liatris* spp. (page 150)

CHAPTER FIVE

Ground Covers

Low-growing plants with a spreading habit serve a number of important purposes in a garden, including defining the boundary of a border or bed, helping to suppress weeds or keep invasives at bay, offering ground-level shelter and food for wildlife, and simply adding another level of interest in a layered landscape.

Since ground cover plantings address needs that come up in various kinds of gardens and landscaping, many of the plants featured in other sections of this book may also work as ground covers. The plants featured here are ones that are typically used anywhere a spreading plant with strong foliage will be useful, but especially in those areas of a yard that we might not even think of as "garden," like under a tree or in a difficult-to-mow spot as a lawn alternative.

It's tempting to take a monoculture approach to ground covers, especially when planting a lawn replacement. Since one objective of a native plant garden is to favor healthier and more beneficial mixed plantings over monoculture, consider combining a compatible mix of ground covers in an area rather than installing a broad expanse of one species.

INSTEAD OF THESE:

Veronica peduncularis

'WATERPERRY BLUE', VERONICA 'WATERPERRY BLUE'

Lamium maculatum

SPOTTED DEADNETTLE

Lysimachia nummularia 'Aurea'

CREEPING JENNY, CREEPING CHARLIE

Thymus species

WOOLY THYME, CREEPING THYME

Liriope muscari and *L. spicata*

LILYTURF

These are some of the most widely planted non-native deciduous ground covers used in North American gardens. In keeping with their hardy reputations, these ground covers grow in full sun to part shade or shade across a wide geographical range. All spread via rhizomes and were initially adopted because of their enthusiastic growth habit and rugged nature. An unintended consequence is that they frequently wander from their intended place in the landscape and require vigilance to keep in check even within garden boundaries. Unfortunately, all are now listed as invasive in some or all of their growing range.

PLANT THESE:

Viola sororia

COMMON BLUE VIOLET

AL, AR, CT, DC, DE, FL, GA, IA, IL, IN, KS, KY, LA, MA, MD, ME, MI, MN, MO, MS, NC, ND, NE, NH, NJ, NY, OH, OK, PA, RI, SC, SD, TN, TX, VA, VT, WI, WV

Viola adunca

WESTERN BLUE VIOLET

AZ, CA, CO, IA, ID, MA, ME, MI, MN, MT, ND, NH, NM, NV, NY, OR, SD, UT, VT, WA, WI, WY

Fragaria virginiana

WILD STRAWBERRY, WOODLAND STRAWBERRY

Throughout the contiguous US

Viola sororia
COMMON BLUE VIOLET

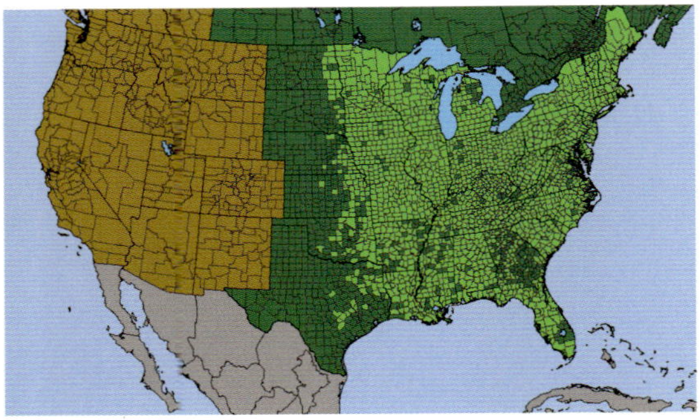

- Upright perennial; 6 to 10 inches.
- Spring purple flowers.
- Sun to part shade; wet to dry soil.
- VHPV: Pollinated by native bees, moths, butterflies, other insects. Host to moth caterpillars.
- Deer resistant.

Viola adunca
WESTERN BLUE VIOLET

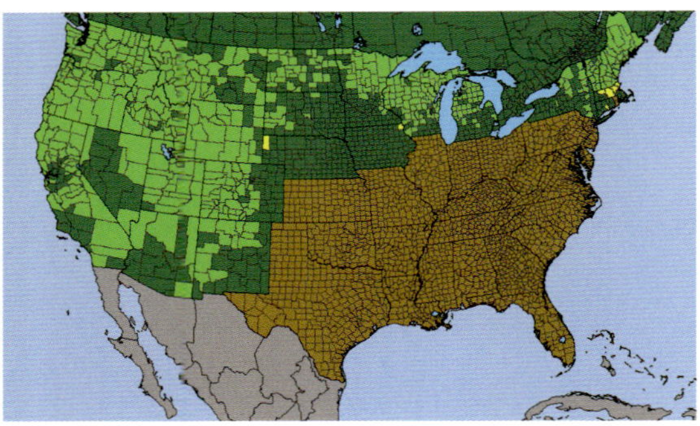

- Upright perennial; 6 to 14 inches.
- Spring purple flowers.
- Sun to shade; moist to dry soil.
- VHPV: Pollinated by native bees, moths, butterflies, other insects. Host to butterfly caterpillars.
- Deer resistant.

Do we take violets for granted because they grow so freely in our gardens and lawns? Heart-shaped leaves and delicate blue and white flowers combine with their tendency to invite themselves into a landscape make violets a great native ground cover. Besides these two widely native violas, there are other commercially available native species to add to your garden, where they will spread by rhizomes to make a pleasant, not very aggressive ground cover. If you're considering lawn alternatives, native violas can make a great lawn addition or replacement, typically blooming before mowing season begins.

Fragaria virginiana

WILD STRAWBERRY, WOODLAND STRAWBERRY

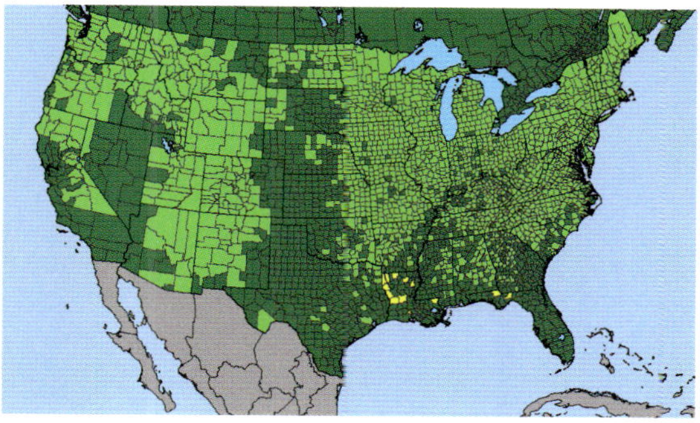

- Herbaceous perennial; 4 to 6 inches.
- Spring to early-summer white flowers followed by small red berries.
- Sun to part shade; moist to dry soil.
- Workhorse. VHPV: Pollinated by native moths, butterflies, other insects. Host to moth and butterfly caterpillars.
- Deer resistant.

The wild strawberry will multiply readily but not too aggressively, and its small white flowers will be covered with berries that ripen from white to red. Much smaller than most market strawberries, the berries are edible to humans—and delicious!—but you'll have to be fast to beat the birds and small mammals to harvest more than a handful.

More great native choices: *Phlox subulata* (page 117), *Polemonium reptans* (page 139), *Geranium* spp. (page 178), *Asarum* spp. (page 187)

INSTEAD OF THESE:

Houttuynia cordata

CHAMELEON PLANT

Galium odoratum

SWEET WOODRUFF

Like their sun-loving counterparts, these widely adopted shade-tolerant ground covers spread aggressively by rhizome and fill a space quickly, soon spilling over to areas outside their intended boundaries. Online discussion forums are full of gardeners who have planted *Houttuynia cordata* for its distinct heart-shaped leaves of red, white, and green, only to find themselves regretting their choice as this plant pops up seemingly forever in unintended places, resistant to chemical controls and even stimulated to further growth by hand removal.

PLANT THESE:

Asarum canadense

WILD GINGER, CANADIAN WILD GINGER

AL, AR, CT, DC, DE, GA, IA, IL, IN, KS, KY, LA, MA, MD, ME, MI, MN, MO, MS, NC, ND, NH, NJ, NY, OH, OK, PA, RI, SC, SD, TN, VA, VT, WI, WV

Asarum caudatum

BRITISH COLUMBIA WILD GINGER, LONG-TAILED WILD GINGER

CA, ID, MT, OR, WA

Asarum canadense

WILD GINGER, CANADIAN WILD GINGER

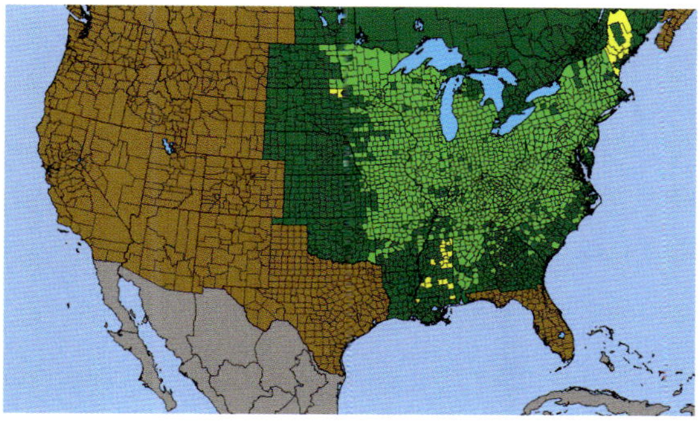

- Herbaceous perennial; 4 to 8 inches.
- Spring to summer inconspicuous purple flowers.
- Part shade to shade; moist soil.
- Workhorse. Pollinated by native bees, other insects. Host to moth and butterfly moth caterpillars.
- Deer resistant.

Another charmer with heart-shaped foliage, wild ginger features unique brownish purple flowers as well as a distinct leaf shape, but you'll have to peek under the glossy leaves to find the blooms. *Asarum* prefers consistently moist soil and will spread happily in the right conditions.

NOTE: This plant is unrelated to the non-native culinary plant that shares the common name ginger.

More great native choices: *Phlox subulata* (page 117), *Tiarella* spp. (page 129), *Carex* spp. (page 172)

Asarum caudatum

BRITISH COLUMBIA WILD GINGER, LONG-TAILED WILD GINGER

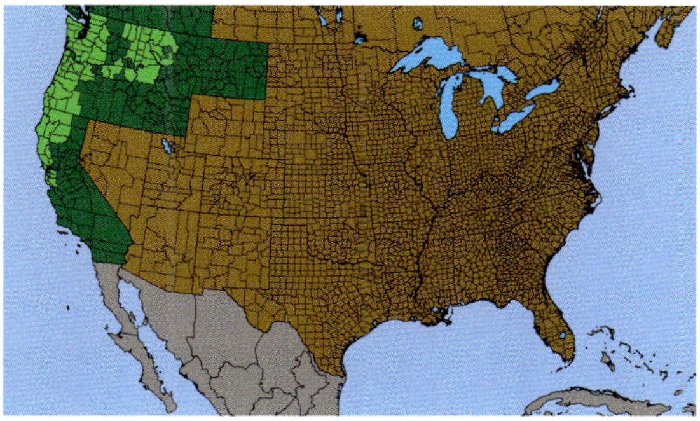

- Herbaceous perennial; 6 to 10 inches.
- Spring to summer purple flowers.
- Part shade to shade; moist soil.
- Workhorse. Provides cover for small mammals.
- Deer resistant.

INSTEAD OF THIS:

Aegopodium podagraria

GOUTWEED

Goutweed is an aggressive grower, spreading by rhizomes across wide areas, often tumbling out of its intended area to take over gardens, yards, and sometimes fields and woods. It shades out other plants and even alters soil chemistry and composition. Once it has colonized an area, it's hard to remove, since any root or rhizome left behind may regrow. While goutweed is still touted for its ability to thrive and produce white flowers even in the dense shade under trees in all but the coldest and hottest US growing zones, this one should be avoided or removed. Its sale is prohibited in some states, and it's a listed invasive in others.

PLANT THESE:

Anemone virginiana

TALL THIMBLEWEED

AL, AR, CO, CT, DC, DE, GA, IA, IL, IN, KS, KY, LA, MA, MD, ME, MI, MN, MO, MS, NC, ND, NE, NH, NJ, NY, OH, OK, PA, RI, SC, SD, TN, VA, VT, WI, WV, WY

Anemone cylindrica

THIMBLEWEED

AZ, CO, CT, IA, ID, IL, IN, KS, MA, ME, MI, MN, MO, MT, ND, NE, NH, NJ, NM, NY, OH, PA, RI, SD, VT, WI, WY

Parthenocissus quinquefolia

VIRGINIA CREEPER

AL, AR, CT, DC, DE, FL, GA, IA, IL, IN, KS, KY, LA, MA, MD, ME, MI, MN, MO, MS, NC, NE, NH, NJ, NY, OH, OK, PA, RI, SC, SD, TN, TX, VA, VT, WI, WV

Parthenocissus inserta

(syn. *P. vitacea*)

WOODBINE

AZ, CA, CO, CT, IA, IL, IN, KS, MA, ME, MI, MN, MO, MT, NC, ND, NE, NH, NJ, NM, NV, NY, OH, OK, PA, RI, SD, TX, UT, VA, VT, WI, WV, WY

Anemone virginiana

TALL THIMBLEWEED

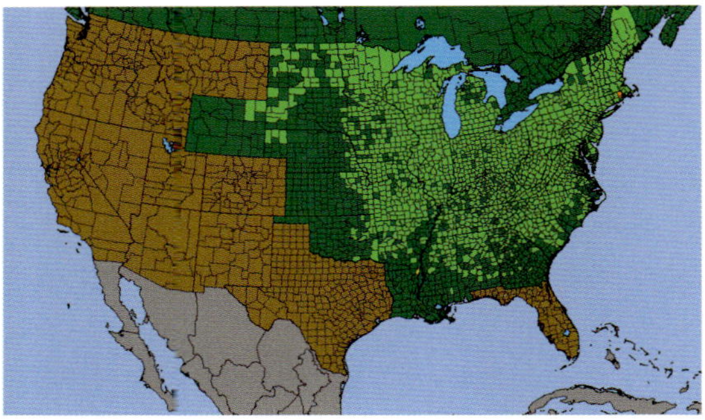

- Herbaceous perennial; 2 to 3 feet.
- Spring to early-summer creamy white flowers with yellow centers.
- Sun to part shade; dry to moist soil.
- Workhorse. Pollinated by native bees, other insects.
- Deer resistant.

Anemone cylindrica

THIMBLEWEED

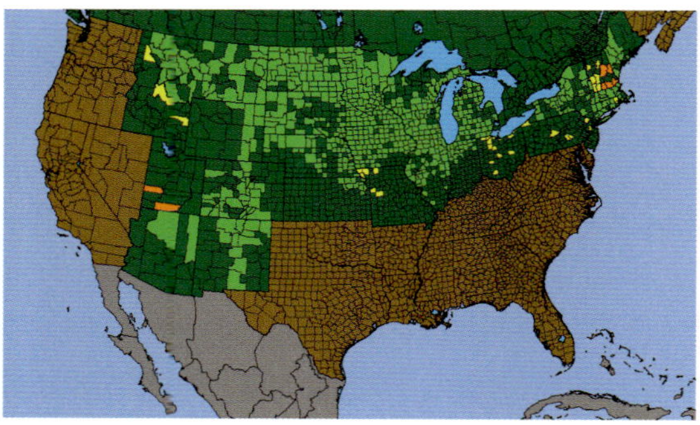

- Herbaceous perennial; 1 to 3 feet.
- Late-spring to summer white flowers.
- Sun to part shade; dry soil.
- Pollinated by native bees, other insects.
- Deer resistant.

These cheerful native anemones can spread assertively, and they are best used alongside other spreading species where crowding out other plants is not a problem, or for filling in a spot with a plant that will keep unwanted aggressors at bay. *Anemone virginiana* has off-white flowers followed by fluffy seed heads. *A. cylindrica*'s greenish white flowers are followed by decorative cones. Both species have deeply cut ornamental leaves that rise up the plant's stem in whorls.

Parthenocissus quinquefolia

VIRGINIA CREEPER

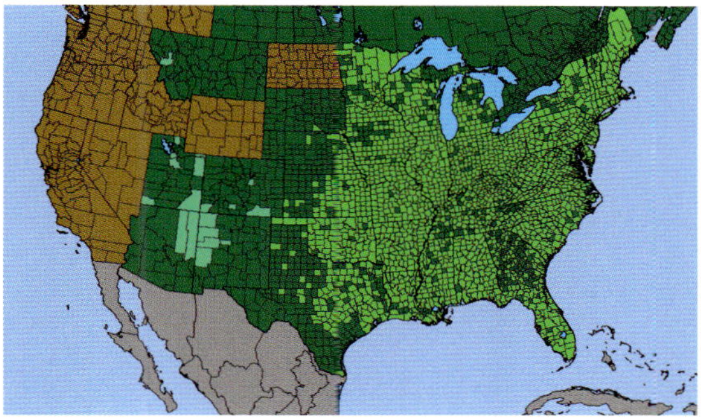

- Deciduous vine; 30 to 50 feet.
- Late-spring to early-summer white flowers followed by dark berries. Red fall foliage.
- Sun to shade; moist to dry soil.
- Workhorse. VHPV: Pollinated by native bees, other insects. Host to moth caterpillars.

Parthenocissus inserta

(syn. *P. vitacea*)

WOODBINE

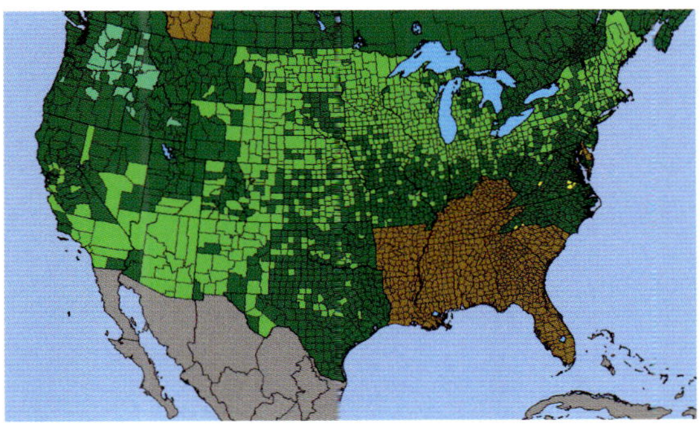

- Deciduous vine; 30 feet.
- Late-spring to summer white flowers followed by dark berries. Red fall foliage.
- Sun to part shade; moist to dry soil.
- Pollinated by native bees.

Both of these native vines are fast-spreading ground covers that also climb via tendrils. They are not damaging to structures the way the aerial roots of some vines, like invasive English ivy, are. Both *Parthenocissus* species have leaves made up of several leaflets, which can cause them to be mistaken for poison ivy. But counting the leaflets makes these plants easy to tell apart: *Parthenocissus* has five leaflets, while poison ivy has three. Both *Parthenocissus* vines have brilliant, deep red fall foliage accented by dark blue berries. *P. inserta* is not as aggressive a climber as *P. quinquefolia*, which often needs watching and pruning to stay in bounds.

More great native choices: *Heuchera* spp. (pages 128–129), *Athyrium* spp. (page 138), *Carex* spp. (page 172), *Polystichum acrostichoides* (page 194)

INSTEAD OF THESE:

Pachysandra terminalis
JAPANESE PACHYSANDRA, JAPANESE SPURGE

Hedera helix
ENGLISH IVY

Euonymus fortunei
WINTERCREEPER

Vinca species
PERIWINKLE

Ajuga species
BUGLEWEED

These commonly used ground covers have two key features in common. They've been garden standards for years because they provide evergreen cover for bare spots in yards and gardens, chiefly under shrubs and trees or in spots near walkways or walls or on slopes where it's difficult to mow. And they are all invasive, growing rapidly and creating an undesirable monoculture environment in a garden, as well as escaping garden boundaries to enter fields and woods where they overtake and displace native species.

PLANT THESE:

Polystichum acrostichoides

CHRISTMAS FERN

AL, AR, CT, DC, DE, FL, GA, IA, IL, IN, KS, KY, LA, MA, MD, ME, MI, MN, MO, MS, NC, NH, NJ, NY, OH, OK, PA, RI, SC, TN, TX, VA, VT, WI, WV

Gaultheria procumbens

WINTERGREEN

AL, CT, DC, DE, GA, IL, IN, KY, MA, MD, ME, MI, MN, NC, NH, NJ, NY, OH, PA, RI, SC, TN, VA, VT, WI, WV

Arctostaphylos uva-ursi

KINNIKINNICK, RED BEARBERRY

AZ, CA, CO, CT, DE, IA, ID, IL, IN, MA, MD, ME, MI, MN, MT, ND, NH, NJ, NM, NV, NY, OH, OR, PA, RI, SD, UT, VA, VT, WA, WI, WV, WY

Polystichum acrostichoides

CHRISTMAS FERN

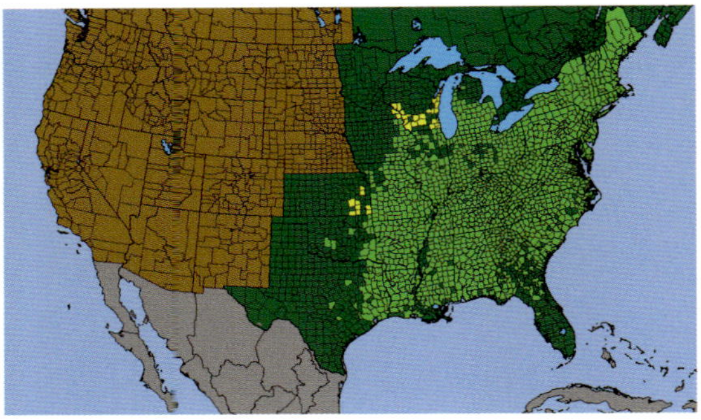

- Evergreen perennial; 1 to 2 feet.
- Part shade to shade; moist acidic soil.
- Workhorse. Larval moth host.

This fern's common name is directly connected to its exceptional role in the garden: Its glossy green leathery leaves keep their color and structure year-round, lying flatter and closer to the ground in winter. New growth unfurls as spring fronds; in late summer brown spores dot the longer fertile fronds. This is a great ground cover plant for a slope where winter erosion is a worry, but it doesn't tolerate heat, liking its soil cool as well as moist and at least somewhat shady. *Dryopteris marginalis* (marginal wood fern) is another evergreen fern, somewhat larger, with a similar native range.

Gaultheria procumbens

WINTERGREEN

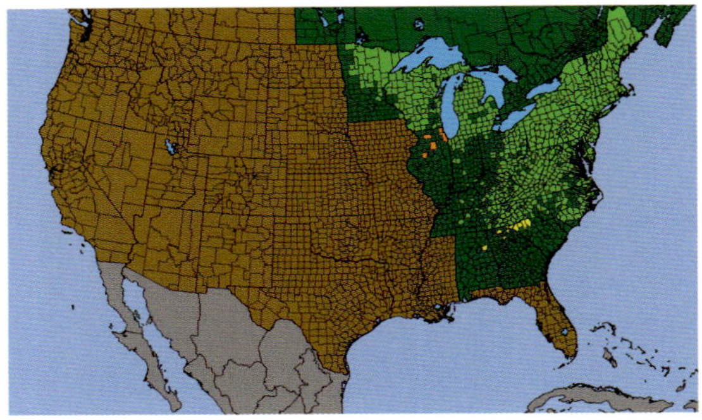

- Evergreen shrub; 3 to 6 inches.
- Spring white flowers followed by red berries. Red fall foliage.
- Sun to shade; moist to dry acidic soil. Drought tolerant.
- Workhorse. VHPV: Pollinated by native bees, other insects.

This shade-tolerant low grower is classified as a shrub, but its shiny green leaves sprout from creeping underground stems, which gives it a vining appearance. It's highly shade tolerant, but its bell-shaped blooms and bright red berries grow best with some sun.

Arctostaphylos uva-ursi

KINNIKINNICK, RED BEARBERRY

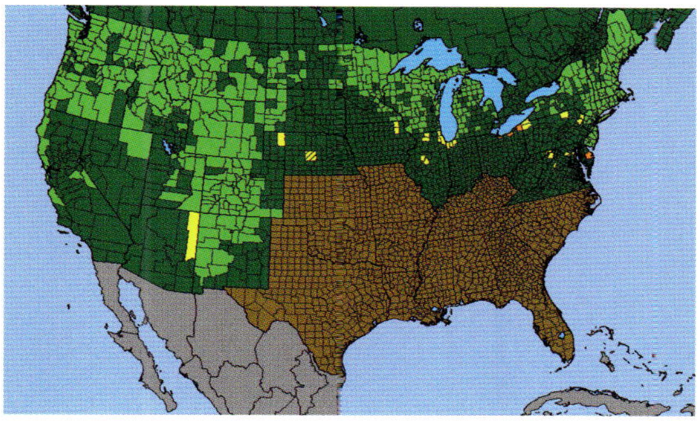

- Evergreen shrub; 6 to 12 inches.
- Spring to summer white to pink flowers followed by red berries. Red fall foliage.
- Sun to shade; moist to dry soil.
- Workhorse. VHPV: Pollinated by native bees, moths, butterflies, other insects, hummingbirds. Host to moth and butterfly caterpillars.
- Deer resistant.

This evergreen is a shrub so low growing that in gardens it's used mainly as a highly adaptable ground cover. Its glossy, thick leaves, topped by delicate bell-shaped flowers, go from pale green to bright green to red over the course of the seasons. Its bright red berries, which often persist through winter, are not palatable to humans but are a favorite of birds and small mammals.

More great native choices: In the southern parts of their ranges where these natives remain evergreen or semi-evergreen, plant *Heuchera* spp. (page 128–129), *Tiarella* spp. (page 129), *Packera* spp. (page 168), *Viola* spp. (page 184), *Fragaria virginiana* (page 185)

CHAPTER SIX

Climbing and Screening Plants

A layered garden provides sustenance for creatures living at all levels of the landscape. There are specialist animals that feed and shelter at specific heights in the garden, from the ground level to the understory of perennials and low shrubs to the middle story of small trees to the treetops of the upper story. Those animals can only live in environments that include plants that meet those needs.

Besides providing food and shelter for insects, birds, and other animals that live in the garden's higher layers, climbing plants provide a strong vertical element in a garden, carrying the eye from one layer of a garden to the next. They are also great for softening structures like posts, fences, and trellises. In some challenging gardening situations, climbing plants have distinct advantages. By growing high, they may avoid lower-level herbivores. And in a shady environment, climbers may reach the sun more efficiently.

INSTEAD OF THIS:

Clematis terniflora

SWEET AUTUMN CLEMATIS

Even admiring descriptions typically describe this Asian vine's growth habit as rampant, adding advice for keeping it under control. It can grow to 30 feet in just a few seasons, climbing structures and clambering over other plants. Its main attraction is its abundant, sweet-scented white blooms, which are the source of its prolifically self-sowing habit. *Clematis terniflora* is now invasive from New Hampshire to Florida, west to Nebraska and Texas. You may also find plants labeled *Clematis paniculata*, with the common name sweet autumn clematis, for sale. Sometimes this is a mislabeled *C. ternifolia*, or it may truly be *C. paniculata*, a New Zealand native that is also invasive in the western United States.

PLANT THESE:

Clematis virginiana

VIRGIN'S BOWER

AL, AR, CT, DC, DE, FL, GA, IA, IL, IN, KS, KY, LA, MA, MD, ME, MI, MN, MO, MS, NC, ND, NE, NH, NJ, NY, OH, OK, PA, RI, SC, SD, TN, TX, VA, VT, WI, WV

Clematis ligusticifolia

WESTERN WHITE CLEMATIS, VIRGIN'S BOWER

AZ, CA, CO, ID, KS, MD, MT, ND, NE, NM, NV, OR, SD, UT, WA, WY

Clematis virginiana
VIRGIN'S BOWER

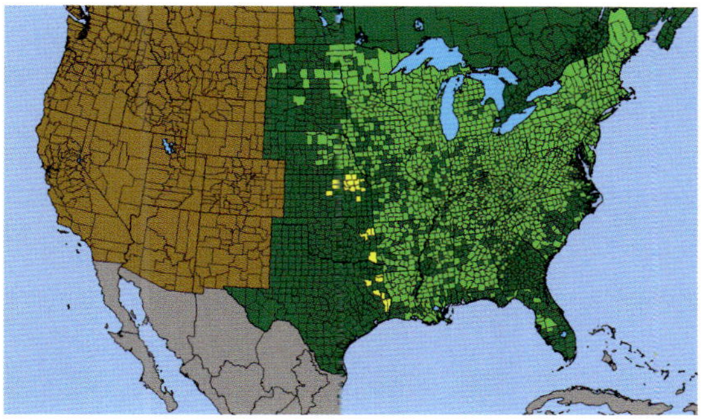

- Deciduous perennial vine; 15 to 20 feet.
- Late-summer to early-fall white flowers followed by ornamental seed heads.
- Sun to part shade; wet to dry soil.
- HPV: Pollinated by native bees, other insects, hummingbirds. Host to moth caterpillars.

Clematis ligusticifolia
WESTERN WHITE CLEMATIS, VIRGIN'S BOWER

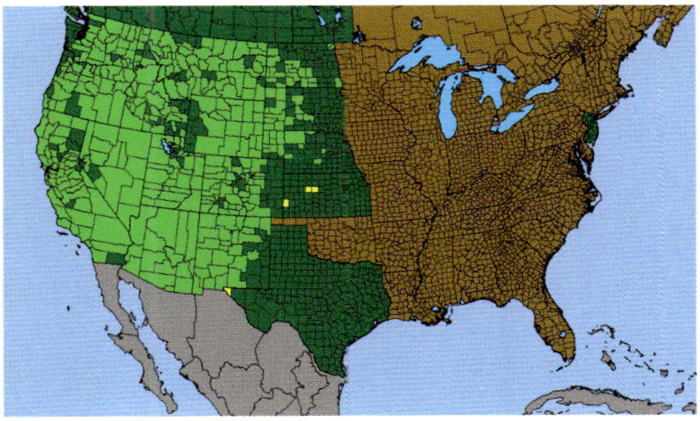

- Deciduous perennial vine; 20 to 30 feet.
- Late-spring to summer white to cream-colored flowers followed by ornamental seed heads.
- Sun to part shade; moist soil.
- HPV: Pollinated by native bees, other insects, hummingbirds. Host to moth caterpillars.
- Deer resistant.

There are native substitutes so similar to the invasive *Clematis terniflora* that it's hard to understand why the non-native is still sold. Both *C. virginiana* and *C. ligusticifolia* have fragrant flowers and reach similar lengths as *C. terniflora* but without the aggression. They may take a year or two to get established, but once they're settled in place, they grow rapidly. Summer flowers are followed by threadlike, almost otherworldly seed heads. Because the plant attaches by tendrils, it climbs best with the support of a trellis or twine. In my garden, *C. virginiana* has self-sown, but not promiscuously, and seedlings are easily transplanted. These clematis can be pruned at virtually any time by cutting down no farther than the first healthy pair of leaves or leaf buds. Because these native plants and *C. terniflora* are so similar, and because common names are often confused or used interchangeably, it's important to double-check what you're buying.

A number of other beautiful native clematis, in a range of colors, will support your local ecosystem and wildlife better than introduced varieties, often with a more surprising, delicate appearance than the assertively showy introduced plants.

INSTEAD OF THIS:

Lonicera japonica

JAPANESE HONEYSUCKLE

The sweet, fragrant nectar of the Japanese honeysuckle combined with its distinctive tubular yellow-and-white flowers have made it a North American landscape standby since its introduction in the nineteenth century. Unfortunately, this adaptable and aggressive vine not only crowds out native plants, it also smothers plants in its path and even encircles and strangles tree saplings. With a preference for shade, *Lonicera japonica* grows in a variety of soils and light conditions. It's listed as invasive in many states and forbidden from sale in several. Happily, there are a number of beautiful native alternatives.

PLANT THESE:

Lonicera sempervirens

TRUMPET HONEYSUCKLE, CRIMSON HONEYSUCKLE, CORAL HONEYSUCKLE

AL, AR, CT, DC, DE, FL, GA, KS, KY, LA, MD, MS, NC, NJ, NY, OK, PA, SC, TN, TX, VA

Lonicera ciliosa

ORANGE HONEYSUCKLE

AZ, CA, ID, MT, OR, UT, WA

Lonicera sempervirens

TRUMPET HONEYSUCKLE, CRIMSON HONEYSUCKLE, CORAL HONEYSUCKLE

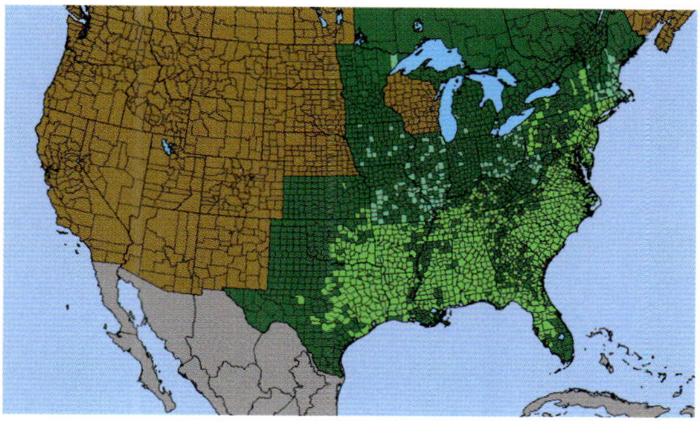

- Semi-evergreen vine; 10 to 20 feet.
- Late-spring to summer; orange to orange-red flowers followed by red berries.
- Sun to part shade; moist soil.
- Workhorse. HPV: Pollinated by native bees, moths, butterflies, hummingbirds. Host to moth caterpillars.

Lonicera ciliosa

ORANGE HONEYSUCKLE

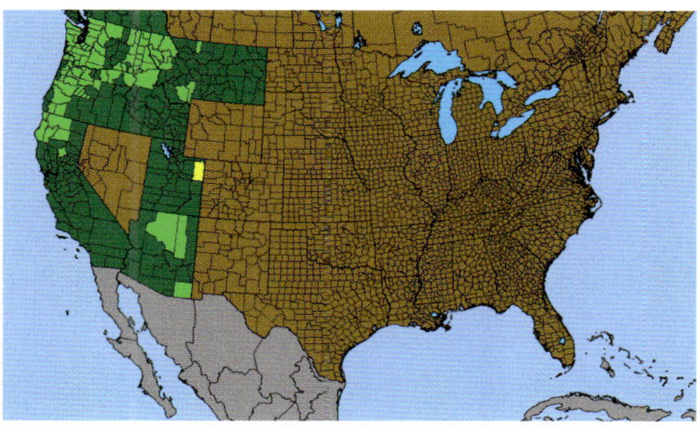

- Deciduous vine; 5 to 20 feet.
- Late-spring to early-summer orange to red flowers followed by red berries.
- Sun to part shade; moist soil.
- Workhorse. VHPV: Pollinated by native bees, butterflies, hummingbirds. Host to moth and butterfly caterpillars.

The large, striking orange-red flowers of these two honeysuckles bloom from spring into summer and sometimes beyond; their leaves are evergreen in warmer areas. Both plants have a twining habit and will support their own new growth, developing an open, shrubby look, but they climb higher in the garden with additional support like a fence or wire. The color and shape of the tubular flowers make both of these reliable hummingbird magnets.

More great native choices: Other native *Lonicera* spp. (pages 80, 201), *Campsis radicans* (page 203)

INSTEAD OF THESE:

Wisteria floribunda

JAPANESE WISTERIA

Wisteria sinensis

CHINESE WISTERIA

The heady fragrance and large purple flowers of Japanese and Chinese wisteria explain why they have been popular full-sun garden plants across much of the United States for more than a hundred years. But homeowners can quickly find themselves overwhelmed by the aggressive growth of these vines, which have been known to crumble walls and collapse downspouts and fences. Both have escaped from gardens into the wild, where their trunks, which may reach several inches in diameter, can girdle and kill trees so effectively that they alter the tree canopy and forest-edge ecology.

PLANT THESE:

Wisteria frutescens

AMERICAN WISTERIA

AL, AR, FL, GA, IL, IN, KY, LA, MI, MO, MS, NC, OK, SC, TN, TX

Campsis radicans

TRUMPET CREEPER

AL, AR, DC, DE, FL, GA, IL, IN, KS, KY, LA, MD, MO, MS, NC, NJ, OH, OK, PA, RI, SC, TN, TX, VA, WV

Wisteria frutescens

AMERICAN WISTERIA

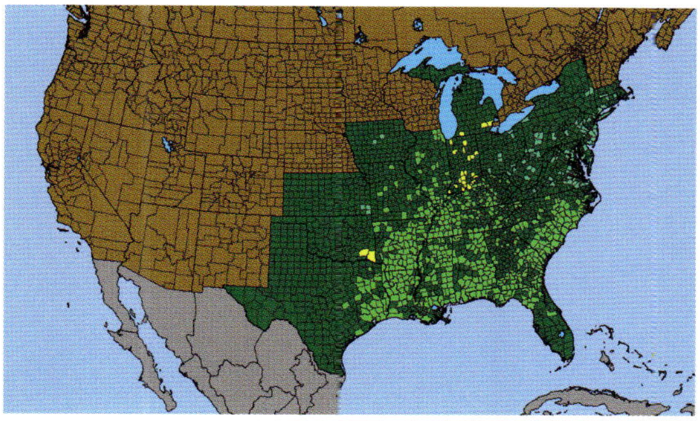

- Deciduous vine; 3 to 10 feet.
- Spring purple flowers followed by purple berries.
- Sun to shade; wet to moist soil.
- Workhorse. VHPV: Pollinated by native bees, butterflies. Host to moth and butterfly caterpillars.

The highly fragrant flowers of native wisteria are similar in color and shape to the Japanese and Chinese species, though *Wisteria frutescens* blooms after its leaves have arrived. Flowers appear only on new wood; pruning will keep blooms plentiful up and down the length of the vining growth. Although mature plants reach 25 to 30 feet, they don't grow as aggressively as their non-native counterparts.

Campsis radicans

TRUMPET CREEPER

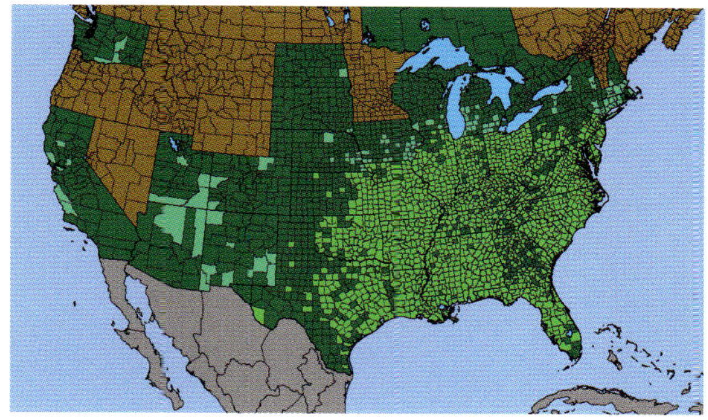

- Deciduous vine; 30 to 45 feet.
- Late-spring to early-summer orange to red flowers.
- Sun to part shade; wet to dry acidic soil.
- Workhorse. VHPV: Pollinated by native bees, other insects, hummingbirds. Host to moth caterpillars.

Quite different in color and form from wisteria's blooms, the vivid orange and red trumpet-shaped flowers of *Campsis radicans* are spectacular in their own way. Be warned that this high climber grows aggressively, and its aerial rootlets mean it should be kept away from wood, stone, brick, or any structure that the roots might infiltrate, so careful consideration must proceed its introduction. Where its growth can be controlled by pruning or mowing, the reward is spectacular blooms highlighted by deep green foliage that are much visited by butterflies and hummingbirds.

More great native choices: *Parthenocissus* spp. (page 191), *Clematis* spp. (page 199), *Lonicera* spp. (pages 80, 201)

CHAPTER SEVEN

Specimen Trees

While a central tenet of native gardening is to replace unneeded lawn and non-native turfgrass with beneficial mixed native trees, shrubs, and bushes, most American gardens will include some lawn for walking, playing, or relaxing. Often these spaces feature specimen plants—single plants that act as a focal point and break up an otherwise monotonous expanse.

Many of the shrubs that appear throughout this book, particularly those with showy or evergreen foliage or large, bright blooms, make good specimen plants. The focus of this section is trees, which have long been valued as specimen plants, particularly on unwooded lots. In fact, this is where many, if not most, of the trees that have now become invasive in American gardens first appeared. Many of these are still being propagated and sold, to the detriment of our ecosystems and natural diversity.

Native trees, thankfully, can be equally showstopping and are the most effective and efficient plants when it comes to assisting local ecosystems, both because of the number of pollinator and insect species they support and because of their other wildlife benefits, including food, shelter, erosion control, and improvements to soil structure.

INSTEAD OF THIS:

Acer palmatum

JAPANESE MAPLE

Japanese maples are popular in American gardens for their distinct serrated foliage, diverse colors, and compact size. They prefer partial shade, but many can tolerate some sun in acidic to neutral soils. Japanese maples typically require close attention to maintain. They may face leaf scorch in hot, dry conditions and some dieback following winter winds. Some varieties are notably prone to pests and diseases. *Acer palmatum* has escaped cultivation and is listed as invasive.

PLANT THESE:

Cornus alternifolia

PAGODA DOGWOOD

AL, AR, CT, DE, FL, GA, IA, IL, IN, KY, MA, MD, ME, MI, MN, MO, MS, NC, NE, NH, NJ, NY, OH, PA, RI, SC, TN, TX, VA, VT, WI, WV

Acer glabrum

ROCKY MOUNTAIN MAPLE

AZ, CA, CO, ID, MT, NE, NM, NV, OR, SD, UT, WA, WY

Cornus alternifolia
PAGODA DOGWOOD

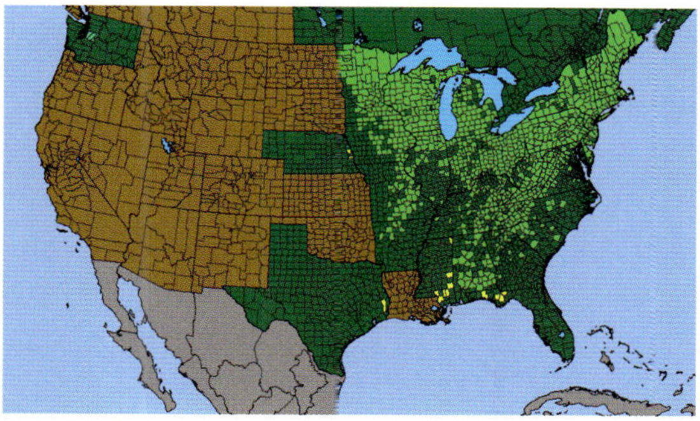

- Deciduous shrub/tree; 6 to 20 feet.
- Early- to mid-spring white flowers followed by purple berries. Purple fall foliage.
- Sun to part shade; moist to dry soil.
- HPV: Pollinated by native bees, butterflies, other insects. Host to moth and butterfly caterpillars. Berries feed birds, mammals.

Its tiered branching pattern gives this plant its common name. *Cornus alterinfolia* can be grown as a multistemmed shrub or as a tree. Flat clusters of small, fragrant white flowers are followed by many dark berries. Green to reddish bark adds interest. It's a favorite of browsing deer, so offer protection while the plant is getting established, after which it will stand up to some deer pressure.

Acer glabrum
ROCKY MOUNTAIN MAPLE

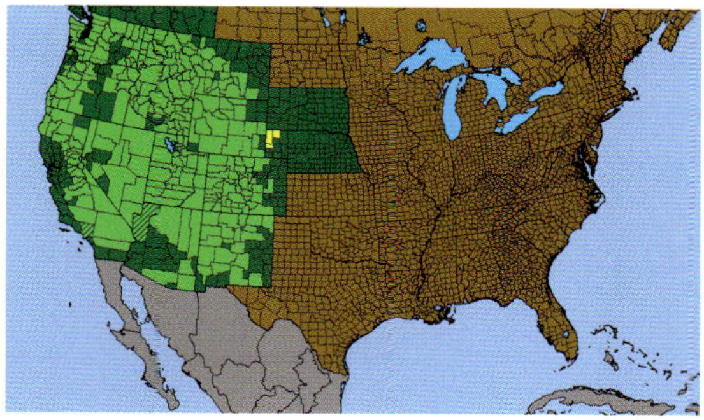

- Deciduous shrub/tree; 8 to 20 feet.
- Spring inconspicuous flowers (catkins). Red, orange, yellow fall foliage.
- Sun to part shade; moist to dry soil.
- Workhorse. Pollinated by native bees. Host to moth caterpillars.

This small native maple usually grows as a multistemmed plant. Its visually inconspicuous catkins make their presence known with a delicious fragrance when they emerge in spring. Fall foliage ranges from bright yellow to orange and red and is complemented by gray bark and red twigs. Winged seeds extend seasonal interest after fall foliage has faded.

More great native choices: *Aronia* spp. (page 27), *Corylus* spp. (page 55), *Viburnum prunifolium* (page 92), *Cornus florida* (page 219), *Cercis* spp. (page 224)

INSTEAD OF THESE:

Magnolia × soulangeana

SAUCER MAGNOLIA

Magnolia stellata

STAR MAGNOLIA

The early, attractive blooms of these introduced magnolias have made them popular in American gardens, where they are grown in full sun in acidic soil from Zones 4 to 8 (or 9 for saucer magnolia), reaching a height of 15 to 20 feet (star magnolia) or 25 feet (saucer magnolia). Toward the northern limit of these magnolias' range, warm spring days will encourage even earlier blooming, only for the open or opening blooms turn to brown mush when seasonably cold weather returns. Native magnolias are better accustomed to spring's fickle nature and wait for true spring's arrival before putting on their own stunning show.

PLANT THESE:

Magnolia virginiana

SWEETBAY MAGNOLIA

AL, AR, DC, DE, FL, GA, LA, MA, MD, MS, NC, NJ, NY, PA, SC, TN, TX, VA

Magnolia acuminata

CUCUMBER TREE, MOUNTAIN MAGNOLIA

AL, AR, FL, GA, IL, IN, KY, LA, MD, MO, MS, NC, NY, OH, OK, PA, SC, TN, VA, WV

Magnolia virginiana

SWEETBAY MAGNOLIA

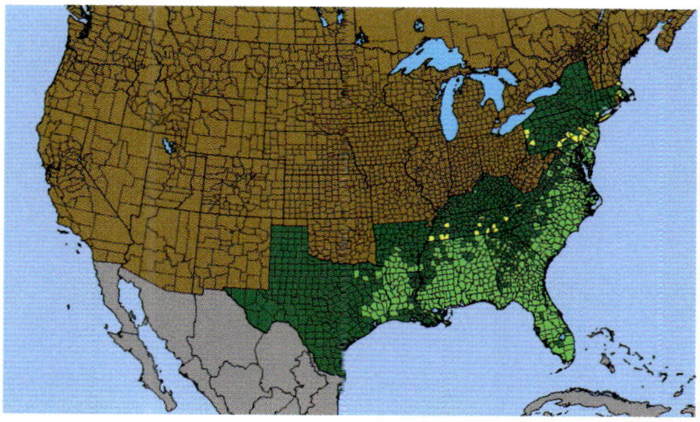

- Evergreen to semi-evergreen tree; 10 to 60 feet.
- Spring to summer white flowers followed by red fruits.
- Sun to part shade; wet to moist acidic soil.
- Workhorse. HPV: Feeds bees, other insects. Host to moth and butterfly caterpillars.

Magnolia virginiana typically grows as a small, multistemmed tree, under 20 feet tall, though it can grow much taller at the southern end of its range. The leaves and twigs have a spicy scent. Its fragrant, creamy white flowers are 4 to 6 inches in diameter, each one blooming for several days, opening in the daytime and closing at night, in a display that can last for several weeks before the conelike red fruits appear.

Magnolia acuminata

CUCUMBER TREE, MOUNTAIN MAGNOLIA

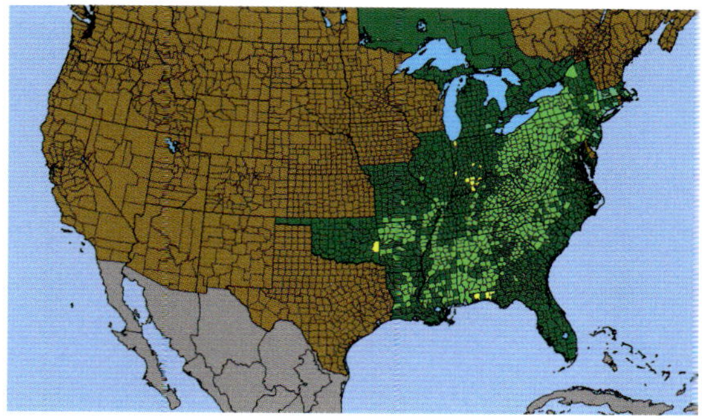

- Deciduous tree; 50 to 80 feet.
- Spring yellow flowers followed by red fruits. Yellow fall foliage.
- Sun to part shade; moist acid to neutral soil.
- HPV: Feeds bees, other insects. Host to moth and butterfly caterpillars.
- Deer resistant.

Magnolia acuminta is exceptional in several ways. Typically reaching 60 feet or taller in a garden setting, this deciduous tree has 6- to 10-inch-long leaves that go from deep green in summer to yellow in fall. Its flowers, which appear high in the tree, may be greenish white or yellow, and are followed by a curious cucumber-shaped fruit that matures from green to red. After falling to the ground, often with its seeds intact, the fruit is a favorite of ground-foraging birds and mammals. This hardy magnolia will grow happily in cold climates where others struggle.

INSTEAD OF THESE:

Malus sylvestris
EUROPEAN CRAB APPLE

Malus floribunda
JAPANESE CRAB APPLE

Prunus serrulata 'Kwanzan'
KWANZAN CHERRY

Prunus × yedoensis
YOSHINO CHERRY

Non-native crab apple and ornamental cherry trees are popular in American gardens for their modest stature; classic, rounded canopy; and early-spring blossoms. While ornamental cherries typically don't produce fruit, crab apple blooms are followed by small red fruits. The manageable size of ornamental fruit trees, typically under 20 feet at maturity, allows for easy integration into diverse garden designs in full sun. By choosing natives to fill this role, you'll be sure to support the widest range of wildlife, with plants that have evolved to thrive in your garden.

PLANT THESE:

Malus angustifolia
SOUTHERN CRAB APPLE

AL, AR, DC, DE, FL, GA, KY, LA, MD, MO, MS, NC, NJ, PA, SC, TN, TX, VA, WV

Malus coronaria
SWEET CRAB APPLE

AL, AR, DC, DE, GA, IL, IN, KS, KY, LA, MD, MI, MO, NC, NJ, NY, OH, PA, SC, TN, VA, WI, WV, WY

Malus ioensis
PRAIRIE CRAB APPLE

AR, IA, IL, IN, KS, KY, LA, MI, MN, MO, NE, NJ, OK, SD, TX, WI

Prunus virginiana
CHOKECHERRY

AR, AZ, CA, CO, CT, DC, GA, IA, ID, IL, IN, KS, KY, MA, MD, ME, MI, MN, MO, MT, NC, ND, NE, NH, NJ, NM, NV, NY, OH, OK, OR, PA, RI, SD, TN, TX, UT, VA, VT, WA, WI, WV, WY

Malus angustifolia

SOUTHERN CRAB APPLE

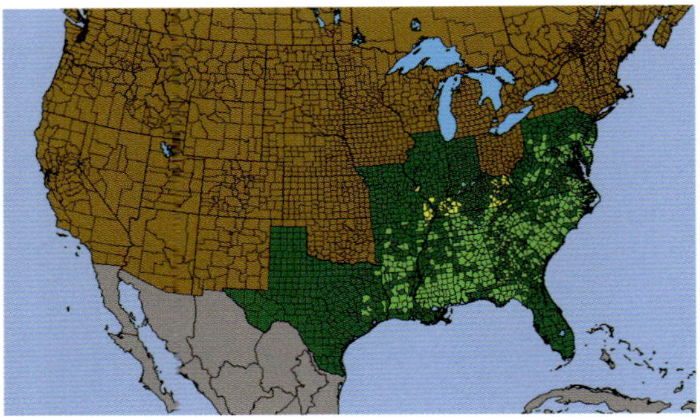

- Deciduous tree; 10 to 20 feet.
- Spring pink flowers.
- Sun to part shade; moist soil.
- HPV: Pollinated by native bees. Host to moth caterpillars. Fruits feed birds, mammals.

Malus coronaria

SWEET CRAB APPLE

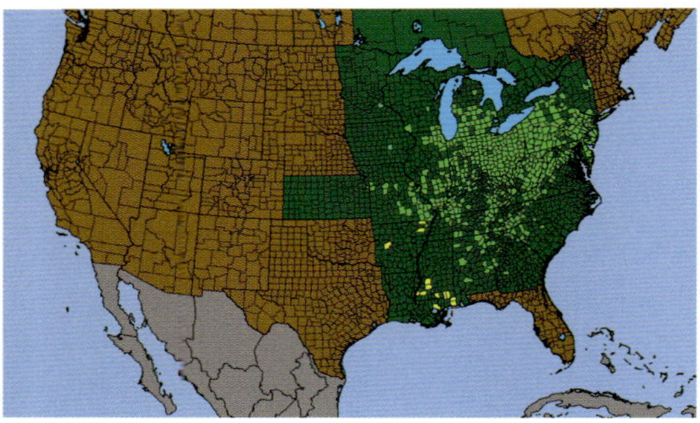

- Deciduous tree; 10 to 25 feet.
- Spring pink flowers followed by red fruits.
- Sun to part shade; moist soil.
- VHPV: Pollinated by native bees, butterflies (including monarchs). Host to moth caterpillars. Fruits feed birds, mammals.

Malus ioensis

PRAIRIE CRAB APPLE

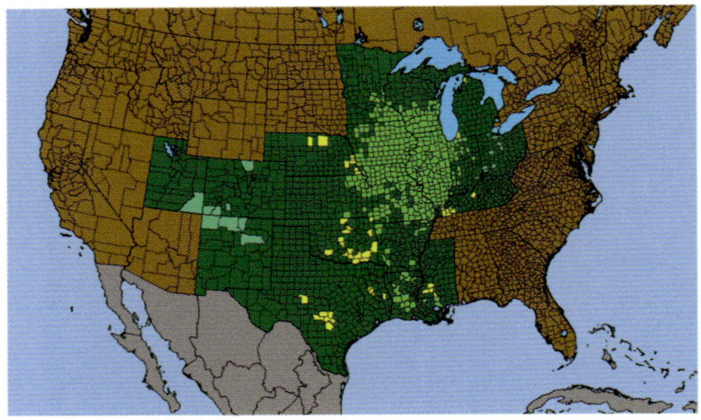

- Deciduous tree; 15 to 25 feet.
- Spring deep pink flowers followed by red fruits.
- Sun to part shade; moist soil.
- HPV: Pollinated by native bees. Host to moth caterpillars. Fruits feed birds, mammals.

All the native North American *Malus* species have fragrant spring flowers that appear after the trees leaf out. Each of these three trees will bloom abundantly, after which small, tart red apples (not palatable to humans but delightful to birds and small mammals) will appear. Watch out for nonfruiting cultivars—though marketed as less messy, these trees are missing one of the plant's key wildlife benefits.

Prunus virginiana

CHOKECHERRY

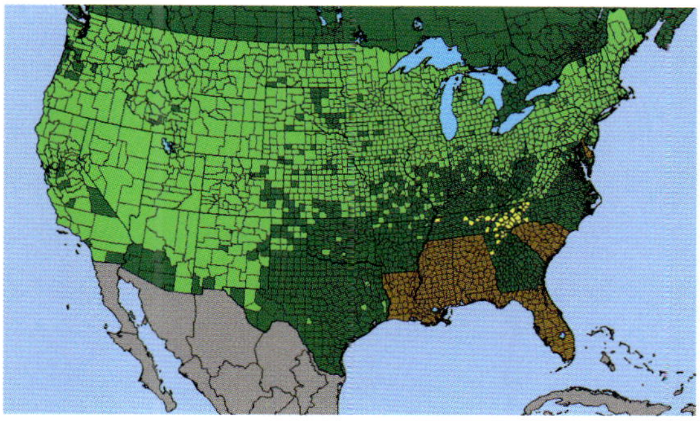

- Deciduous shrub/tree; 10 to 25 feet.
- Spring white flowers followed by dark red fruits.
- Sun to part shade; moist to dry soils.
- Workhorse. VHPV: Pollinated by native bees, moths, butterflies, other insects. Host to moth and butterfly caterpillars. Berries feed birds, mammals.

Of all the cherry species, *Prunus virginiana* is perhaps most versatile in home landscapes, topping out at a reasonable 25 feet but often maturing to a lower height in a garden setting. The shiny oval leaves make a lovely, high-contrast backdrop first to delicate white spring flowers and then to clusters of small, dark cherries that are loved by birds and small mammals. Chokecherry can form thickets if left to sucker, but suckers are easily controlled by pruning.

More great native choices: *Amelanchier alnifolia* (page 53), *Crataegus* spp. (page 218), *Cercis* spp. (page 224)

INSTEAD OF THIS:

Paulownia tomentosa

EMPRESS TREE, PRINCESS TREE

Valued as a fast-growing shade tree with ornamental heart-shaped leaves, *Paulownia tomentosa*, introduced from eastern Asia, can grow as much as 15 feet in a season, reaching a mature height of 50 feet in a few years in full sun in a variety of soils in Zones 5 to 8. A downside to fast growth is wood that tends to be weak and is prone to breakage and limb loss. The many seeds produced by its clustered flowers, along with an ability to resprout aggressively from the remaining roots when cut, have made *P. tomentosa* an invasive tree to be avoided in North American landscapes.

PLANT THESE:

Catalpa speciosa

NORTHERN CATALPA

AR, IL, IN, KY, MO, TN

Catalpa bignonioides

SOUTHERN CATALPA

AL, FL, GA, LA, MS, TX

Catalpa speciosa

NORTHERN CATALPA

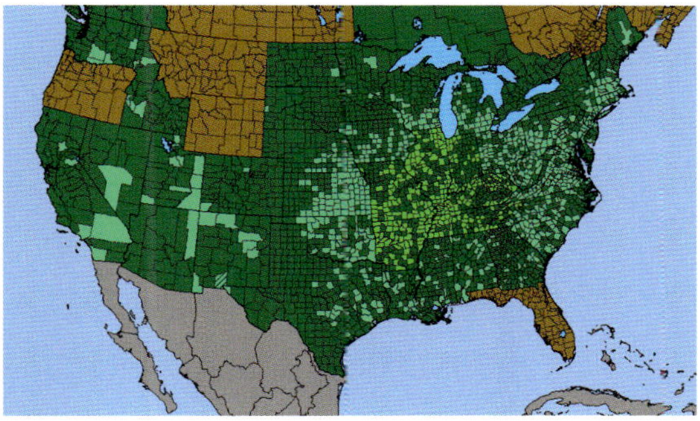

- Deciduous tree; 40 to 60 feet.
- Summer white-and-red flowers.
- Sun to part shade; moist to dry soil.
- VHPV: Pollinated by native bees, moths, butterflies, other insects. Host to moth and butterfly caterpillars.
- Deer resistant.

Catalpa bignonioides

SOUTHERN CATALPA

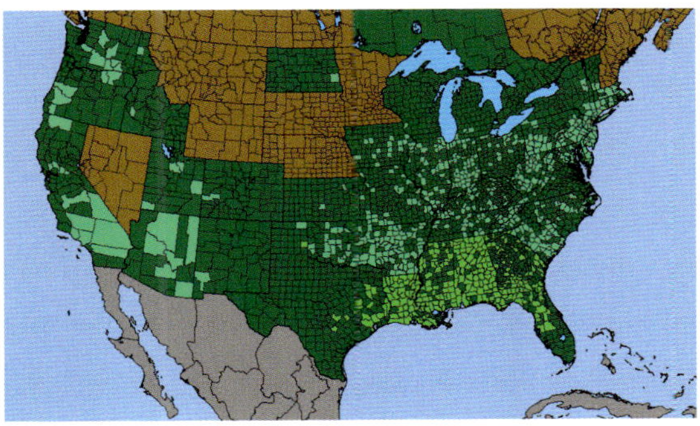

- Deciduous tree; 25 to 40 feet.
- Summer white-and-red flowers.
- Sun to part shade; moist to dry soil.
- VHPV: Pollinated by native bees, moths, butterflies, other insects. Host to moth caterpillars.
- Deer resistant.

In summertime, the heart-shaped leaves of catalpa trees make them lookalikes for *Paulownia tomentosa*. The white spring flowers are different but equally beautiful and more distinct, sitting in profusion above the leaves, where their internal dark red stripes are visible. Like *P. tomentosa*, a catalpa is a rapid grower. What it lacks in fall color it makes up in winter interest, with flaking bark and decorative hanging brown seedpods.

Catalpa bignonioides is slightly less cold tolerant and doesn't reach the same mature heights as *C. speciosa*. Both will grow in some shade but flower best in more sun.

More great native choices: *Magnolia virginiana* and *M. acuminata* (page 209)

INSTEAD OF THIS:

Pyrus calleryana

CALLERY PEAR, 'BRADFORD' PEAR

The Callery pear, specifically its 'Bradford' cultivar, gained popularity in twentieth-century American gardens because of its rapid growth, attractive spring blossoms, and adaptability to various soil conditions in Zones 4 to 9 (almost the entire contiguous United States). The Callery pear's drawbacks soon appeared, however: Although the popular 'Bradford' cultivar is self-sterile, it cross-pollinates with other varieties, and the offspring has made it into the wild, colonizing disturbed areas in particular and crowding out natives. It's now listed as invasive. In addition, while the plant's oval shape and white blooms have spring appeal, its wood is fragile and highly susceptible to damage, making it high maintenance and typically short-lived.

PLANT THESE:

Crataegus chrysocarpa

YELLOW FRUIT HAWTHORN

AL, AR, CT, DC, FL, GA, IA, IL, KS, KY, LA, MA, MD, ME, MI, MN, MO, MS, NC, NJ, NY, OK, PA, RI, SC, TN, TX, VA, VT, WI, WV

Crataegus crus-galli

COCKSPUR HAWTHORN

AL, AR, CT, DC, DE, FL, GA, IA, IL, IN, KS, KY, LA, MA, MD, ME, MI, MN, MO, MS, NC, NH, NJ, NY, OH, OK, PA, RI, SC, TN, TX, VA, VT, WI, WV

Crataegus douglasii

BLACK HAWTHORN

CA, ID, MI, MN, MT, ND, NV, NY, OR, SD, UT, WA, WI, WY

Cornus florida

FLOWERING DOGWOOD

AL, AR, CT, DC, DE, FL, GA, IL, IN, KS, KY, LA, MA, MD, ME, MI, MO, MS, NC, NH, NJ, NY, OH, OK, PA, RI, SC, TN, TX, VA, VT, WV

Crataegus chrysocarpa
YELLOW FRUIT HAWTHORN

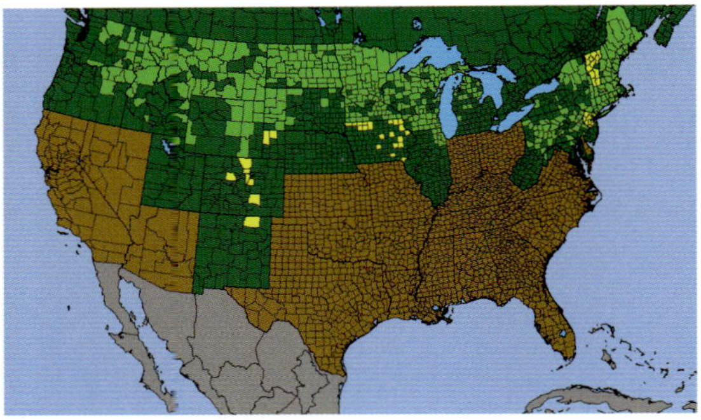

- Deciduous shrub/tree; 15 to 25 feet.
- Spring white to pink flowers followed by orange fruits. Yellow fall foliage.
- Full sun to shade; wet to moist soil.
- VHPV: Pollinated by native bees, moths, butterflies (including monarchs), other insects. Fruits feed birds.

Crataegus douglasii
BLACK HAWTHORN

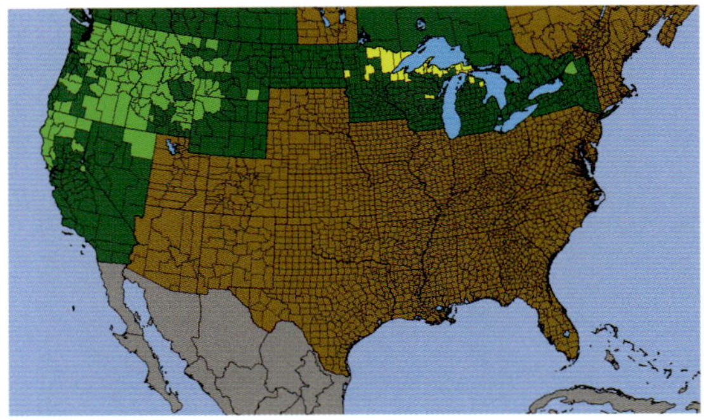

- Deciduous shrub/tree; 12 to 15 feet.
- Spring white flowers followed by dark fruit. Yellow, orange, red fall foliage.
- Sun to part shade; wet to dry soil.
- Workhorse/HPV: Pollinated by native bees, moths, butterflies. Host to moth and butterfly caterpillars. Fruits feed birds.

Crataegus crus-galli
COCKSPUR HAWTHORN

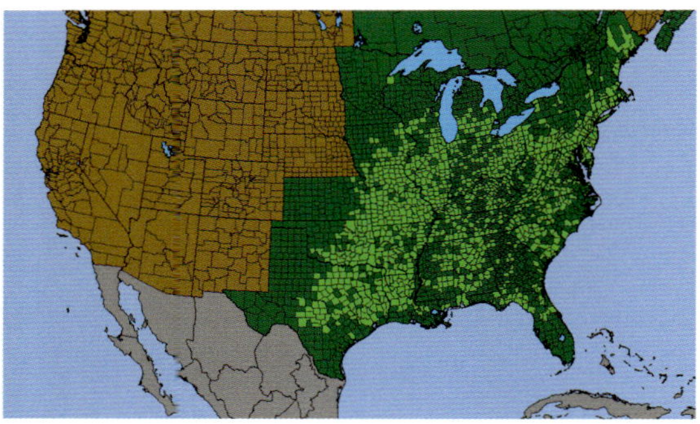

- Deciduous shrub/tree; 15 to 25 feet.
- Spring white flowers followed by red fruit. Orange to red fall foliage.
- Sun to shade; wet to dry soil. Drought tolerant once established.
- Workhorse. VHPV: Pollinated by native bees, moths, butterflies (including monarchs), other insects. Host to moth caterpillars. Fruits feed birds.

These apple relatives produce fragrant flowers in dense clusters along thorny branches. Small, red, applelike fruits shine brightly against dark green leaves, after which a brilliant fall foliage show takes place. Hawthorns are a host for cedar-hawthorn rust, which can be avoided by planting them far from cedars, but damage from the disease is more cosmetic than harmful to the underlying health of hawthorns.

Cornus florida

FLOWERING DOGWOOD

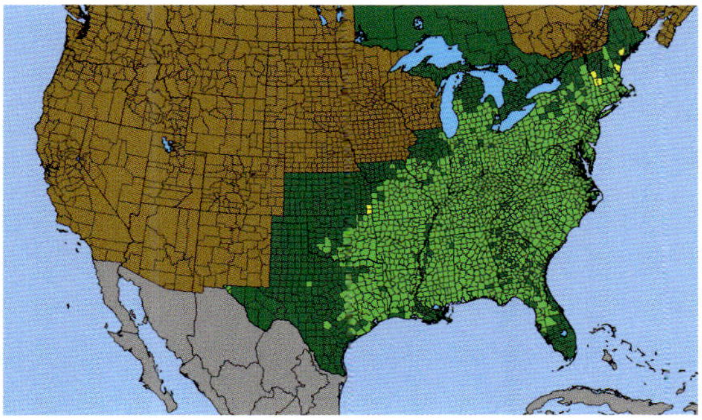

- Deciduous shrub/tree; 15 to 40 feet.
- Spring white flowers.
- Full sun to part shade; moist to dry soil.
- Workhorse. VHPV: Pollinated by native bees, moths, butterflies, other insects. Host to moth and butterfly caterpillars. Fruits feed birds, small mammals.

This quintessentially American spring bloomer has made its way back into gardens and natural spaces after being nearly eliminated by anthracnose, a fungal disease, in the late twentieth century. While wild populations have not recovered, *Cornus florida* is returning to nurseries and gardens. A number of cultivars bred specifically for disease resistance have been introduced; these include varieties with 'Appalachian' or 'Cherokee' in their name. Look for those rather than the hybrids developed from crosses with the nonnative *C. kousa*, whose names are often star related, such as 'Milky Way', 'Constellation', and 'Stellar Pink', among others. Finding the right dogwood can be confusing, and your best bet is to get help from a knowledgeable nurseryperson and then double-check sources before you buy.

More great native choices: *Amelanchier alnifolia* (page 53), *Malus* spp. (page 212)

INSTEAD OF THIS:

Salix babylonica

WEEPING WILLOW

These iconic trees have arched branches that bend to the ground to form a rounded canopy up to 40 feet in diameter. They are typically found in moist or wet sites but are adaptable to a variety of soil conditions in sun to light shade in Zones 4 to 10. The roots of a *Salix babylonica* will reach far and wide underground in their search for water and have been known to damage foundations and especially sewage and water lines.

PLANT THESE:

Salix nigra

BLACK WILLOW

AL, AR, CT, DC, DE, FL, GA, IA, IL, IN, KS, KY, LA, MA, MD, ME, MI, MN, MO, MS, NC, NE, NH, NJ, NY, OH, OK, PA, RI, SC, TN, TX, VA, VT, WI, WV

Salix scouleriana

SCOULER'S WILLOW

AZ, CA, CO, ID, MT, NM, NV, OR, SD, UT, WA, WY

Salix nigra

BLACK WILLOW

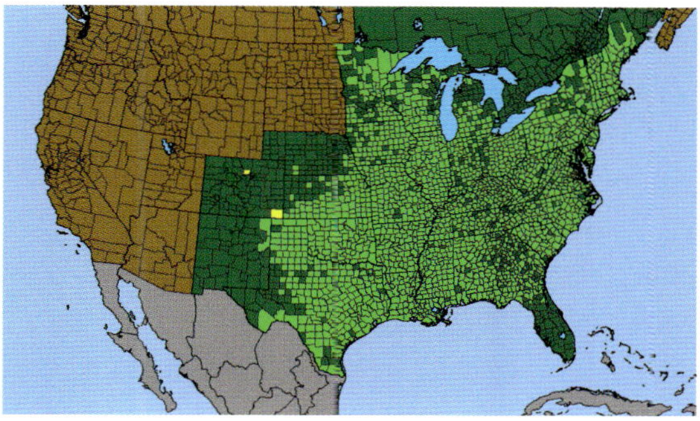

- Deciduous tree; 12 to 60 feet.
- Early-spring inconspicuous yellow flowers. Fall yellow foliage.
- Full sun to part shade; wet to moist soil.
- Workhorse. VHPV: Pollinated by native bees, moths, butterflies, other insects. Host to moth and butterfly caterpillars.

A fast-growing, multistemmed tree, *Salix nigra* is the largest and most widely native of the North American salixes, reaching its tallest heights in the southern part of its range. *S. nigra* typically matures to make a fine shade tree, with a rounded, almost cloudlike canopy, in consistently moist soil. Like other willows, it has water-seeking roots so shouldn't be planted near waste or water lines.

Salix scouleriana

SCOULER'S WILLOW

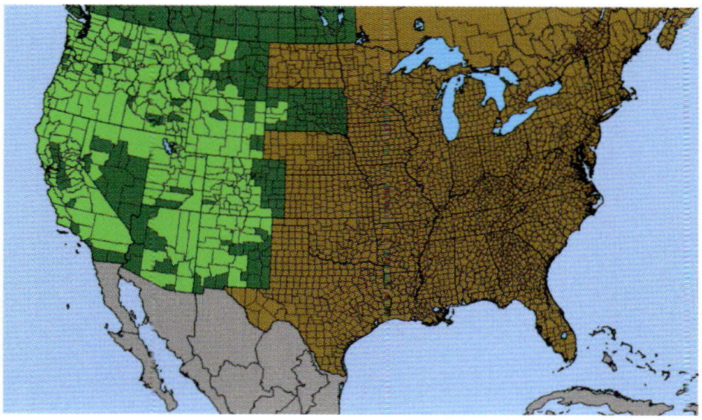

- Deciduous shrub/tree; 10 to 30 feet.
- Early-spring yellow flowers; yellow fall foliage.
- Full sun to part shade; moist to dry soil.
- Workhorse. HPV: Pollinated by native bees, hummingbirds. Host to moth and butterfly caterpillars.

A multistemmed large shrub or small tree, *Salix scouleriana* tolerates drier soil than many other willow species. Its oval leaves are wide compared to other willows, giving it a pleasingly full shape. Its prominent spring catkins, reddish bark, deep gold fall foliage, and the velvety undersides of its leaves add to its appeal.

NOTE: Both these willows can form thickets, and the wood is sometimes weak and prone to break, but they can be pruned or coppiced to limit their size and keep them in shape.

INSTEAD OF THESE:

Syringa vulgaris

COMMON LILAC

Lagerstroemia indica

CRAPE MYRTLE

Both lilacs and crape myrtles are grown primarily for their dramatic flower clusters. Lilacs are also prized for their rich fragrance, which is multiplied in a classic lilac hedge. Once the lilac's pink or purple blooms have passed, though, their foliage is not particularly remarkable; older plants can get leggy without proper pruning. Lilacs grow 12 to 15 feet tall, preferring full sun; and resent wet feet or poor air circulation, which makes them prone to powdery mildew that can disfigure their foliage.

Commercial growers have created dozens of variations of the crape myrtle, from shrub forms to small trees, all of which are covered in pink or nearly purple blooms in summer in full sun in Zones 6 to 10. Crape myrtles have escaped cultivation, especially in the southern part of their range, where they may crowd out more beneficial native plants. Though these trees have an appealing exfoliating bark, crape myrtle bark scale has become a serious threat to the health and appearance of these plants.

PLANT THESE:

Cercis canadensis

EASTERN REDBUD

AL, AR, CT, DC, DE, FL, GA, IA, IL, IN, KS, KY, LA, MD, MI, MO, MS, NC, NE, NJ, NM, OH, OK, PA, SC, TN, TX, VA, WV

Cercis orbiculata

(syn. *Cercis occidentalis*)

WESTERN REDBUD, CALIFORNIA REDBUD

AZ, NV, UT

Chionanthus virginicus

FRINGETREE, WHITE FRINGETREE

AL, AR, DC, DE, FL, GA, IN, KY, LA, MD, MO, MS, NC, NJ, OH, OK, PA, SC, TN, TX, VA, WV

Cercis canadensis

EASTERN REDBUD

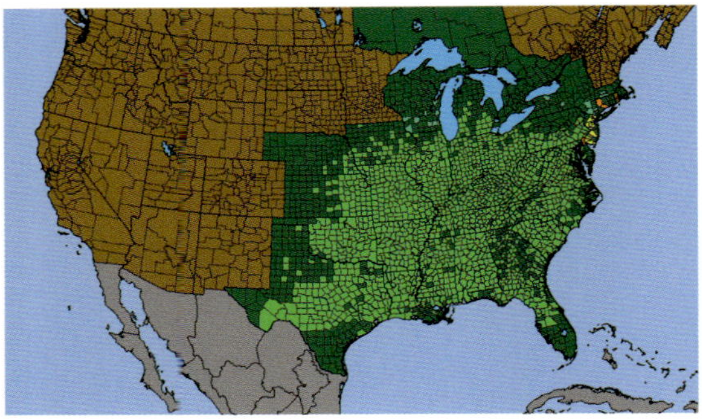

- Deciduous shrub/tree; 10 to 30 feet.
- Early-spring pink flowers.
- Sun to part shade; moist soil.
- Workhorse. VHPV: Pollinated by native bees, butterflies (including monarchs), other insects, hummingbirds. Host to moth and butterfly caterpillars.

Cercis orbiculata

(syn. *Cercis occidentalis*)

WESTERN REDBUD, CALIFORNIA REDBUD

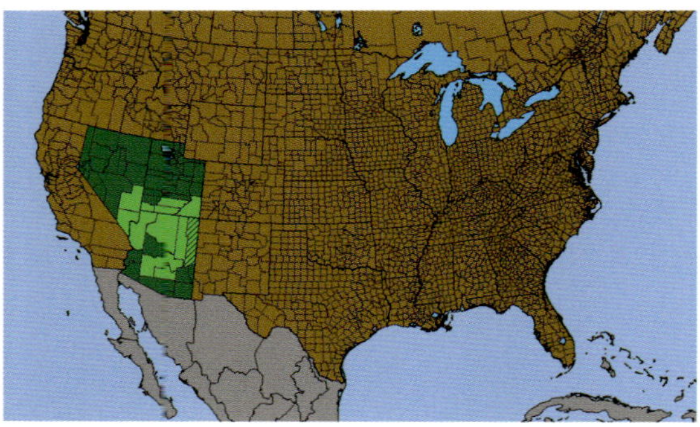

- Deciduous shrub/tree; 10 to 20 feet.
- Early-spring pink flowers. Yellow fall foliage.
- Sun to part shade; moist to dry soil.
- VHPV: Pollinated by native bees, butterflies, other insects, hummingbirds. Host to moth and butterfly caterpillars.

The eastern and western varieties of *Cercis* are very similar. But even in their own ranges, there are small differences from place to place among the leaves, flowers, and fruits of the plants—important mainly to botanists, but highlighting just how local a plant's true native range may be. Everywhere it grows, this harbinger of spring is high on many people's favorite plants list. In late winter or early spring, bright pink to magenta pea-like flowers appear along the branches and trunk of the single- or multistemmed plant. After the initial flush of flowers, distinctive, heart-shaped leaves appear, reddish at first and then settling into their dark green seasonal color before turning yellow in fall.

NOTE: The popular 'Forest Pansy' cultivar of *C. canadensis* has red leaves all summer long, which are distinct and attractive, but may not be as valuable to pollinators as the straight species.

Chionanthus virginicus

FRINGETREE, WHITE FRINGETREE

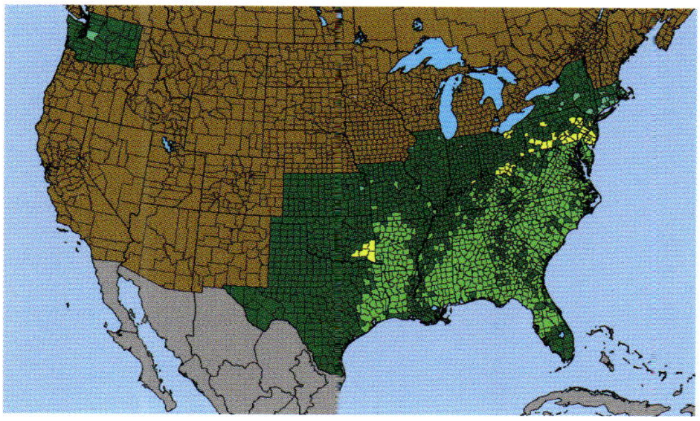

- Deciduous shrub/tree; 10 to 20 feet.
- Spring white flowers followed by blue fruits on female plants.
- Sun to part shade; moist to dry soil.
- Workhorse. VHPV: Pollinated by native bees, butterflies, other insects. Host to moth caterpillars. Fruit feeds birds.

Chionanthus virginicus typically grows as a multi-stemmed shrub but can also develop into a small, slender tree with a single trunk. The leaves are dark green, glossy, and elliptical in shape. The bark is smooth and light gray when young, becoming scalier with age. *C. virginicus* is one of the last trees to break dormancy, but it's worth the wait: Come late spring, the delicate, fringelike flowers are a highlight, providing a unique and beautiful display. *Chionanthus* is dioecious, with separate male and female plants. Both plants flower, with males having slightly showier blooms, but only females will produce fruits when both male and female are present.

More great native choices: *Physocarpus* spp. (page 24), *Hydrangea arborescens* (page 30), *Ceanothus* spp. (page 31), *Amelanchier alnifolia* (page 53)

INSTEAD OF THIS:

Acer platanoides

NORWAY MAPLE

This fast-growing, sturdy, pollution-resistant maple native to Europe and Asia was introduced as an adaptable ornamental for American landscapes. But this same adaptability has also made it a notorious problem plant. Its extensive shallow roots make it difficult for other plants to survive under its canopy, and it has spread widely beyond cultivation via prolific production of the winged seeds typical of maples, which can travel far from the parent tree. When it arrives in woods, it can crowd out other plant populations and threaten the diversity of the local ecosystem. It's known to be invasive in the Northeast, Southeast, Midwest, and Pacific Northwest. Luckily, there's an abundance of beautiful native maples to choose from.

PLANT THESE:

Acer rubrum

RED MAPLE

AL, AR, CT, DC, DE, FL, GA, IA, IL, IN, KY, LA, MA, MD, ME, MI, MN, MO, MS, NC, NH, NJ, NY, OH, OK, PA, RI, SC, TN, TX, VA, VT, WI, WV

Acer grandidentatum

BIGTOOTH MAPLE, CANYON MAPLE

AZ, CO, ID, MT, NM, NV, OK, TX, UT, WA, WY

Acer macrophyllum

BIGLEAF MAPLE

CA, OR, WA

Acer rubrum
RED MAPLE

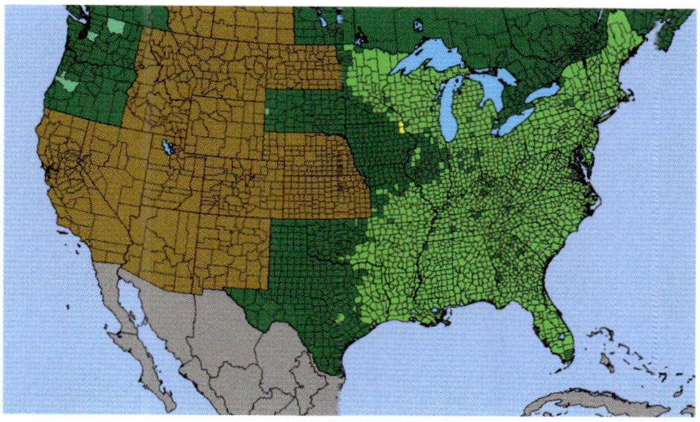

- Deciduous tree; 40 to 60 feet.
- Yellow to orange to red fall foliage.
- Sun to part shade; moist soil.
- Workhorse. VHPV: Pollinated by native bees, other insects. Host to moth caterpillars.

Acer macrophyllum
BIGLEAF MAPLE

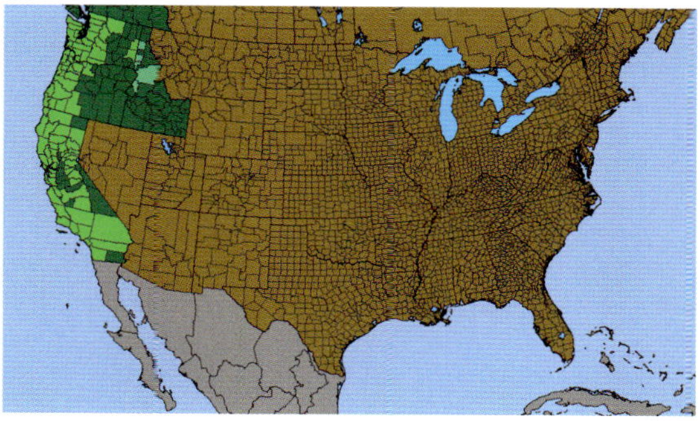

- Deciduous tree; 50 to 70 feet.
- Orange fall foliage.
- Sun to part shade; moist to dry soil.
- Workhorse. Pollinated by native bees. Host to moth caterpillars.

Acer grandidentatum
BIGTOOTH MAPLE, CANYON MAPLE

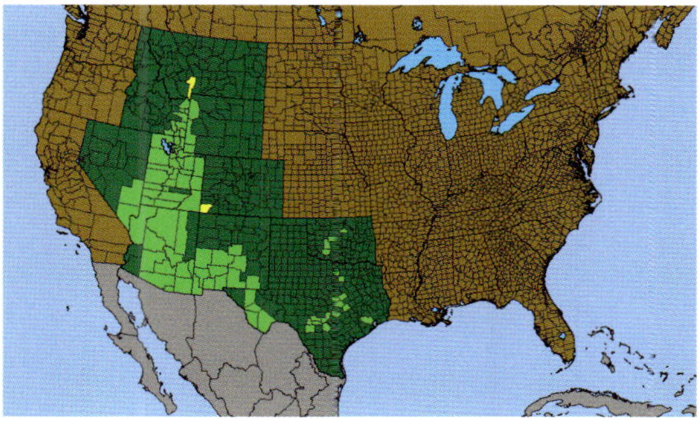

- Deciduous tree; 25 to 50 feet.
- Yellow to red fall foliage.
- Sun to part shade; wet to dry soil.
- Host to moth caterpillars.

These three maples represent some of the garden-friendliest, most widely native species in their regions. All feature the iconic, lobed leaves with pointed tips that make maples so easy to spot, as well as brilliant fall foliage, ranging from bright, clear yellow to burgundy red, depending on the species. Other *Acer* species may also work in your ecoregion, but note that many maples are considerably shorter than these and may have different light and water requirements. As horticulturist William Cullina has noted, tree species may vary across their native range, so for the best success, it makes sense to plant locally grown trees if you can find them.

Beyond Plant Swaps

Choosing native plants over non-natives is a key first step in native plant gardening. But in important ways, it's only the beginning of your journey. To match your shift in perspective about what kinds of plants you choose and what you value in a garden plant, you'll want to reevaluate what's important in garden maintenance and make changes in how you care for your garden in every season. And then gradually (or all at once!), you may find yourself rethinking the fundamental place and purpose of our home yards, gardens, and landscapes, making further changes to have a bigger impact on biodiversity and our broader environment.

Maintaining a Native Plant Garden

Along with *what* you plant, *how* you care for those plants is important. One of the big benefits in growing a native plant garden is that the best practices are mostly low intervention, especially when compared to the maintenance involved in creating a garden of non-native species. Native plants succeed in their range because they are well suited to soil, light, and water conditions naturally occurring there. Once you take the initial time to match your plants to the existing conditions where you plan to garden, you are already free of the time-consuming work of amending soil and supplementing water (at least after root systems are initially established).

Bear in mind that native plants thrive in communities. So rather than plan for the back-breaking work of seasonally surrounding your isolated plants with a frame of mulch, if you plant abundantly (and then tolerate the appearance of some volunteer seedlings), you'll gain the benefits of green mulch, where a wealth of plants covers the soil and suppresses weeds.

If you're used to relying on an annual mulching, this new way of gardening may require a shift in perspective. Successful native plant gardens are typically a little less formal, maybe a little more exuberant, than the residential standard passed down from the twentieth-century American landscape. But you'll soon find more rewards than saying goodbye to labor-intensive and expensive practices. Most native plants depend on interconnected root systems and the support of nearby plants to thrive. By allowing your garden to get to this point, rather than positioning plants too far apart or ruthlessly eliminating volunteer seedlings, you may find you no longer need to intervene with staking or other artificial supports, since plants get what they need from one another.

As you learn to take into account the needs of the plants you are growing, rather than force them into a less natural garden scheme, there are other practices to (re)consider, as well.

The Chelsea Chop/Perennial Pruning

You'll still find lots of discussion, even in native plant forums, about how the "Chelsea chop"—i.e., cutting back perennials midway through the season—can keep a garden tidy and extend the bloom period of perennials. Before you make it standard practice, however, consider that the coevolution of beneficial plants and animals means that the growing stages of plants are well matched with the needs of the animals that depend on them. Straight species plants that are allowed to complete their life cycle undisturbed will be the most beneficial to wildlife.

Deadheading

Deadheading, or removing spent blossoms before they produce seed heads, has traditionally been done to extend the garden season and keep plants looking tidy. But seeds are a great way to multiply the plants in your garden, and they are often an important source of winter food for birds.

Seasonal Cleanup

We have been accustomed to cleaning up our gardens for fall, putting them to bed for winter. But cutting stems back to the ground eliminates not only food but also winter shelter for many bees and other pollinators. And raking leaves disturbs or eliminates habitat for overwintering caterpillars and mature insects as well as small mammals. That decaying plant matter also feeds the health and structure of the soil in just the right way for native plants to use, freeing gardens and gardeners from the practice of adding fertilizer or other amendments.

Similarly, cleaning up the garden in spring can disturb creatures overwintering among plants and in leaves before they are ready to emerge. The conventional wisdom is to wait until air temperatures reach 50°F, but garden designer and writer Benjamin Vogt points out that many garden creatures are still slumbering at that temperature and may be harmed by disturbance. Vogt asks us to prioritize a garden's value to the ecosystem over tidiness, and he advocates setting aside many of those traditional practices—removing leaves, cutting back stems, thinning seedlings, etc.—to let nature take its course once the garden is established and close to self-sustaining.

"Pest" Control

One more serious shift in perspective that comes with native plant gardening—one that may take some time to get accustomed to—is recognizing the role of insects in your garden's health and support of the ecosystem. Some of the traditional appeal of non-native plants, as presented in twentieth-century garden catalogs, was freedom from pests. But freedom from pests typically means freedom from pollinators and larval insects (like caterpillars) that use plants as food and shelter. It's common to see newcomers to native plant forums ask how they should treat the milkweed tussock moth caterpillars or aphids or other insects that show up on their *Asclepias* species (milkweeds) in order to make room for the monarch caterpillars they had been looking for. But even a benign intervention like insecticidal soap or dish soap can disturb the circumstances that allow monarch caterpillars to get established while getting rid of insects a gardener may perceive as less welcome.

Instead, patience and tolerance for all the creatures who make use of a plant will soon reveal their own rewards as your garden reaches a more natural balance. Ladybugs, ants, larger insects, and birds will show up to make a meal of smaller insects. It became part of my annual ritual to wait for aphids to appear on my *Lonicera sempervirens* (crimson honeysuckle), knowing ladybugs and hummingbirds soon would follow. You'll realize how deep into your journey as a native plant gardener you have traveled when you find yourself recognizing—and delighting in—the distinctive shape of a leaf-cutter bee's nibbles on your plants' leaves.

Cues to Care

Many gardeners work in suburban communities, where not everyone may be ready for a less-formal approach to landscaping and garden maintenance. Native landscape designers use "cues to care," a concept and term first defined by Joan Nassauer in 1995, to mean practices that indicate a garden (often one that doesn't meet traditional expectations for design and style) is being cared for. This can refer to the inclusion of elements like well-defined paths, benches, or sculpture that say this is a designed and maintained space. It can also include making sure the spaces where the garden connects with public pathways, neighboring properties or other traditional boundaries are tidier than the garden's more interior spaces: for example, with edges defined by shorter plants, without branches or leaves spilling onto walkways, or with more traditional seasonal cleanup taking place in these spaces than elsewhere in the garden. These practices alone may be enough to let your neighbors and community know that you are working with thought and intention. If you want to go a step further and invite questions and conversations about your garden, you might even post a sign announcing your garden's purpose. Many organizations—including Homegrown National Park, National Wildlife Federation, Wild Ones, the Xerces Society, and others—sell these signs, often to fundraise. Of course, your presence in your garden is both the best cue to care *and* conversation starter of all.

The Next Steps in Your Native Garden Journey

My own growth as a native plant gardener really began when, as a volunteer in New York City's Riverside Park, I was asked to work with native plants as much as possible because the garden area entrusted to me was adjacent to the park's Forever Wild native plant area. I began restoring a long-neglected space by working with native plants in place of non-native ones in a very traditional public-garden planting scheme. As the garden grew and changed, my point of view changed, too. My focus, which had once been almost entirely on color and bloom time, shifted to noticing leaves and plant structure and the winter shapes of shrubs and trees, as well as the way insects and birds flocked to the space.

By the time I had the chance to make a brand-new garden in Maine, I was prepared for plants and wildlife to lead the way. I began my planning by asking how I could be a steward of the local ecosystem and make a contribution to the natural plant and animal beauty around me. It was a gradual process, but within a couple of years, the pleasures of my native plant garden included not just the color, shape, and scent of individual plants but the daily visits from bees, butterflies, dragonflies, songbirds, birds of prey, turkeys, frogs, salamanders—and yes, even groundhogs and deer, because an abundance of plants through dense planting and the removal of lawn area meant the garden could withstand a little mammal browsing.

There are members of the native plant community who feel that we need to be more radical in our actions, that we need to give up the traditional American approach to landscape (i.e., a lawn surrounded by or dotted with beds for shrubs and perennials) right now. That's a big leap to make for a variety of reasons, ranging from our collective long-held ideas about North American gardens to community pressure and regulation to the effort and expense of altering an existing landscape all at once.

My hope for readers of this book is that it might first persuade you to incorporate more native plants into your home landscape, ideally until you have reached at least 70 percent native plants, and then to go deeper with your journey. After a number of years of reading Douglas Tallamy's and Benjamin Vogt's and other authors' works on the subject, for me it boils down primarily to the following steps.

Eliminate Invasives

Some days in the garden, I find myself spending more time removing plants than adding them. I joke that if only there were a market for an invasive plant nursery, I could make my fortune. Not one but two homes had been built in the last forty years on the Maine property where I gardened for ten years, making it a textbook definition of disturbed land, which is a favorite landing spot for many invasive species.

In addition to the opportunist plants that appeared—knotweed, five kinds of vetch, Morrow's honeysuckle, Asian bittersweet, and others—invasives like barberry, forsythia, daylilies, and burning bush had been purposely planted in the garden. So it sometimes felt as though half my gardening time there was spent removing invasives. Invasive plants are resilient by definition. As important as it is to do your part in minimizing their presence in the landscape, it's also important to understand that their complete elimination may be (and probably is) an unreachable goal. I've sat in on many discussions where gardeners, myself included, lamented the ineffectiveness of removal methods or the reappearance of a plant they thought had been eliminated. The first objective is not to bring invasives into your garden, by carefully researching any non-native plant you are considering. Then you can work to reduce the presence of existing invasive plants or at least prevent their proliferation.

You can start with the removal of invasives introduced to your garden as ornamentals. If you are not sure whether a plant you've identified is invasive in your area, the Invasive Plant Atlas of the United States (invasiveplantatlas.org) is a great place to find out. It will tell you where plants are listed as invasive, where they have been banned from sale, and where they are problematic but not yet classified as invasive. Many states also have continually evolving lists of invasive species; search online or contact your local Cooperative or Agricultural Extension Office. If you need first to identify an unfamiliar plant, a plant ID app, like the one created by the nonprofit organization iNaturalist, can be a great tool. (There are also many printed plant identification guides available, though nowadays they are usually less comprehensive and more cumbersome to use than digital ones.)

The methods you adopt (whether mechanical or chemical) to remove invasives will depend on the plant's physiology and growth characteristics, where it is found, and your own comfort with various methods. Because my Maine garden was on the water, the only methods I used were mechanical, but even the recommended mechanical methods may differ from plant to plant. Digging plants like honeysuckles or Asian bittersweet, which reproduce via long runners that send up new growth along their length, may have the opposite of the intended effect, stimulating new growth many feet or yards away from the original plant. The recommended treatment for these plants is often to starve them of nutrients through seasonal mowings (often three a season) over the course of several years. In some cases, smothering plants through solarization or the use of physical barriers and wood chips or mulch may be recommended, but I've had trees survive years of solarization, and I've watched vetch send a stem many feet horizontally beneath a layer of cardboard to find the exact single spot where time and weather had created a tiny opening for it to pop through. Several years ago, when I began this work, the use of clean cardboard was frequently recommended. More recently, evidence of unexpected chemicals in cardboard has called its advisability into question. The newer recommendation is to cover the ground—bare or mowed as short as possible—with several inches of arborist wood chips, often available for free.

There's tremendous debate around the use of chemicals, with reputable proponents arguing that *used properly*, chemical herbicides are most effective at killing invasives (or lawn) and not harmful to nearby plants and animals.

However, because chemicals are so easily misused and important factors like wind and rain can be unpredictable, some gardeners and experts believe they should never be employed.

It's not within the scope of this guide to make specific recommendations about removing invasive plants. There are printed guides to invasive plant removal and many guides on the internet, and most regional native plant organizations and many university agricultural extensions include advice about invasive plant removal on their websites. My advice is to focus on the specific invasive plant to be eliminated, and research methods appropriate to that plant, taking into consideration your particular soil and climate conditions and making sure you are reading the most up-to-date materials or hearing from sources using current information and research. Then arm yourself with patience and persistence and a willingness to try different approaches until you find one that works.

Lose the Lawn

Turfgrass is likely to be by far the largest non-native planting in your garden by percentage. Before colonization, short, clipped lawns didn't exist on the continent now called North America. Like many features of our landscapes, the concept is a European import, along with the plants we use to create lawns. It's also usually the most high-maintenance feature of a landscape, requiring mowing, weeding, and ongoing chemical treatments to meet the established standards for looks.

If you are ready and able to turn your entire yard over to native plants, fantastic. But there are plenty of reasons—practical, social, economic, and even legal—for not removing your entire lawn. Eliminating even some lawn will make a big impact on meeting the goals of a native plant garden. The first step in shrinking your lawn is to identify how you use it and consider maintaining only what you really require for leisure, play, foot traffic, or other purposes. Then think about how you might incrementally convert more lawn to garden use. (As with removing invasives, you can find advice on a variety of mechanical or chemical methods to eliminate turfgrass depending on your conditions.) I was inspired by the story of a couple who started at the outside limits of their property and over the course of twenty years added to their border gardens in concentric circles toward the center until their once all-lawn yard became a garden with many winding paths through it.

Another interim option is letting go of traditional notions of what makes a great lawn, eliminating the use of fertilizers and herbicides (remembering that even organic supplements alter the natural balance of your ecosystem) and learning to live with the plants that find their way into your yard. In the lawn area that remained on my property, I was excited to see the violets, blue-eyed grass, geraniums, Canada mayflowers, blueberries, bunchberries, sedges, and other natives that appeared. Non-natives like clovers and dandelions showed up, too, but since they are benign species held in check by the beneficial plants, I tolerated their presence and saved my energy for battling invasives and introducing more beneficial natives elsewhere. Even the simple practice of leaving the remaining grass longer is helpful to the insects, birds, and small mammals that shelter at or near ground level.

Plant Keystone Species in a Layered Landscape

The focus of this book has been on understanding how native plants can fill the role of classic garden plants. As long as the plants you are adding to your garden are native to your area, there's no doubt you are boosting the benefits of your garden to its larger ecosystem. But keystone plants are the way to supercharge your garden's ecological value. An ecoregion's keystone plants are the ones that support the life cycles of the most native animal species, from feeding pollinators to sheltering mammals. The specific plants vary in every region, and can include trees, shrubs, and perennials, with trees generally supporting the most species. Homegrown National Park (homegrownnationalpark.org), the National Wildlife Federation (nwf.org), and many local plant organizations feature level I ecoregion maps that link to lists of keystone plants and the species they support.

While there are many adaptable generalist insects and birds who feed and shelter on various plants, some species depend on a single plant or live in and on certain plants found only near the ground, middle, or upper layer of the landscape. So after establishing a foundation of keystone species, you'll want to layer in other plants at every level of your garden—ground, middle, and treetop—to benefit the full range of native animal species.

Once you have reached your goal of growing (at least) 70 percent native plants, with as many keystone species as possible, consider making the balance of your plantings natives from nearby, or other North American natives, rather than non-natives from abroad. Some plants in this guide, particularly those that have naturalized outside their native ranges, grow well in other regions and support generalist insect and pollinator species—oakleaf hydrangea in large parts of the East, for example, or the many California plants truly native to a small ecoregion that thrive in other parts of the West and Southwest. Hollies and mountain laurels native to the East may be a better solution in the Upper Midwest, where few native evergreens are found, than introduced evergreen species.

A number of North American native plants whose narrow range kept them from being featured in this guide, like *Fothergilla* (witch alder), *Amsonia hubrichtii* (narrowleaf bluestar), and *Heuchera villosa* (hairy alum root), are already popular in American gardens well beyond their native range because they grow well, are distinctly attractive, and do not crowd out their neighbors.

But even with nearby natives, a caution: *Juniperus virginiana*, a valuable plant in its eastern native range, has become invasive in the Great Plains, where overplanting and disruption of the historical natural fire patterns have supported its takeover of grasslands. Other natives, including *Iris* and *Asclepias* species, may behave similarly. So before planting anything from outside your local range, consult the Invasive Plant Atlas or other guides to make sure what you plant will be beneficial.

FURTHER READING AND ADDITIONAL RESOURCES

Books on the Benefits and Importance of Native Plants

Kimmerer, Robin Wall. *Braiding Sweetgrass: Indigenous Wisdom, Scientific Knowledge, and the Teachings of Plants* (Minneapolis, MN: Milkweed Editions, 2013).

—. *The Serviceberry: Abundance and Reciprocity in the Natural World* (New York: Scribner, 2024).

Lawson, Nancy. *The Humane Gardener: Nurturing a Backyard Habitat for Wildlife* (New York: Princeton Architectural Press, 2017).

Renkl, Margaret. *The Comfort of Crows: A Backyard Year* (New York: Spiegal and Grau, 2023).

Tallamy, Douglas. *Bringing Nature Home: How You Can Sustain Wildlife with Native Plants: Updated and Expanded* (Portland, OR: Timber Press, 2009).

—. *Nature's Best Hope: A New Approach to Conservation That Starts in Your Yard* (Portland, OR: Timber Press, 2019).

—. *The Nature of Oaks: The Rich Ecology of Our Most Essential Native Trees* (Portland, OR: Timber Press, 2021).

Vogt, Benjamin. *A New Garden Ethic: Cultivating Defiant Compassion for an Uncertain Future* (Gabriola Island, BC: New Society Publishers, 2017).

Books on Identifying and Gardening with Native Plants

Adelman, Charlotte, and Bernard L. Schwartz. *The Midwestern Native Garden: An Illustrated Guide* (Athens, OH: Ohio University Press, 2011).

—. *Midwestern Native Trees and Shrubs: An Illustrated Guide* (Athens, OH: Ohio University Press, 2016).

Cullina, William. *Native Trees, Shrubs, and Vines: A Guide to Using, Growing, and Propagating North American Woody Plants* (Brattleboro, VT: Echo Point Books and Media, 2019).

Diboll, Neil, and Hilary Cox. *The Gardener's Guide to Prairie Plants* (Chicago, IL: University of Chicago Press, 2023).

Smith, M. Nevin. *Native Treasures: Gardening with the Plants of California* (Berkeley: University of California Press, 2006).

Various authors. The Native Plant Primer series (Portland, OR: Timber Press, various years). Includes titles on the Midwest, Northeast, Pacific Northwest, the Southeast, the Southwest, and Texas.

Books on Native Garden Design

Darke, Rick, and Douglas Tallamy. *The Living Landscape: Designing for Beauty and Biodiversity in the Home Garden* (Portland, OR: Timber Press, 2014).

Vogt, Bejamin. *Prairie Up: An Introduction to Natural Garden Design* (Champaign, IL: 3 Fields Books/University of Illinois Press, 2023).

Weaner, Larry, and Thomas Christopher. *Garden Revolution: How Our Landscapes Can Be a Source of Environmental Change* (Portland, OR: Timber Press, 2106).

Online Resources

Here are some of the richest and most reliable nationally focused sources for information on native plants and gardens in the United States, with highlights of the features of each one. Many have membership programs that support their work and enable sharing of information and resources.

The Biota of North America Program (BONAP)
bonap.org
The source for the native plant maps in this volume, the searchable BONAP website includes maps of county and state distributions of native plants in its North American Plant Atlas; its data are used by many guides and institutions as well as nurseries for identifying native ranges.

Facebook
facebook.com
This site hosts many highly active state and regional native plant groups. Search for the state or region you're looking for followed by "native plant," and you're likely to find an abundance of forums with active conversations, delivering useful information almost in real time. As with any public group, it's important to read critically and consult other sources to confirm what's posted in these spaces (usually because someone with good intentions is mistaken about a plant's native range or identification).

Homegrown National Park
homegrownnationalpark.org
The place to identify your ecoregion and find a guide to its keystone plants: the trees, shrubs, and forbs that provide the most benefit to pollinators. You can also add your garden to the Homegrown National Park map.

The Invasive Plant Atlas of the United States
invasiveplantatlas.org
The key resource for identifying plants that do not belong in your native plant garden,

this collaborative project of the National Park Service and several other organizations offers tools for the identification and reporting of invasive plant species across the United States. Because safe methods of invasive plant removal vary depending on geography and climate, a local native plant society (found through the North American Native Plant Society, below) or local Agricultural Extension Office may offer the best guidance on techniques once you've identified the undesirable plant.

National Wildlife Federation
nativeplantfinder.nwf.org
Here you can search for plants native to your area by zip code, including keystone plants, and find out about additional ways to support pollinators, birds, and other animals that sustain ecosystems.

North American Native Plant Society
nanps.org/native-plant-societies
This Canada-based organization is four decades old and offers a wealth of resources, including a list of local plant societies across Canada and the United States. Virtually every state has a native plant society or organization, and almost all of them have websites. These are invaluable for finding information on locally native plants and nurseries that sell them.

Pollinator Partnership
pollinator.org
This site offers guides to planting the most beneficial trees, shrubs, and perennials in more than thirty-five US ecoregions, which can be located by zip code, with information on the specific pollinators they support.

Pollinator Pathway
pollinator-pathway.org
This organization promotes community efforts to plant natives and create unbroken pathways across home gardens to feed and shelter pollinators throughout their lifecycle, wherever they live or migrate.

Prairie Up
prairieup.com
Prairie Up is the online hub of garden designer, educator, and writer Benjamin Vogt, the heart of whose work is "unlawning America through design and education." Here you'll find Vogt's extensive blog posts, articles, garden guides, and educational offerings, including live and self-paced workshops. If you want to take your native plant philosophy and practice as far as they can go, Benjamin Vogt is the person to know.

University of Texas Lady Bird Johnson Wildflower Center
wildflower.org
Officially the Botanic Garden of Texas, the Lady Bird Johnson Wildflower Center maintains a comprehensive, easy-to-use national native plant database.

Wild Ones
nativegardendesigns.wildones.org
This national organization includes local chapters that meet in person. Their site hosts a unique resource: sample regional native plant garden designs, donated by their creators for the use and inspiration of those just getting started.

The Xerces Society
xerces.org
Dedicated to the conservation of invertebrate species, including butterflies and other insects, this site offers information about invertebrates and focuses on pollinator-safe native plant gardening.

Native Plant Nurseries

As with all businesses, native plant nurseries are opening and closing all the time. Rather than name local businesses, this list includes online directories of brick-and-mortar retailers as well as several trustworthy online sources for native plants. I encourage you to look for local nurseries propagating, growing, and selling local ecotypes, which are plants genetically adapted to the conditions in your area, giving them the best chance to thrive and to benefit your ecosystem. Once you find a nursery, don't hesitate to ask for the origins of plants for sale (never harvested from the wild!) as well as assurances that plants for sale are pesticide-free.

Beech Hollow Farms
beechhollowfarms.com/native-plant-nurseries
This Georgia-based native plant nursery maintains a growing list of native plant nurseries nationwide.

Garden for Wildlife
gardenforwildlife.com
This site is affiliated with the National Wildlife Federation. They offer shopping by zip code, a quiz to match plants with your garden goals, and curated collections of plants.

Homegrown National Park Native Plant Resource Directory
homegrownnationalpark.org/directory
You can filter this site's resource directory to locate retail or wholesale native plant nurseries. Their listings are extensive; there's a map to help home in on your area.

The Plant Native
theplantnative.com/resources/order-native-plants-online
This site publishes a list of online native plant nurseries nationwide, by region.

The Xerces Society
xerces.org/pollinator-conservation/native-plant-nursery-and-seed-directory
Their annually updated directory of state-by-state sources for native plants includes sources for seeds and milkweed plants to support monarchs.

Wild Ones
nativegardendesigns.wildones.org/nursery-list
This site invites users to contribute to their state-by-state list of native plant nurseries.

INDEX

Entries in red indicate non-natives. Page numbers in **bold** indicate a native's featured presentation in the book, including a photograph.

R

STATE-BY-STATE INDEX OF NATIVE PLANTS

Refer to the BONAP map accompanying each plant listing for a more precise county-by-county native range.

PHOTOGRAPHY CREDITS

Alamy: A. LaRue p. 222 (right); Allen Creative/Steve Allen p. 167 (top right); John Anderson p. 211 (bottom left); AngieC p. 131 (bottom right); Avalon.red pp. 28 (top), 152 (top left), 222 (left); AY Images p. 188 (right); Karina Azaretzky p. 50 (left); B. Christopher pp. 111 (bottom right), 220 (top right); Anna Babii p. 78 (bottom); Todd Bannor p. 78 (middle); Robert E. Barber p. 141 (top left); Gerry Bishop pp. 137 (bottom right), 141 (bottom left); blickwinkel pp. 41 (top left), 45 (top right), 56 (middle left), 57 (bottom right), 66 (top right), 71 (bottom left), 79 (right), 145 (top left), 156 (left), 164 (right), 189 (right), 202 (top right); Donna Bollenbach p. 4; Botanic World pp. 71 (top left), 90 (right), 182 (top left); Botany Vision pp. 19 (bottom left), 62 (top right), 71 (bottom right), 91 (right), 94 (left), 136 (bottom), 149 (bottom right), 200 (top right); Florin Brezeanu p. 44 (top); Geraldine Buckley p. 44 (bottom); Anett Bulano p. 183 (right); Roberta Canu p. 216 (left); Nigel Cattlin p. 182 (bottom left); CharlineXia Ontario Canada Collection p. 60 (top right); Chocoholic/Stockimo p. 182 (top right); D. Merrimon Crawford p. 71 (middle right); Derek Croucher p. 122 (left); Adrian Davies p. 198 (left); Daybreak Imagery p. 15; deefish p. 126 (left); Danita Delimont p. 193 (top); Don Johnston_GA p. 119 (right); Peter Eckert p. 104 (right); Jonathan Eden p. 64 (middle right); Elen p. 104 (left); Everyday Artistry Photography pp. 177 (bottom right), 208 (top right); Clint Farlinger pp. 115 (right), 131 (middle left); Simona Flamigni p. 171 (top left); Florapix pp. 19 (top left), 76 (bottom left), 192 (top left), 214 (bottom right); Florida Images p. 18 (right); flowerphotos p. 223 (left); franconiaphoto p. 9; Diane Friend pp. iv–v; Brian & Sophia Fuller p. 210 (bottom right); Clare Gainey pp. 144 (bottom left), 170 (left), 176 (right), 182 (middle right); Tim Gainey pp. 66 (top left), 76 (bottom right), 131 (bottom left), 164 (top); David Gater p. 135; Bob Gibbons pp. 64 (bottom right), 85 (right), 149 (left); GKSFlorapics pp. 56 (top left), 166 (left), 192 (middle left); Agata Gładykowska p. 202 (bottom right); Alexandra Glen p. 140 (top right); Alan Gregg back cover (middle), pp. 23 (top left), 90 (bottom left); Robert Harding p. 226 (middle); Jani-Markus Häsä p. 90 (top); Carmen Hauser p. 51 (bottom left); Steffen Hauser/botanikfoto pp. 26 (top right), 70 (top right), 111 (bottom left), 114 (left), 118 (bottom right), 127 (bottom left), 182 (middle left), 189 (bottom left), 210 (top left); Frank Hecker pp. 144 (bottom right), 193 (right); Robert Henno p. 228; Miriam Heppell p. 164 (bottom); HHelene p. 148 (bottom left); Penny Hicks p. 210 (bottom left); Historic Collection p. 36 (right); Holmes Garden Photos p. 177 (top right); Janet Horton p. 88 (left); Donna Ikenberry/Art Directors p. 183 (bottom left); Image Source Limited p. 108 (top right); imageBROKER.com pp. 66 (bottom left), 123 (bottom right), 127 (right), 130 (left), 186 (top left), 208 (top left), 220 (left); imageBROKER.com GmbH & Co. KG p. 22 (bottom); Mike Jarman p. 193 (bottom left); Peter Jordan_NE p. 226 (bottom right); Antoniya Kadiyska p. 33 (bottom left); R. Ann Kautzky p. 84 (right); Linda Kennedy p. 70 (left); Samantha Kent p. 211 (top right); Natallia Khlapushyna p. 88 (middle right); krolya25 p. 37 (bottom left); Nick Kurzenko p. 76 (top right); Jonathan Larsen/Diadem Images p. 141 (top right); Jesse Lee pp. 70 (bottom right), 100 (top right); Lorenza Photography p. 50 (middle right); Kateryna Maksymenko p. 167 (bottom right); Piotr Malczyk p. 82 (left); David Mann p. 91 (top left); Jeff March p. 211 (bottom right); Oleg Marchak p. 22 (top); John Martin pp. 124 (top left), 206 (left); Gunter Marx/NR p. 186 (bottom right); mauritius images GmbH pp. 186 (bottom left), 210 (top right); Jordana Meilleur p. 153 (top right); Tony Mills p. 226 (left); Raquel

Mogado p. 82 (bottom right); Skip Moody/Dembinsky Photo Associates pp. 130 (top right), 177 (top left), 183 (top left); Paul Mozell p. 85 (left); Peter Murray p. 56 (bottom left); MusicMan5Photos p. 145 (bottom left); Elisabeth Myers pp. 98-99; Natural History Archive pp. 105 (left), 156 (bottom), 198 (bottom right); Nature Picture Library p. 105 (right); Roberto Nistri p. 200 (left); Organica p. 158 (top left); Organics Image Library p. 60 (left); George Ostertag pp. 23 (bottom left), 29 (bottom right), 37 (right), 41 (bottom left), 82 (top right), 131 (top left), 141 (middle left), 223 (top right); Panther Media Global pp. 126 (bottom right), 141 (bottom right), 174 (top right); Diana Pappas p. 131 (middle right); Michael Peters p. 144 (top right); piemags/nature pp. 19 (right), 41 (right), 50 (bottom right), 51 (middle right, bottom right), 127 (top left), 159 (bottom right), 171 (bottom left, top right), 174 (bottom right), 211 (top left), 216 (right), 220 (bottom right); psychoshadow p. 214 (top right); Puffin's Pictures p. 118 (top right); Jason Pulley p. 137 (bottom left); RUPENDRA RAWAT p. 62 (left); Jon Reaves p. 79 (left); Lee Rentz p. 186 (top right); Bryan Reynolds pp. 29 (top right), 37 (top left), 122 (top right), 153 (top left), 167 (left); John Richmond pp. ii–iii, 158 (right); Anne Rippy p. 159 (left); RM Floral pp. 108 (left), 174 (left); Susan A. Roth pp. 56 (bottom left), 57 (bottom left); Nick Scott p. 214 (left); Sea2Sea Photography p. 149 (top right); Eugene Sergeev p. 26 (bottom right); Onur Sezer p. 164 (middle); shapencolour p. 91 (bottom left); Jarvis Shirky p. 131 (top right); Daniel Shumny p. 200 (bottom right); Gary K. Smith p. 40 (left); Sue Smith p. 177 (bottom left); Nadya So p. 110 (left); Klaus Steinkamp p. 126 (top right); Stocktaker p. 76 (top left); Kiki Streitberger back cover (top), p. 64 (top right); STUDIO75 pp. 33 (top left), 56 (top right); Sundry Photography p. 111 (top left); Rosanne Tackaberry pp. 23 (bottom right), 51 (top left); Sharon Talson pp. 66 (bottom right), 137 (top right), 217 (bottom left); Emanuel Tanjala pp. 94 (top right), 156 (top right), 166 (right); Kenneth Taylor p. 26 (left); Matthew Taylor pp. 28 (bottom), 118 (left); Nik Taylor p. 45 (left); Jennifer Tepp p. 78 (top); thrillerfillerspiller pp. 64 (left), 148 (top left); P. Tomlins pp. 36 (left), 100 (left), 102 (top left), 136 (top), 140 (bottom right), 202 (top left); Masa Uemura p. 140 (top left); Universal Images Group North America LLC/DeAgostini pp. 33 (right), 140 (bottom left); Andrew Vanhooser p. 71 (top right); Greg Vaughn p. 119 (top left); Deborah Vernon p. 226 (top right); vgarfotos p. 208 (bottom left); vivoo p. 57 (top left); Michael Wheatley pp. 108 (bottom right), 110 (right), 130 (bottom right); C. J. Wheeler p. 192 (bottom left); WILDLIFE GmbH pp. 32 (top, bottom), 60 (bottom right), 153 (bottom left); Ray Wilson p. 176 (left); Wirestock, Inc. pp. vi–vii, 102 (bottom left); Feng Yu p. 90 (middle left); Zoonar GmbH pp. 23 (top right), 29 (top left), 62 (bottom right), 66 (middle right), 84 (left), 94 (bottom right), 95 (bottom left, top right), 114 (bottom right), 189 (top left), 223 (bottom right). **Getty Images:** mtreasure p. 206 (bottom right). **Shutterstock:** Vahan Abrahamyan p. 57 (top right); Denis Achberger p. 145 (right); Bankiras p. 102 (top right); Algimantas Barzdzius p. 158 (bottom left); Al Bittler p. 123 (top left); butterfly's dream p. 170 (right); dilamita26 p. 159 (top right); Sukanya Dluzak front cover (bottom); F_studio p. 123 (top right); Lea Fritz p. 152 (bottom left); Kabar p. 152 (top right); KSCHiLI p. 188 (left); Alex Manders p. 122 (bottom right); Tom Meaker p. 102 (middle right); Anton Nikitinskiy p. 153 (bottom right); nnattalli pp. 202 (bottom left), 217 (top left); Pictures_for_You p. 111 (top right); Picunique p. 95 (top left); Sergey and Marina Pyataev front cover (top); Sanjiv Shukla p. 18 (left); teddiviscious p. 137 (top left); Trxiswan back cover (bottom), p. 81; Brian Woolman p. 198 (top right).

Courtesy Use: Leo Chapman pp. 16, 256; Elise Howard p. 114 (top right); Mark Turner pp. 48, 162, 196, 204; Mackenzie Younger pp. viii, 29, 40, 45, 50, 51, 68, 88, 100, 115, 119, 122, 148, 171, 180, 206, 216.

ACKNOWLEDGMENTS

I must begin my acknowledgments with a shout-out to my book group. When I retired from my publishing career, they asked what I wanted to do with the rest of my life. I told them about my idea for this book, and they immediately said, "Do that!" And here we are.

Going back even further, I owe a debt to three people who were essential to my time as a volunteer gardener in New York City's Riverside Park. The park's then-head of horticulture Lynda Tower assigned me a garden area near the park's "Forever Wild" area, and asked if I'd please work strictly with native plants there. Park gardener Stephen Zelno helped educate me on native plant IDs, but more importantly, he worked energetically to restore long-neglected areas with a native plant palette that demonstrated how beautiful a garden of all natives could be. Laurie Strawgate Kanefsky was my volunteer gardening partner at that time, and she smiled through our hours-long efforts to get water by whatever means available from the volunteer house a block away to our newly planted shrubs and flowers. She also became a cherished friend, because gardening together will do that to you.

Big thanks to Mary Ellen O'Neill, the editor who championed this book through its acquisition; to Bridget Monroe Itkin, who took the manuscript on enthusiastically and made it tighter, clearer, smarter, and more approachable; to publisher Lia Ronnen, who felt this book could and should be a Workman book; to art director and designer Suet Chong, who made it elegant beyond my wildest dreams; to Julia Perry, who helped make sure some of the most fiddly details were correct and consistent; to Paula Brisco, who painstakingly checked every plant name, cross-reference, abbreviation, and botanical term; to production editor Samantha Gil and her invaluable care and problem-solving; to photo researcher Sophia Rieth; and to the whole Workman publishing team.

Native plant folks are generous with their knowledge and their resources, eager to spread the word and share the beauty of native plants. Thanks to the Lady Bird Johnson Wildflower

Center for sharing their resources and references, and to John Kartesz and Misako Nishimo of BONAP. Misako not only made sure I had the most up-to-date information and maps but helped correct some mistakes and misspellings that had made it past several other sets of eagle eyes. Huge thanks to Mackenzie Younger of New York Flower Farm, who offered up his large library of images as soon as he heard this book was taking shape. Mackenzie is also a member of the Native New York Gardens crew, whose owner, Johnny Kunen, runs the only truly native plant garden firm who were excited to implement a native plant vision in the shared gardens of my Manhattan apartment community in 2020. My conversations with Johnny about how homeowner needs and visions combine and sometimes conflict with the goals of native plant gardening have been helpful in shaping my conversations with gardeners new to the benefits of native plants. The same goes for the members of our garden committee, whose stalwarts include Hilary Reis, Sarah Durham, Cynthia Holden, Chelly Jones, Olya Shevchenko, and Francisco Quesada.

Thanks to the family who made me a gardener. I first puttered with Pansy (yep, true!) and Bill Howard in our home gardens in Maryland and Virginia. During his retirement, my dad became a keen horticulturist and plant hunter, and he enthusiastically shared his finds with me, including sources for the plants I admired on garden trips home and abroad. He loved fritillaries best of all, so my mother and I were only a little surprised when one somehow appeared in each of our gardens, 225 miles apart, the spring after we lost him. My siblings Bill, Elena, and Jonathan Howard listened to me talk (and talk and talk . . .) about native plants, and now I delight in getting their latest native garden updates, complete with pollinator news.

My husband, Leo Chapman, and son, Tristan Chapman, have put up with decades of my heading into the garden for a planned twenty minutes only to return hours later, confounded by the passage of time. They have dug holes, carried heavy tip bags, unloaded pots, dragged hoses, reached for high branches, endured side trips on family vacations to botanical gardens, nurseries, and garden supply companies famous and obscure, and cheerfully made room for grow lights in the hallway; leaves, buds, and bugs in the kitchen sink; and seed starts all over the place. To them, all my love and gratitude.

Megan Howard, my soul sister, was my partner in all things, lawful and criminal, including the journey from *Alchemilla mollis* to *Heuchera americana*. I carry her heart in my heart always, especially in the garden.

ELISE HOWARD has grown a garden everywhere she has lived since childhood, up and down the Eastern Seaboard between Virginia and Maine. She has gardened in window boxes, suburban backyards, apartment courtyards, and on the rural coastline. Her native plant journey began more than fifteen years ago, when she became a volunteer gardener in New York City's Riverside Park. She currently gardens and lives with her family in New York City and western Massachusetts.